@ home with your
Ancestors.com

If you want to know how . . .

The Beginner's Guide to Tracing Your Roots
An inspirational and encouraging introduction to discovering your family's past

Writing Your Life Story
How to record and present your memories for friends and family to enjoy

How To Research the History of your House
Every home tells a story . . .

How To Research Local History

howtobooks

For full details, please send for a free copy
of the latest catalogue to:

How to Books
Spring Hill House, Spring Hill Road
Begbroke, Oxford OX5 1RX
e-mail: info@howtobooks.co.uk
www.howtobooks.co.uk

@ home with your
Ancestors.com

HOW TO
RESEARCH FAMILY HISTORY
USING THE INTERNET

DIANE MARELLI

howtobooks

Published by How To Books Ltd
Spring Hill House, Spring Hill Road
Begbroke, Oxford OX5 1RX
Tel: (01865) 375794 Fax: (01865 379162
info@howtobooks.co.uk
www.howtobooks.co.uk

First published 2007
Reprinted 2007

British Library Cataloguing in Publication Data
A catalogue record for this book is available from the British Library

ISBN: 978 1 84528 177 9

Cover design by Mousemat Design Ltd
Produced for How To Books by Deer Park Productions
Typeset by Kestrel Data, Exeter, Devon
Printed and bound in Great Britain by Cromwell Press Ltd, Trowbridge, Wiltshire

NOTE: The material contained in this book is set out in good faith
for general guidance and no liability can be accepted
for loss or expense incurred as a result of relying in particular
circumstances on statements made in the book. The laws and
regulations are complex and liable to change, and readers should
check the current position with the relevant authorities before making
personal arrangements.

In loving memory of

Lilian (Peggy) Hughes
Previously Moloney, née Reynolds
28 February 1929 – 14 February 2005
'Your love for us lives on'

Dedicated to

Lisa Castle, née Garbett
'You lifted us when nothing else could'
Our love and grateful thanks to you Lisa

Special mentions

My husband Brian for being my husband
My brothers, sisters, their partners and children for their unconditional love
My stepfather Garry and his eldest son and wife for their support
My friend Sue Bevan for the tears and laughter
&
The Witches of Wix Hill, outrageous

Acknowledgements for permission to reproduce material in this book

Contents

Introduction

It is remarkable how things have changed in the short time since 1998 when I first began researching family history. No longer do I have to travel to London week after week, using up my free time in the pursuit of my ancestors. I now research when it suits me and from the comfort of my home. Since writing my last book there has been a heartbreaking change in my family history. My mum developed a brain tumour and after a traumatic time fighting for her life we lost her on Valentine's Day in 2005. Due to these circumstances, I stepped away from researching, thinking I would never get back into it, yet a year on from Mum's death I started to remember some treasured moments including two in particular. Her joy when I presented her with her own family history providing some answers to difficulties she faced as a child, and her pride when *Meet Your Ancestors* was published in 2003. My only consolation is that I was able to share my findings with Mum, in complete contrast to the sadness I felt at not being able to share similar results with my father-in-law.

So here I go again wending my way down the never-ending path of discovery to my ancestors and although I am still unable to record the final detail of Mum to my family tree, I am once again hooked by the yearning to learn more about the life and times of my family. The journey continues.

Picking up the threads is not as difficult as you might imagine because although your life moves on and you will have new additions, marriages or deaths in your present-day family, the history of past generations remains exactly the same. The beauty of this pastime is that temporary abandonment does not change what history has recorded; in fact a break from research can prove to be an advantage, as I found out.

After selecting which branch of the family I was going to work on, I logged into some of my favourite websites and discovered a wealth of additional information. Amazingly, within a relatively short time I had solved a few mysteries regarding my own family and filled the gaps in a five-generation pedigree of my husband's family history. Delighted with my findings I began investigating other ancestors that had previously eluded me and again started producing favourable results. It was then that I began to question why I was suddenly able to achieve so much so quickly. Perhaps I was just more experienced. Or maybe the break from research had cleared the debris of facts from my head enabling clear-minded focus on the task in hand. I accept I am more experienced and admitted, my head isn't spinning with thousands of names and dates, as it was over two years ago, but the real answer is that due to the Internet, researching is much more accessible now. Having so much information available at the touch of a button, the time to think and analyse and with all my research to hand, I can manipulate information quickly and efficiently without worrying about whether I will find what I am looking for before the Family Record Centre or the Society of Genealogists closes that day. The great thing about researching today is that the Internet never shuts and at any given time – day or night, seven days a week – I can choose when I want to research. I could even take my laptop on holiday and with the help of technology I could research sitting on a beach! Not that I have, well not so far. Obviously, there will only be so much I can achieve via the Internet before I will have to venture out from the comfort of my home, but for now I am fully occupied with the wealth of material available on the Internet.

It was then that I began to wonder how many of you out there would love to research your own histories but cannot because you do not have the luxury of living in the area of your research or near the locations where archives are held. Maybe you are confined to home because of family commitments, as I am at the moment. You might have poor health or time constraints holding you back. All of these circumstances a few years ago would have made it difficult to embark upon your ancestral search, but not any more. I am going to show you how you can make real inroads into your own histories without having to put a foot outside your own front door.

This book will show you how to start building the history of your ancestors. Using only the Internet and working with several browsers at once you will source Birth, Marriage and Death registers (BMD) and order certificates; locate and access Census and Parish Record information, build and expand your tree through a combination of other resources and finally, record and store your findings. By the end of this book you will be able to provide your children and future generations with a picture of how their families evolved over at least five generations.

1

The Internet, births and marriages

I am sure you will agree that the history of your family is straightforward in as much as your parents had parents, and their parents had parents, taking you back to the beginning of time, or at least until we were humanised, or not as the case might be. But locating historical information about your forebears might prove a little more difficult in reality. If you have read my first book, you will understand exactly what I mean if embarking on this journey as a complete novice. But with the benefit of hindsight I can now show you how to create your first pedigree chart following a logical process using only the resources of the Internet and working more efficiently and productively than I did in my earlier research.

For the benefit of this exercise I am going to start from scratch, as if just beginning my research, and trace the pedigree of my father-in-law, Albert William Marelli, the inspiration behind my first book, using only the resources of the Internet. At his death we inherited various documents containing family information, including Bert's (Albert William) birth certificate.

Step 1 - Acquire a birth certificate of a parent or grandparent

1. If you have only a marriage certificate, see Chapter 2, Step 1.
2. If you have only a death certificate, it will give you their age at death or the date of birth on later certificates. See the Tips section at the end of this chapter and Chapter 4, Step 1.
3. If you don't have a birth certificate (or any other certificate) of a close relative such as parent or grandparent then ask family members. If the relative is deceased someone somewhere will have a copy either of the birth or of the death certificate, usually the eldest child. Ask for a photocopy or at least the information recorded on the certificate.

4. If you don't have any way of obtaining documented evidence of an ancestor then see the Tips section at the end of this chapter.

> It is always preferable to work backwards in family research, although sometimes not always possible.

Birth certificate for Albert William Marelli

Birth certificate for Albert William Marelli

What information does a birth certificate give us?

1. The names of the person's parents.
2. The address where s/he was born.
3. The address of the parents at the time of birth.
4. Father's occupation.
5. Mother's maiden name.

But what else should we pay attention to on birth certificates?

Birth certificates in more detail

The top of the birth certificate gives the district name and this information is important when searching indexes. It is important to remember that boundaries were constantly changing, including not only counties but parishes. For instance, I knew that an ancestor died in Brixton but the registration district in the indexes is Lambeth. Also villages in rural areas such as Devon could share the registration district of the nearest large town, even though situated some distance away. This can be very misleading and it is always worth looking up registration districts in Genuki (http://www.fhsc.org.uk/genuki/reg/).

GENUKI Contents

REGISTRATION DISTRICTS IN ENGLAND AND WALES (1837-1930)

These pages show composition of the civil registration districts in England and Wales between 1st July 1837 and 31st March 1930*. The same districts were also used to compile the decennial census for the years 1851, 1861, 1871, 1881, 1891 and 1901.

The following information is given for each district:

- Name of the district
- Registration county - many districts crossed county boundaries, but were classed wholly in one registration county for registration and census purposes.
- Date of creation
- Date of abolition (if before 1930)
- Names of the sub-districts.
- The General Register Office (GRO) volume numbers used for the district in the national indexes of births, marriages and deaths
- A list of the civil parishes or townships included within its boundaries.
- The name(s) of the district(s) which *currently* hold the records. If two or more offices are listed, the one which holds most records is named first, and the one with least is given last. Click here for addresses of current register offices.

There is also an Alphabetical List of Districts and an Index of Place-Names for the whole of England and Wales.

Any comments or queries regarding these listings should be sent to Brett Langston.

NB: The coverage of these listings is gradually being extended up to 1974. This is being done on a county-by-county basis, and those counties marked with an asterisk below have now been so extended.
The remaining areas will be completed by the end of 2006.

ENGLAND

- Bedfordshire *

Details of contents on GENUKI

First column on your birth certificate is the GRO reference

Numbered 1 to 500 the GRO reference is for a complete page in a register. Twins on the same page will have the same reference number, but if the twins were the last entry on one page and the first on the next they will have consecutive reference numbers. Another point to remember is that some families may have two births that appear as if they are twins when in fact they could be cousins or not even related.

Column 1: Date and place of birth

The date of birth is not always accurate, for a number of reasons, including:

♦ Parents were not above telling lies when registering a child outside the six-week rule of registration.

♦ Parents often became confused about the various dates of birth for their children as you will find on the Census (for example, you sometimes find brothers' and sisters' ages switched in error).

The place of birth can be helpful during later registrations, but in earlier ones you will find that in some instances only the name of the village is given, as with earlier Censuses.

When finding a full address a useful check is to see if the mother or father has registered the birth and given the same address as the place of birth for the child. It is important to remember some women went home to their mother's to give birth, but even if a child was born in an institution, there could be a clue to the location of the family if the address of the informant is listed. If there is no address other than the institution then the area itself could be a clue or an old map might show the nearest institution to where the family resided, although this could be many miles from the family home.

Column 2: Forenames/given name
The forename or names are in this column. A child can be registered without a first name due to the fact that the child died before registration, or because they do not as yet have a name, or because the child was abandoned, born into poverty or going to be adopted.

Where there are no father's details in the register you might be lucky enough to find two Christian names with the latter proving to be the surname of the father.

Remember that a person might be registered with a given name, as with one of my ancestors Alice Amy Plummer, who was known as Amy throughout her life. Or perhaps they were known by a nickname bearing no resemblance to their given name.

Column 3: Sex
Mistakes have been made in recording the sex of the child when a name can be used for either sex, such as Francis and Frances if spelt incorrectly. Unusual names also get recorded incorrectly. Another ancestor of mine, Stephen, had two baptism registrations, one for Stephen in FamilySearch.com and one for Stephanie in the National Burial Index. At first I thought they were twins as both were christened at the same time but further investigation at the original church records of the Surrey History Centre proved there was a mistake made in the transcription in the National Burial Index and Stephanie was in fact Stephen. Always allow for human error!

Column 4: Father's name

At the beginning of Civil Registration, 1837, the rules of registration were open to interpretation. They stated that a birth should be registered within 42 days, but it wasn't necessary to record the name of the fathers of bastard children. This meant that some registrars recorded the names of both parents even if not married and others recorded only the mother if the parents were unmarried. This situation was clarified in the mid 1800s with clear instructions for registrars and stated that if parents were not married, the father's name should be left blank. Towards the third quarter of the 19th century the father of illegitimate children could be added if both parents were in agreement.

Even when the name of the father is recorded on a birth certificate it is open to question when a couple are not married. This can also cause problems when no father is named on a birth certificate and can carry on for generations.

My five times great grandfather, Frederick, after the death of his first wife, became involved in a second relationship, so far no record of a marriage has been found. He inherited two children by the surname Webber, neither child had the name of the father on their birth certificates, but I am aware this does not mean that Frederick was not the father of her earlier children. Both of her children used the name Pudvine and when the boy married he actually named his children Pudvine when they should have been know as Webber. The name Pudvine continues in that family to this day.

Column 5: Mother's name

Column 5 gives the mother's name and will also include previous names if married. For instance, I found one birth certificate with the mother's married surname as Garbett, late Burnett, formerly Clarke, as she had been previously married.

In later records it is possible to find a mother registered a birth with the name she has adopted, when unmarried. My great grandmother, Azor Zoar, is shown on the birth certificates of her children as Azor Zoar Brown, formerly Walker, although she never married the father of her children. Again it is important to remember that, as with the stepson of my five times great grandfather, a female could also record herself formally by her previous name if married more than once.

Column 6: Father's occupation

Sometimes this can be blank either because the informant did not know the occupation of the father, or the father was unemployed, i.e. not in paid employment. Sometimes the occupation may be listed as a labourer, but there were many forms of labourers. My husband's great grandfather is recorded as being a carman on one birth certificate, an ice merchant on the next, then back to carman on the next. His occupation was a carman delivering ice.

Column 7: Signature, description and residence of the informant
Once the entry has been checked by the informant, s/he signs Column 7 with their usual signature. If the informant can't write, they will put their mark, usually an X, and the registrar will add 'the mark of . . .'. When you see that the informant cannot write, it probably means they cannot read, so they are relying on the registrar to record everything correctly, which can cause problems. The first wife of Martino Marelli, my husband's great grandfather, could not write and one of her children was recorded as Ellen Morrelli, and in my early days of research this caused me great trouble. Because I searched, understandably, under the surname Marelli but had no luck, I had to try Morelli, Merelli, Murelli, and so on, back and forth, again and again. Finally I thought of another variant of the surname, Morrelli! I cannot express enough how important it is not to give up looking for an ancestor until you have explored every spelling variant you can think of. It is also worth remembering that a signature is not always proof that they were literate as many people learnt to write their names but that was as far as their education went.

Informants can be the mother, the father if married to the mother, both parents if not married to each other (this came into being in the last quarter of 1800s), someone present at the birth (grandparents, aunt, midwife etc.), or the owner or occupier of a property or institution, such as a master at a workhouse, or a person with responsibility for a child, a relative or family friend, or the master of an institution if the mother died in childbirth.

Addresses given can be misleading especially if the mother goes to the home of a friend or relative to have her child. You could also have the address where the child was born recorded as the same as the residence of informant, and you think you have the correct address for the family, but the mother might be recording her residence at the time of the birth. Also, when someone else is registering the birth, the address will be that of the informant and the place of birth could be the address where the child was born and not the family address. The address given could also be many miles away from the true family residence.

Column 8: Date of registration
The date of registration is important as this will be the date recorded in the indexes and not the date of birth. My own mother was born on the 28 February 1929 but her birth was not registered until 16 April 1929 so when

searching for a copy of her birth certificate we found her not in the March quarter but in the June quarter of the indexes.

If the child was not registered within the given period required by the law, it is possible the child was never registered at all, as with my husband's maternal grandmother. Sometimes a birth was registered up to a year later, or longer if there was acceptable proof of birth from relatives, doctors etc. We must not forget, a parent may give an incorrect date of birth in order to escape paying penalties for late registrations.

Column 9: Signature of registrar

The registrar's signature is of little genealogical benefit unless of course the registrar bears the same family name meaning there could be a family connection.

Column 10: Name given after initial registration

You might find a correction of the given name in this column if the name is changed at baptism. Usually a child would be baptised after Civil Registration which could cause problems searching the indexes if the Christian name/s were changed and not corrected on the birth certificate.

So, as you can see, there is a lot more to be considered when analysing birth certificates.

Step 1 - Continued . . .

At this stage I can choose my next step. I could estimate the ages of both of Albert's parents and start a search for their birth certificates or I could estimate the year of his parents' marriage based on the birth date of Albert Marelli.

♦ To estimate a birth, remember that either parent could be as young as 18 or younger and as old as 40 years of age or older when Albert was born, giving me a search period of 22 years or more, i.e. the years from 1875 to 1897. I personally would assume they married young and choose 1897 to begin my search and work backwards.

♦ To estimate this second marriage, I would start at the date of their first child born in 1915 and work backwards.

I have chosen to find the marriage certificate of Albert and Lilian next as the information on this document will give me further clues to finding their individual birth certificates as I will show you.

♦ Remember that BMD registers are split into four quarters per year, March, June, September and December, and the registers began in the September quarter of 1837.

As Bert was born in November 1915, I am going to start searching from this year as they could quite easily have married shortly before his birth. But don't forget they could also have married later.

Step 2 - Choose an Internet site to source BMD

My favourite sites that provide access to the Civil Registration Index for BMDs housed at the Family Record Centre (FRC) are as follows:

FreeBMD	http://freebmd.rootsweb.com
Ancestry.co.uk	http://www.ancestry.co.uk
Find my Past	http://www.findmypast.com

> Work with several browsers open at once to save logging in and out all the time.

FreeBMD

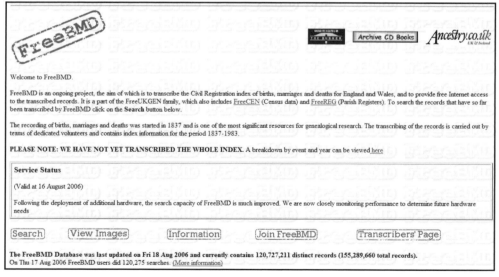

Copyright © 1998-2005 The Trustees of FreeBMD, a charity registered in England and Wales, number 1096940

FreeBMD is exactly what name implies, a free resource for finding transcriptions of the Civil Registration Index for births, marriages and deaths for England and Wales housed in total at the FRC, or in part at local history centres, libraries and so on. This site is easy to use and provides you with a transcription of the index you will need to obtain your certificate and it also allows you to view and print a scanned copy of the original register, if scanned into the FreeBMD site, in a variety of formats. The only drawback is that this wonderful store of information is not yet complete.

FreeBMD is always my initial port of call because first, it is free and second, you can search more specifically by name which is of particular use when looking for that elusive ancestor without having to scrawl through pages of registers.

> The cost of using FreeBMD = Zilch!

Ancestry.co.uk

Another great source and one I use constantly, is Ancestry.co.uk. Although this site is chargeable it offers true value for money. What it costs me per year to use this site, I could easily spend over a weekend travelling to family history archive centres, so it is definitely worth it.

Ancestry.co.uk offers:

UK Census records

1901 England	1901 Wales	
1891 England	1891 Wales	
1881 England	1881 Wales	
1871 England	1871 Wales	
1861 England	1861 Wales	1861 Scotland*
1851 England	1851 Wales	1851 Scotland*
1841 England*	1841 Wales*	1841 Scotland*

*new

UK and Ireland Parish and Probate Records
England and Wales, BMD Index (Beta)
Pallot Marriage Index
Irish Immigrants: New York Port Arrival

For a further charge you can access a variety of other records from such places the USA, Canada and Ireland.

The cost of using Ancestry.co.uk, as of April 2006

12 months UK Deluxe Membership is £69.95.
12 months World Deluxe Membership is £199.95.
You can trial World Deluxe for a month for £24.99.
You can also choose Pay-Per-View which costs £4.95 for 10 records over 14 days.

Find my Past

Findmypast.com formerly 1837online, proved to be a real lifesaver for me; my first experience accessing BMDs on the Internet. Again findmypast.com is a very straightforward, easy to use website constantly requesting feedback from its users for ideas for improvement, which they achieve on a regular basis. Findmypast.com is another excellent resource offering a flexible payment plan to suit everyone's pocket.

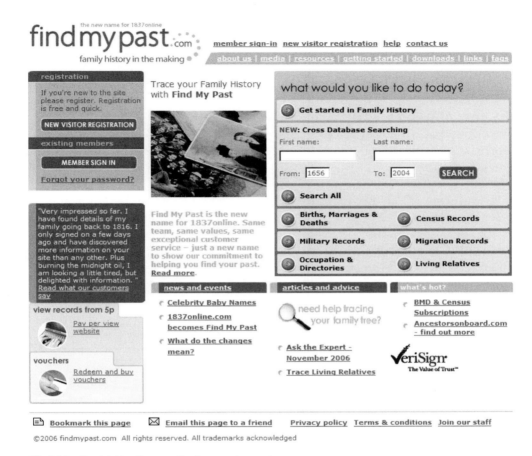

Find My Past http://www.findmypast.com/

Findmypast.com offers the following:

Births, marriages and deaths

Births	1837–1983	1984–2004
Marriages	1837–1983	1984–2004
Deaths	1837–1983	1984–2004 (Also BMDs overseas)

Census records

1861 Census
1891 Census

Military Records

WW1 soldiers died
War deaths WW1, WW2, Boer War

Living relatives
Person, address and business search

'Living Relatives' is a premium database available only to subscribers who have purchased a price plan of £25 or more.

The cost of using Findmypast.com as of April 2006
Subscription (Changes in price ongoing)
1 year's subscription for unlimited access to BMD indexes for England and Wales is £50.00.

3 years' subscription for unlimited access to BMD indexes for England and Wales is £125.00.

BMD and Census subscriptions
Unlimited BMD and Census access for 1 year is £65.
Unlimited BMD access for 3 years is £160.

Unit Plan

90-day plan	(50 units @ 10 pence)	£5.00.
120-day plan	(176 units @ 8.5 pence)	£15.00.
365-day plan	(313 units @ 8 pence)	£25.00.
365-day plan	(810 units @ 7.5 pence)	£60.00.
365-day plan	(2400 units @ 5 pence)	£120.00.
365-day plan	(4800 units @ 5 pence)	£240.00.

With all of the above websites, additions, improvements and price changes occur regularly and although I have endeavoured to keep apace with all changes while writing this book, you may find some additions or changes when you visit the sites at a later date.

Step 3 - Search for your ancestor

As FreeBMD is free, I am going to search their facility for the marriage certificate for Lilian Chappell and Albert Marelli before I log into a paying site. If I was going to use Ancestry.co.uk or findmypast.com as Albert was born in 1915, my first search would take in 1915 and the preceding 5 years, as you will see later in this book. For this search I will be using FreeBMD and will search by name; a very convenient way to search.

Go to FreeBMD website: http://freebmd.rootsweb.com then select 'search'.

If you know of other siblings born at an earlier time than the relative you have a certificate for, then their birth date would be the starting point for your marriage search.

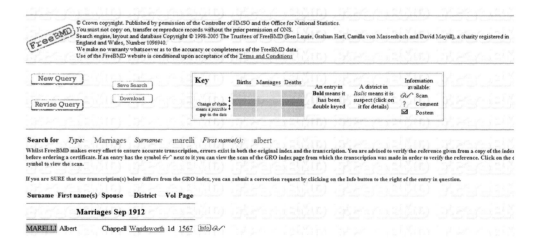

As you can see I selected marriages and Albert Marelli – with an unusual surname it is not necessary to use other criteria. Now select 'find'.

Search for *Type:* Marriages *Surname:* marelli *First name(s):* albert

Whilst FreeBMD makes every effort to ensure accurate transcription, errors exist in both the original index and the transcription. You are advised to verify the reference given from a copy of the index before ordering a certificate. If an entry has the symbol next to it you can view the scan of the GRO index page from which the transcription was made in order to verify the reference. Click on the symbol to view the scan.

If you are SURE that our transcription(s) below differs from the GRO index, you can submit a correction request by clicking on the Info button to the right of the entry in question.

Surname	First name(s)	Spouse	District	Vol	Page
Marriages Sep 1912					
MARELLI	Albert	Chappell	Wandsworth	1d	1567

I have found the marriage details for Albert Marelli, spouse Chappell, married in Wandsworth in the September Quarter, Vol. 1d, Page 1567. At this stage print the details below or record the information you will need to purchase a copy of the marriage certificate. Look at the information at the bottom. The 'spectacles' symbol means that on this particular search FreeBMD has the facility for me to view the original Register of Marriages for this particular record. Click your mouse on the spectacles.

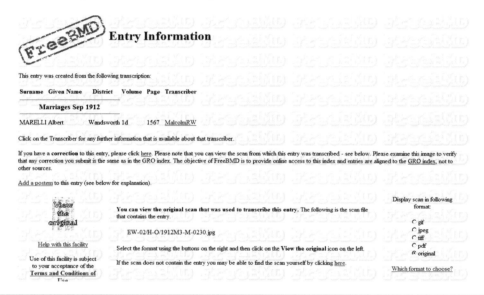

If you don't find what you are looking for then try other spellings of the names, such as Chappell, Chapple, Chapel.

You now have the facility to view the original register and choose the format you prefer to view the document. This time, I decided on jpeg to view the original.

This is what I received. When viewing online you can choose to enlarge the view and print a copy for your records. Below is the enlarged view of the information I require.

Marelli, Albert   Chappell   Wandsworth   1 d   1567

In later registers you will find the page records the 'event' (B, M or D), quarter and year. If you are printing off an early record it does not record the information on the page so remember to write event (B, M or D), year and quarter on the top of the page otherwise you will not have enough data to enable you to order the original certificate.

Step 4 - Ordering certificates online

I now want to order the original certificate and to do this I am going to access the GRO (General Register Office) online: www.gro.gov.uk. Select 'ordering certificates online'.

Step 1: GRO home page © 2006 Office for National Statistics

Step 2: Here you can either register or put in your login details once you have registered.

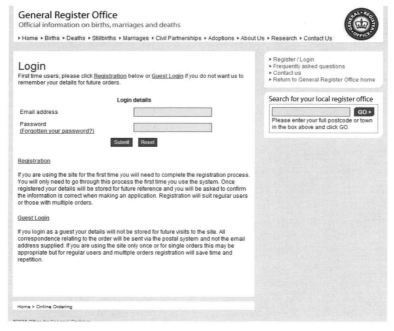

Step 3: Once you have registered or logged in you will find a screen like this. As you can see I have put in the criteria relating the Albert Marelli and Lilian Chappell's marriage.

General Register Office
Official information on births, marriages and deaths

▸ Home ▸ Births ▸ Deaths ▸ Stillbirths ▸ Marriages ▸ Civil Partnerships ▸ Adoptions ▸ About Us ▸ Research ▸ Contact Us

Certificate choice

Please select a certificate type and provide any additional information requested. We can then choose the appropriate application form.

▸ Logout
▸ Types of certificate
▸ My details
▸ Frequently asked questions
▸ Contact us
▸ Return to General Register Office home

Certificate Types

For events registered in England and Wales

1. Birth Certificate (England & Wales) ○

2. Marriage Certificate (England & Wales) ◉

3. Death Certificate (England & Wales) ○ Age at death in years [   ]

4. Adoption Certificate (England & Wales) ○ Current age of adoptee [   ]

For overseas events which were registered with the British authorities

5. Birth Certificate (Overseas events) ○

6. Marriage Certificate (Overseas events) ○

7. Death Certificate (Overseas events) ○ Age at death in years [   ]

For all events

Is the General Register Office Index known? Yes ◉ No ○
(Explanation)

Year in which the event was registered [1912]

Age at death must be given for applications where event was registered in last 50 years. Applications for events registered within the last 18 months cannot be made via this site. Please refer to the Obtaining Certificates page

[Submit] [Reset]

Step 4: Select 'submit'. The next page will ask for your delivery details.

This will be the delivery address for this individual application only.

After completing, please press the 'Submit' button to continue.

Delivery address details

Title	Mrs
Forenames*	Diane
Surname*	Marelli
DX address (not sure what this is? see our faqs. if you have one, you will not need to complete postal details below)	
Address line 1*	No Where Land
Address line 2	
Town*	
County / State	Surrey
Country*	United Kingdom ▼
Post / Zip Code	1837 abc
E-Mail Address	dianemarelli@tiscali.co.uk
Telephone number (daytime)	0000 00000
Telephone number (evening)	00000 000000

Submit   Reset

Home > Online Ordering

Step 5: Fill in the full particulars of the certificate you are purchasing.

Required fields will be followed by the * character.

Please complete the form and press the "Submit" button to add the application to your basket.

Particulars of the person whose certificate is required

Either the man's surname and forename or woman's surname and forename must be given.

Year marriage was registered	1912
Man's surname	Marelli
Man's forenames	Albert
Woman's surname at marriage	
Woman's forenames	

Reference information from GRO Index

Year	1912
Quarter*	July, Aug, Sept ▼
District name*	Wandsworth
Volume Number*	1d
Page Number*	1587

Step 6: You do not have to put in both names unless you are unsure that you have the correct certificate. I have not put in the name of Albert's wife because I know I have the correct reference information taken from the original register. This is useful to remember when you are searching broadly for an ancestor but you can request further checks from the GRO by selecting reference checking shown on the next image.

Scrolling down the screen will allow you to order either by standard delivery and price, or priority delivery and price. But, as you can see at the bottom of this screen, there is an option for reference checking.

Service Options

Please choose the service you require:

Standard :
Despatched on the 4th working day from receipt of order. Cost: £7.00 per certificate.

Priority :
Despatched next working day from receipt of order. Cost: £23.00 per certificate.
Please note that orders received, on Saturday or Sunday, will be classed as received on Monday (except those received on Bank Holidays, which will be classed as received on the following working day).

Priority applications received after 16.00 and standard applications after 17.00 will result in the order date being that of the next working day.

Delivery service *

Standard ⦿

Priority ○

Number of Certificates

Number of certificates *

Full | 1 |

Please note additional copies will be charged at £7.00 each.

Your reference for the application

Please type your personal reference for this application

Your reference

Reference Checking Options

If you would like more than one GRO Index reference checked for this certificate application or have checking points you wish to be checked against the entry please click on the button marked "Reference Checking"

[Reference Checking]

Step 7: By using reference checking you will be charged only a checking or search fee and you will be refunded the difference along with a letter or email of explanation. As you can see, reference checking gives you the option to add further information if unsure and you don't want delivery of a certificate that bears no relation to your family.

Application for an England and Wales marriage certificate

▸ Logout
▸ Types of certificate
▸ My details
▸ Frequently asked questions
▸ Contact us
▸ Return to General Register Office home

Below is an England and Wales Marriage Certificate Application Form for a certificate quoting the GRO index reference number.

Required fields will be followed by the * character.

Please complete the form and press the "Submit" button to add the application to your basket.

Form Errors

Man's full name or woman's full name must be given
Quarter must be given for the GRO reference
District Name must be given for the GRO reference
Volume Number must be given for the GRO reference
Page Number must be given for the GRO reference

Particulars of the person whose certificate is required

Either the man's surname and forename or woman's surname and forename must be given.

Year marriage was registered	1912
Man's surname	
Man's forenames	
Woman's surname at marriage	
Woman's forenames	

Step 8: Further down on this screen will be all the GRO information for the particular certificate you want checking. Please note the box to the right of the above screen. FAQs will provide you with most of your queries if you are unsure about what you are doing.

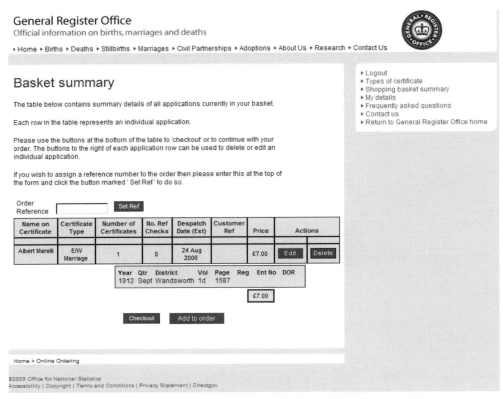

Step 9: After completing all the information select 'submit' and you will be taken to a summary screen and at this point you can choose to checkout or add details to order and continue shopping.

Recap

1. Acquire a birth certificate for a parent or grandparent.

2. Estimate the approximate year of your parent's or grandparent's marriage (if born in 1912 then search the preceding years working backwards from the date on the certificate).

3. If unsuccessful after searching backward for a sensible time-frame, then work forward from the birth-date.

4. Select the Internet source you will use to find the index details or a copy of the original register for ordering your certificate from the GRO.

5. Search for ancestor and GRO index.

6. Print a copy of your sourced register, then print or write down the GRO index.

Name	Event	Year	Quarter	Vol.	Page
A. Marelli	Marriage	1912	September	1d	1567

7. Register or log in to the GRO website and order your certificate.

8. Using FreeBMD is economical. The cost so far for a marriage certificate for Albert Marelli and Lilian Chappell would be £7.00.

The copy inherited below is quite different in appearance from a copy purchased from the GRO.

Marriage certificate for Albert Marelli and Lilian Chappell.

Step 5 - Your first family tree

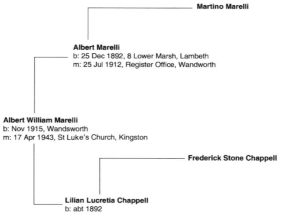

An A4 starter tree is available as a free download at www.dianemarelli.co.uk

You will soon be able to start building your family tree. The above tree was produced using Family Tree Maker, more of this later in the book.

➤ Tips

1. If you have no information about a grandparent or great grandparent move forward a generation and follow the actions above.
   a Start with yourself if necessary.
   b Start with the birth year of an older sibling to assess the marriage year of a parent.

2. Refer back to living memory.
   a When was the last time you or a relative can remember the person you are looking for was living?
   b Can anyone remember roughly a death-date or age at death?
   c If you have a death-date you could start by acquiring a death certificate (age at death will give you a birth-date).
   d Can you remember a big family event of the relative, such as a milestone birthday, wedding, anniversary?

3. Was the person living at the time the 1901 Census was taken?
   a The 1901 Census is accessible online, see Chapter 2, Step 4.

4. Has anyone in the family stored old letters, postcards, photographs with dates, newspaper cuttings, bills etc. that could provide you with clues?

5. It is always preferable to work backwards in family research, although sometimes not always possible.

6. Remember to try variations in the spellings of names.

7. Find the right payment method for acquiring information on the Internet. Read through the first few chapters of this book before committing to paying for Internet resources.

8. When working with various sites open a new browser for each website, this way you can switch between sites without forever logging in and out.

2

The next generation and the 1901 Census

Hopefully, you will now have a copy of a marriage certificate that will take you through to the next generation and provide clues for an even earlier generation.

Step 1 - Marriage certificates

What information does a marriage certificate give us?

1. Marriage date
2. Names of those married
3. Ages of those married
4. Condition – widow, single etc.
5. Occupation of those married
6. Addresses of those married
7. Names of both fathers
8. Occupation of both fathers
9. Witnesses

Example of a marriage certificate

Heading

This gives the place where the marriage was solemnised, usually the church or register office, and the registration district or parish, and the county. It is important to remember that the registration district will not always match the village or parish where the couple were living, especially in rural areas.

Directly beneath the details of the married couple you will be given more information about the religious denomination of the couple. For instance, Martino Marelli married Amy Plummer in 1891 at St George's Catholic Church according to the rites of Roman Catholics. Some of their children have similar information but others have 'according to the rites of the Established Church' (the Church of England).

Entry number

A church will have two identical registers and when they are complete one book is deposited with the superintendent registrar, but the other is kept by the church authorities and may finish up in the county record office or in the local church.

Some 500 entry registers are as yet incomplete and it is quite possible that the information has never been passed to a superintendent registrar who will therefore have no record of the marriages in a church in their district. The GRO however takes this type of information quarterly which is why you will often find a certificate via the GRO where you may have failed via your local registrar.

Column 1: Date of marriage

A marriage entry is dated on the day a marriage took place. There are various ways of recording the dates of marriages as I found with the following:

> 27th April 1931
> Sept 14th 1932
> Twentieth January 1926
> November 16 (with the year 1851 in the header)
> May 1 1879

Column 2: Name and surname of bride and groom

It is important to remember that the name and surname of the bride and groom are not always as recorded on their birth certificates. Until later years they were not asked for proof of identity at the time of their marriage, simply the names they were known as. Therefore, they could use different Christian names as with Alice Amy Plummer who married using the name of Amy Plummer. Or in the case of Henry George Webber, who not only was known as George Henry on his marriage certificate, but also used the name of his stepfather rather than his birth-name. Some people were known by aliases for many different reasons and hid their true identities, others for bigamous reasons.

Column 3: Age at the date of marriage

Again the couple were not asked to prove their age or identity, so these dates could vary enormously from the truth. Reasons might be that they were under age, the bride might be older than her husband, or maybe they had to guess their ages as they did not have copies of their birth records. Also, if a couple stated they were 21 years of age or over, they were not required to give their ages and if they were in fact under age and married without the consent of their legal guardian, the marriage itself could be classed as illegal.

I have a marriage record dated May 1 1879 with the ages of the couple simply recorded as 'full', and another as 'both of full age'. Interestingly, I have one ancestor Asor Zoar who had children previously from a relationship in which she was unmarried, but went on to marry someone else in 1911 aged 28 years. However, she records her age as 33 years maybe because the man she married was 50 years of age, or for reasons we can only speculate.

Column 4: Condition

This column records the marital status of the persons getting married, usually spinster, bachelor, widow or widower.

Of course, we have to allow for the possibility that one or the other might be lying as they might record themselves as single to avoid accusations of bigamy, or maybe they record themselves as a widow or widower when not actually married to the previous partner that they shared a home, life and children with.

If for some reason a previous marriage was annulled because of age or because the marriage was never consummated, or the female lied about being pregnant, they would revert to their previous condition and be recorded as single.

Divorce during the 19th century was a drawn-out and expensive process forcing couples to either stay together but live separate lives, to move into another relationship without marriage, or to marry bigamously.

Column 5: Occupation

The next column shows the occupation of both parties at the time of their marriage. If left blank or there is a line through this column it does not mean that the person concerned was not employed, especially if the marriage took place during the 19th century and the party concerned was female. Again, as with birth certificates, occupations could be embellished. One of my ancestors records himself as a provision dealer when he was a shop assistant.

Column 6: Residence at the time of marriage

The address at the time of the marriage can often be a misleading column. Couples would frequently marry away from the districts in which they lived for a variety of reasons. Maybe there was no suitable church where they resided, or perhaps there wasn't a church of the correct religion locally. Also we have to remember that one or both parties would have to establish residency in the locations they wished to get married. Maybe they both went to stay with a relative, or maybe they both give the same address although one might be living elsewhere. Maybe one or both parties did not have a static address and lied about their place of residence or gave that of a friend or relative in order to get married. Sometimes you will find only the village or street recorded as the address in earlier certificates, such as one I have for my three times great grandfather that records the address for both parties as simply Stoke (Guildford).

Columns 7 and 8: Fathers' names, surnames and rank or professions

These two columns relate to the fathers of the bride and groom. The information in these columns should relate to the natural fathers of the couple in question but again the information can be misleading. My George Henry or Henry George Pudvine, although using the surname of his stepfather, does not record his father's details on his marriage certificate. There could be several reasons for this – he knew that Frederick Pudvine was not his father, maybe he'd lost touch with Frederick or believed him to be deceased, and of course there is the possibility that he was never told who his true father was. Legally, he was required to add only the details of his natural father, but legally he wasn't really a Pudvine.

Sometimes couples chose not to record the names of their fathers for personal reasons and although these columns were to be used only for natural parents, they were not obliged to fill in this information. However, I imagine that many people fabricated details of fathers where none existed to save embarrassment. Martino Marelli was brought up in a foundlings home in Milan and his parents are recorded as unknown, yet on his first marriage certificate he records his father as Martino Marelli, a carman (identical to himself), but on his second marriage certificate he records his father as Angelo Marelli, a farmer. Was there any truth in this? Maybe he was told his father's name as a child in Milan. Maybe he fabricated a father, as he was of the Catholic faith and to be illegitimate was a stigma.

If a father was deceased at the time of the marriage it was usually recorded as such under the name but not always.

The occupation is the last column that will give the occupation of the father but if retired it will usually state that he is retired. Again, occupations are open to interpretation. For Martino, I have his occupations listed on his children's marriage certificates as fishmonger, master fishmonger, shopkeeper, tradesman and restaurant proprietor. I know that he was a carman, then ice merchant, then fishmonger and finally he owned a chain of fish and chip shops, so all of the descriptions are correct although different.

When relying on occupations to verify an ancestor it is wise to remember that some occupations had several descriptions but the meaning could be the same.

The line beginning with 'married in'

After rites and ceremonies underneath the details of the couple married, the last part starting with the word 'by' and followed with 'by me' or 'after and by me' will have the following possibilities:

♦ 'by certificate' = found on a register office marriage and shows that the couple gave three weeks' notice,

♦ 'by licence' = means the couple may have married with less than three weeks' notice. Maybe they needed to marry in a hurry or maybe there was another reason for the short notice, such as moving away,

♦ 'after banns' = Church of England marriage,

♦ 'by common licence' = Church of England marriage meaning a licence has been granted by the Bishop of the diocese,

♦ 'by special licence' = Church of England, with the licence issued by the Archbishop allowing the couple to marry in a church of their choice,

- 'by registrar generals' = found on any denomination except if a marriage was by the Church of England rites, the licence was issued for special reasons allowing a couple to get married at any time or place due to the impending death of one of the party,

- 'by superintendent registrars certificate' = a Church of England marriage but instead of banns being called in the church publicly, notice of marriage has been given to the superintendent registrar. Reasons for this could include a need to keep the marriage private by the church or for the party in question. Having banns read out meant that anyone could view these records and create problems for the couple in question if perhaps one was of another religion or latterly if a couple was divorced.

The signatures at the bottom of the certificate

These signatures include those of the married couple and their witnesses. Although they are supposed to be signatures, their names are frequently written in full and do not give a true indication of a proper signature for verification purposes.

Generally, witnesses should be personally known to the bride or groom but again it is possible that the witnesses have been hired or pulled in from the street in some instances. Witnesses should be carefully scrutinised as more often than not they can be family members, married sisters, nieces or nephews, brothers or sisters, mothers, aunts and uncles. Usually there are two witnesses but sometimes you will find several witnesses on a certificate.

The last signature on the certificate is for the person or persons conducting the ceremony. Register office marriages have two signatures which are those of the superintendent conducting the ceremony and that of the registrar who is doing the registration. The Church of England marriages have just the signature of the cleric, in the main.

The certificate has the date the certificate was issued, the same day usually. If there are any corrections to be made on a marriage certificate you will find these in the space to the right of the certificate, otherwise you will find a line drawn through it. Although it is possible to find corrections have been added after a line was drawn through this space.

Step 1 - Continued . . .

Each piece of information is a valuable source and should be studied at length. We now have the exact date of the marriage. We also have the age at the time of the marriage of both parties giving us a huge clue to finding birth certificates but also the names of each of their fathers, taking us to another generation.

As stated earlier, witnesses should not be discounted. In the case of Albert Marelli the witnesses appear to be no relation, but a female member of the Marelli family may have married someone by the name of Spiller. Quite often you will find that witnesses are other family members and therefore should always be investigated.

An interesting point to the Marelli family is the fact that Albert was a motor mechanic, as was his son, grandson and great grandson. Facts like these provide a window into the lives of your ancestors.

What this marriage certificate doesn't give us is the birthplace of both Lilian and Albert.

Step 2 - Options available to source birth records

I now have two options to follow:

1. The 1901 Census – as both parties were living at this time or as both parties have unusual names, i.e. Marelli and Lilian Lucretia, I could try the birth index.

2. For this exercise I am going to search births and my first port of call again is going to be FreeBMD.

Search

To search FreeBMD enter the details of the search below. A fuller explanation of how to get the most out of your search is here. To hold down CTRL as you click the mouse. The earliest possible date is 1837.

Service Status

(Valid at 16 August 2006)

Following the deployment of additional hardware, the search capacity of FreeBMD is much improved. We are now closely monitoring performan needs

---

Type	All Types / Births / Deaths / Marriages	Districts	All Districts / Aberayron (to Jun1936) / Aberconwy (from Sep1975) / Abergavenny (to 1958) / Aberystwyth (to Jun1936) / Abingdon / Acle (1939-Mar1974) / Alcester / Alderbury (to Jun1895) / Aldershot (Dec1932-Mar1974) / Aldridge & Brownhills (Jun1966-Mar1974) / Aled (Dec1935-Mar1974) / Alnwick (to 1936) / Alresford (to Sep1932)
Surname	Marelli		
First name(s)	Albert		
Spouse/Mother surname			
Spouse first name(s)			
Death age/DoB			
Date range	Mar ▼ to Dec ▼		
Volume/Page	/	Counties	All Counties / Anglesey (to Mar1974) / Avon (from Jun1974) / Bedfordshire / Berkshire
Options	☐ Mono / ☐ Exact match on first names / ☐ Phonetic search surnames		

Step 1: Search by name. As Albert's surname is uncommon in the UK this was the only search criteria I used.

New Query   Save Search

Revise Query   Download

Key

	Births	Marriages	Deaths	An entry in **Bold** means it has been double keyed	A district in *Italic* means it is suspect (click on it for details)	Information available: ↗ Scan ? Comment ✉ Postem
Change of shade means a *possible* gap in the data						

Search for *Type:* Births *Surname:* Marelli *First name(s):* Albert

Whilst FreeBMD makes every effort to ensure accurate transcription, errors exist in both the original index and the transcription. You are advised to verify the reference given from a copy of the inde: before ordering a certificate. If an entry has the symbol ↗ next to it you can view the scan of the GRO index page from which the transcription was made in order to verify the reference. Click on the · symbol to view the scan.

If you are SURE that our transcription(s) below differs from the GRO index, you can submit a correction request by clicking on the Info button to the right of the entry in question.

Surname First name(s) District Vol Page

Births Mar 1893

Marelli   Albert   Lambeth 1d 363   Info ↗

Step 2: Here he is. Albert's birth certificate index details.

I can be fairly certain that this is my Albert as he married in 1912, aged 19. Taking 19 from 1912 = 1893, but looking at his birth certificate you can see although his birth-date is 1892 he was not registered until 1893.

I wonder if locating Lilian's birth details will be as simple – apparently so, this time.

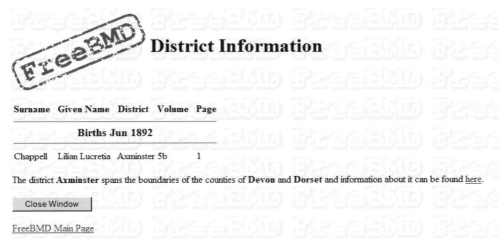

District Information

Surname	Given Name	District	Volume	Page
Births Jun 1892				
Chappell	Lilian Lucretia	Axminster	5b	1

The district **Axminster** spans the boundaries of the counties of **Devon** and **Dorset** and information about it can be found here.

[Close Window]

FreeBMD Main Page

Step 3: Lilian's birth details.

Do I have the correct record? Yes, I think so. There was only one birth that came up on my search for Lilian Lucretia but it is important to remember that FreeBMD is an ongoing project and not yet complete. Therefore I have a seed of doubt at this juncture even though the year is correct, i.e. 20 – 1912 = 1892, because the birthplace is Axminster! So where is Axminster and how did Lilian end up in Wandsworth? I decided to click on the spectacles and save a PDF file of this index for Lilian and then look into the registration district by clicking on 'Axminster' on the information line, to find out more about the registration district of Axminster.

> It is important to remember facts you collect along the way such as that Lilian was born in Axminster but married in London. I would discover later that she moved to work in service.

Step 3 - Sourcing district information

  GENUKI Contents  List of Counties

REGISTRATION DISTRICTS IN DEVONSHIRE

The list below shows the civil registration districts in the county of Devon (Devonshire) between 1st July 1837 and 31st March 1930. The same districts were used to compile the censuses returns for the years 1851, 1861, 1871, 1881, 1891 and 1901.

Click on a district name to see the places and dates covered, or see the Index of Place-Names for the whole of England and Wales (1837-1930).

- Axminster
- Barnstaple
- Bideford
- Chard
- Crediton
- Devonport
- Dulverton
- East Stonehouse
- Exeter
- Holsworthy
- Honiton
- Kingsbridge
- Launceston
- Newton Abbot
- Okehampton
- Plymouth
- Plympton St. Mary
- St. Thomas
- South Molton
- Stoke Damerel
- Taunton
- Tavistock
- Tiverton
- Torrington
- Totnes
- Wellington

Step 4: Select Axminster or the district of interest.

  GENUKI Contents List of Districts

AXMINSTER REGISTRATION DISTRICT

Registration County : Devonshire.
Created : 1.7.1837.
Sub-districts : Axminster; Chardstock; Colyton; Lyme.
GRO volumes: X (1837-51); 5b (1852-1930).

Parishes in Devonshire (1837-1930):

Axminster, Axminster Hamlets, Axmouth, Beer, Chardstock (from 1896), Colyton, Combpyne, Dalwood (from 1844), Hawkchurch (from 1896), Kilmington, Membury, Musbury, Rousdon, Seaton, Shute, Stockland (from 1844), Thorncombe (1844-96), Uplyme.

Parishes in Dorset (1837-96):

Chardstock (1837-96), Charmouth (1837-96), Dalwood (1837-44), Hawkchurch (1837-96), Lyme Regis, Stockland (1837-44), Thorncombe (1837-44).

Registers now divided between East Devon *and* South & West Dorset *districts.*

Step 5: This information comes from GENUKI http://www.genuki.org.uk/contents/ a wonderful site offering masses of information for the family historian.

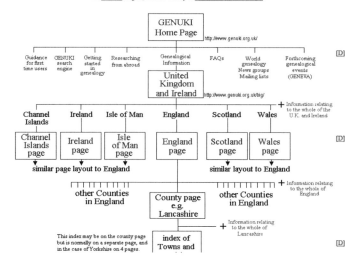

GENUKI site map

As I have details from Lilian's marriage certificate, I know that she was alive in 1901. I also know that she would have been roughly 9 years old and that her father was Frederick Stone Chappell. So the next step will be to search the 1901 Census for Lilian Chappell with a father called Frederick Stone Chappell in the Axminster area, presuming that she might still be living there as a child, unless the whole family moved to the Wandsworth area.

Step 4 - 1901 Census

Go to the www.Ancestry.co.uk site on the Internet. You will need to register to view records on this site but there are cost options available. See the tips at the end of this chapter.

Once you have registered, select the 1901 Census for England.

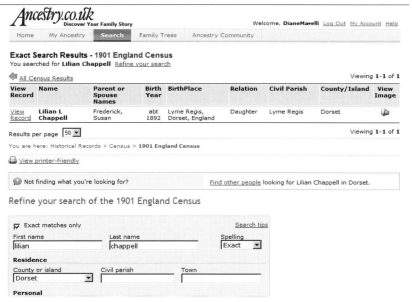

Copyright © 1998–2006, MyFamily.com Inc. and its subsidiaries

Step 6: Key in your search criteria.

Copyright © 1998–2006, MyFamily.com Inc. and its subsidiaries

Step 7: The details. Unusually, only one match has come up in this instance.

1901 England Census Record
about Lilian L Chappell

Name:	**Lilian L Chappell**
Age:	9
Estimated Birth Year:	abt 1892
Relation:	Daughter
Father's name:	Frederick
Mother's name:	Susan
Gender:	Female
Where born:	Lyme Regis, Dorset, England
Civil parish:	Lyme Regis
Ecclesiastical parish:	Lyme Regis St Michael the Archangel
Town:	Lyme Regis
County/Island:	Dorset
Country:	England
Street address:	
Occupation:	
Condition as to marriage:	View image
Education:	
Employment status:	
Registration district:	Axminster
Sub-registration district:	Lyme
ED, institution, or vessel:	2
Neighbors:	View others on page
Household schedule number:	246

View Original Record

View original image

View blank form

Household Members:

Name	Age
Frederick Chappell	50
Frederick R Chappell	13
Lilian L Chappell	9
Susan Chappell	49

Step 8: Select to view the record.

As you can see the age and year of birth is right.

Step 9: View the original. Other family members are shown if you scroll down the screen.

This looks as if it could be the correct record because it lists a Frederick Chappell as head of the family, as per her marriage certificate, and Lilian L. Chappell as daughter. You can now print a copy or save to file.

Lyme Regis is listed in the Genuki information above as being part of the registration district of Axminster. Let's take a closer look at the information recorded on the 1891 Census compared with the 1901 Census.

Copyright © 1998–2006, MyFamily.com Inc. and its subsidiaries
The 1891 Census form

Copyright © 1998–2006, MyFamily.com Inc. and its subsidiaries
The 1901 Census form

If you compare the two you will see how little information was taken in 1841 compared with the later census.

1841 Census Form

Ancestry.com

For more family history charts and forms,
visit www.ancestry.com/save/charts/census.htm

PLACE	HOUSES		NAMES of each Person who abode therein the preceeding Night.	AGE and SEX		PROFESSION, TRADE, EMPLOYMENT, or of INDEPENDENT MEANS.	Where Born		
	Uninhabited or Building	Inhabited		Males	Females		Whether Born in same County	Whether Born in Scotland, Ireland, or Foreign Parts.	

Country: _____ H.O./ _____ Book: _____ Folio: _____ Page: _____ E.D.: _____

Copyright © 1998–2006, MyFamily.com Inc. and its subsidiaries
Detail of 1841 Census form

But by as early as 1851 the information recorded on the census had become more informative.

Ancestry.com

1851 Census Form

For more family history charts and forms,
visit www.ancestry.com/save/charts/census.htm

Country: _____ Piece #: H.O./ _____ Folio: _____ Page: _____ Enumeration District: _____

The undermentioned Houses are situate within the Boundaries of the

	Name of Street, Place, or Road, and Name or No. of House	Name and Surname of each Person who abode in the house, on the Night of the 30th March, 1851	Relation to Head of Family	Condition	Age of		Rank, Profession, or Occupation	Where Born	Whether Blind, or Deaf and-Dumb
					Males	Females			

Parish or Township of	Ecclesiastical District of	City or Borough of	Town of	Village of

Copyright © 1998–2006, MyFamily.com Inc. and its subsidiaries
The 1851 Census form

The 1851 Census forms offer a lot of important information to be gleaned about your ancestors and their neighbours. When recording information taken from the Census it is important to document the following:

Piece: RG13/ and the number following, i.e. RG13 / 1567
Folio number
Page number
Enumeration district
Administrative county
Civil parish
Parish
Town or hamlet

If for any reason the information you source is different from what you expected or what your family expected, don't forget to write an explanation as to why you believe you have the correct ancestor and how you sourced them.

Don't neglect to look at surrounding Census pages as sometimes you will find other family members. Also other pages will provide you with information about their social history and status in a community. Types of things to look for would be size and type of property, did they share accommodation and were they the lodgers or the landlords. In what kind of accommodation did their immediate neighbours reside? What kind of occupations did your ancestors have and their neighbours? These and other facts are all great indicators of the social history of your ancestors.

I now have details of Lilian's brother and his age, her father's age and the name of her mother, Susan, and Susan's age. Having produced such a result for the Chappell family on the 1901 Census, the next most obvious step is to look for information concerning the Marelli family in 1901 and this is what I found.

Employment status:	♪
Registration district:	Wandsworth
Sub-registration district:	Southwest Battersea
ED, institution, or vessel:	14
Neighbors:	View others on page
Household schedule number:	227

Household Members:

Name	Age
Ada Marelli	20
Albert Marelli	8
Amelia Marelli	6
Amy Marelli	33
Amy Marelli	3
Kathleen Marelli	1
Martine Marelli	49
Matilda Marelli	18
William Marelli	5
William Plummer	56

Copyright © 1998–2006, MyFamily.com Inc. and its subsidiaries
Ages of the Marelli family

What an amazing outcome! When I viewed the original Census, I found Albert Marelli and his whole family. What is more thrilling is the name of Martino's father-in-law, William Plummer.

> The relationship of persons is always related to the head of the household, although you do get errors.

So Albert's mother is Amy Marelli née Plummer, and yes, thanks to the Census, we can go back another generation on this branch of the family tree, as we now have the name of Amy's father.

There is a bit of a mystery though. Amy Plummer was born in 1868 but Ada, her daughter, was born in 1881 and Matilda, another daughter, in 1883. That means Amy would have been only aged 13 and 15 respectively when they were born. Martino must have been married previously or Amy was a child bride!

Step 5 - Reading certificates and types of certificates

Again, I already had copies of these certificates and we are going to look at them next for two very interesting reasons.

As you can see, Lilian Chappell's certificate is typed and provides us with the information required to trace another branch of our tree, that of Susan Chappell née Lugg who is the mother of Lilian. What is of particular interest to me is that this certified copy of her birth was issued for the purposes of Widow's Orphan's and Old Age Contributory Pensions on 19th March 1948.

Lilian Chappell's birth certificate

The next birth certificate for Albert Marelli was produced in compliance with the National Insurance Act of 1911 as required by The Oddfellows Society. The schedule was filled in by the person concerned, then sent to the superintendent registrar of the district of Albert's birth where the birth certificate details were copied onto the back of the form.

Albert Marelli's birth certificate

Birth certificate in compliance with the National Insurance Act, 1911

When searching for a birth certificate record in Civil Registration it is important to remember that a child was not always registered at the time of birth. Very often it was a few months or a few years later, or in some cases you will discover that a birth was never registered.

Certificates should be studied meticulously for information that will help you build the story of your ancestry.

Step 6 - Updated family tree

Although I am tempted to add other family members I have discovered via the Census, for the benefit of clarity I have resisted the temptation!

I still think it's pretty impressive for the amount of work carried out this far.

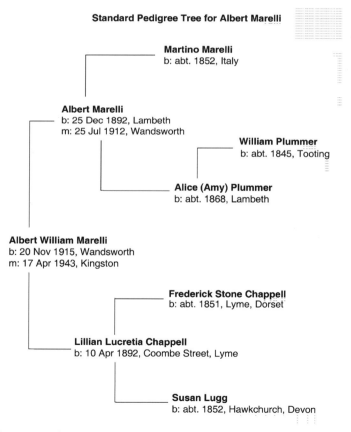

Standard Pedigree Tree for Albert Marelli

- **Martino Marelli**
  b: abt. 1852, Italy

Albert Marelli
b: 25 Dec 1892, Lambeth
m: 25 Jul 1912, Wandsworth

- **William Plummer**
  b: abt. 1845, Tooting

Alice (Amy) Plummer
b: abt. 1868, Lambeth

Albert William Marelli
b: 20 Nov 1915, Wandsworth
m: 17 Apr 1943, Kingston

- **Frederick Stone Chappell**
  b: abt. 1851, Lyme, Dorset

Lillian Lucretia Chappell
b: 10 Apr 1892, Coombe Street, Lyme

- **Susan Lugg**
  b: abt. 1852, Hawkchurch, Devon

Updated family tree so far

There are many facts that should be added to our database, such as sources like the Census and certificates we have gathered, but we will look at storing and recording your family history later in this book.

Recap

1. Resource a marriage certificate from information taken from a birth certificate, or acquire a marriage certificate of parent, grandparent etc.

2. A marriage certificate will provide you with ages of both parties, enabling you to source their birth certificates and the names and occupations of their fathers, which in turn will enable you to source their fathers' marriage certificates.

3. Choose the most cost effective option, i.e. FreeBMD to source records before moving on to paying sites.

4. If a person you are looking for was alive at the time a Census was taken, use this resource to help you find other documents.

5. Record all the reference information found on a Census page for future generations to source, and for referral purposes.

6. Keep all your records together with a sketched tree of your findings if you don't already have relevant software.

7. The total cost so far is:

Annual UK Deluxe Membership with Ancestry.co.uk	£69.95
Cost of three certificates	£21.00
Total	**£90.00**

Tips

1. Remember, if you plan to use Ancestry.co.uk on a regular basis, then an annual membership is far more cost-effective. There are cheaper options such as monthly or pay-per-view. Alternatively you can pay via findmypast.com which I will show you in the next chapter.

2. Don't run out and purchase software to store your information without investigating the various packages available. More information about software in Chapter 5.

3. Study the pages surrounding the address of your ancestor. Viewing other Census pages (neighbours) could produce other family members and will provide information about their social history.

4. Study certificates thoroughly. When purchasing several at once, it is easy to miss a valuable piece of information. Keep going back over documents every so often. It is amazing what comes to light as you become more experienced.

5. Study the sites available and find out what other resources they offer; they are being updated on a regular basis.

6. Try to remain focused on the person or persons you are searching for. It is easy to get sidelined into other members of the family such as finding siblings on the Census. Print off copies or record the information for researching or adding to your family histories when you have completed the task in hand.

7. If for any reason the information you source is different from what you expected or what your family expected don't forget to write an explanation as to why you believe you have the correct ancestor and how you sourced them.

8. When searching for birth certificate records in Civil Registration remember that a child was not always registered at the time of birth, very often it was a few months, a few years later, or in some cases you will discover that a birth was never registered.

3

Births, marriages and the Census

Step 1 - The 1901 Census analysis

My next step is to find the marriage certificate for Martino Marelli and his
wife. Thanks to the 1901 Census, I will also source Amy's birth certificate,
as I have learnt her maiden name, approximate year of birth and birthplace.
Hopefully, you will have similar information about your own family.

Employment status:	
Registration district:	Wandsworth
Sub-registration district:	Southwest Battersea
ED, institution, or vessel:	14
Neighbors:	View others on page
Household schedule number:	227

Household Members:

Name	Age
Ada Marelli	20
Albert Marelli	8
Amelia Marelli	6
Amy Marelli	33
Amy Marelli	3
Kathleen Marelli	1
Martine Marelli	49
Matilda Marelli	18
William Marelli	5
William Plummer	56

Information from the 1901 Census to further my research

Before heading off to search for a marriage or other certificate, I suggest you analyse the information you found on the 1901 Census. In my case it raised some questions. Was Amy only 13 years old when her first child was born? If so, then why was there a ten-year gap between the ages of two of their children? (Matilda born in 1883 and Albert born in 1893). Could Martino have been married twice?

If the ten-year gap indicates a possible second marriage I have to presume that the second marriage took place close to 1893. Therefore, I have decided to look at the 1891 Census for Martino and family for clarification of my suspicions.

Step 2 - 1891 Census analysis

Log on to your chosen Census resource website, in my case Ancestry.co.uk, and select the Census year 1891.

Keying in the name Martino Marelli produced no results. So I tried using just the surname of Marelli. This produced five persons with the surname Marelli. Unfortunately, none was related to my family.

Now I had two choices. I could search the whole parish of Battersea in the district of Lambeth, and hope that he was living there at the time, or I could try some surname spelling variations. I keyed in Marelli and chose to have a Soundex search (a search that would produce spelling variations of the surname Marelli), which gave me over 29,000 results. So I tried again using varying information about the location such as Battersea and Lambeth, using spellings such as Mirilli, Morrelli, Murelli etc. and still nothing! Did this mean trawling through 29,000 results or, worse, searching the whole of Lambeth in the hope that the Marelli family was living there in 1891. With a name like Marelli, I expected this to be far simpler, so what other information do I have that is uncommon that would help my search?

Eventually, it hit me like a sledgehammer! I decided to try anyone born in Italy now living in Lambeth.

This produced 33 results and only one that looked possible, Martins Marcelli:

| View Record | Martins Marcelli | abt 1854 | Italy | Head | Lambeth | London | |

Clicking on 'View Record' produced the following information:

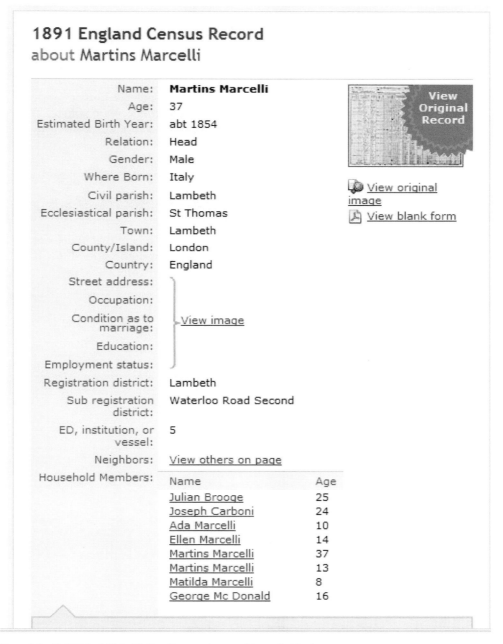

1891 England Census Record
about Martins Marcelli

Name:	**Martins Marcelli**
Age:	37
Estimated Birth Year:	abt 1854
Relation:	Head
Gender:	Male
Where Born:	Italy
Civil parish:	Lambeth
Ecclesiastical parish:	St Thomas
Town:	Lambeth
County/Island:	London
Country:	England
Street address:	
Occupation:	
Condition as to marriage:	View image
Education:	
Employment status:	
Registration district:	Lambeth
Sub registration district:	Waterloo Road Second
ED, institution, or vessel:	5
Neighbors:	View others on page

View Original Record

View original image
View blank form

Household Members:

Name	Age
Julian Brooge	25
Joseph Carboni	24
Ada Marcelli	10
Ellen Marcelli	14
Martins Marcelli	37
Martins Marcelli	13
Matilda Marcelli	8
George Mc Donald	16

Census record for Martins Marcelli

Viewing the original told me I had the correct record, even though transcribed incorrectly. Not only had I found another daughter of Martino born in 1877, making it impossible for Amy to be her mother, the original document also told me that Martino was a widower. There is also information about a nephew, George McDonald.

Always check as many variations of a spelling as possible before going through laborious searches of districts – although this does produce results, it is time consuming. Even when you have a rare surname it does not mean searching will be straightforward.

Look for information pertaining to your family that makes them stand out from the norm when having difficulty searching.

Ancestry also provides a sample of handwriting used in the original Census returns. Select a Census year and on the right of the screen you will find downloadable blank Census forms and sample handwriting.

ORIGINAL IMAGES

The **1891 Census**
is provided in
association with:

A

the national archives

This database contains images of original records. The following resources may be helpful to you.

Sample Forms
Download blank Census forms
You can fill out the form with information on your ancestor, or just use it to better read the column headings.

Handwriting Help
View a sampling of handwriting examples
The examples should help you read the text on the original images more easily.

Aa	Bb	Cc	Dd	Ee	Ff	Gg	Hh	Ii	Jj	Kk	Ll	Mm	Nn	Oo	Pp	Qq	Rr	Ss	Tt	Uu	Vv	Ww	Xx	Yy	Zz

Handwriting sample

The information I now have about Martino is that he was previously married probably pre-1877, when his daughter Ellen was born, and between 1891 (Martino is a widower on the 1891 Census) and 1893, when Albert Marelli was born. I decided to look for both marriage certificates, because the second marriage provides direct ancestors to my husband, and, from the first marriage, the children of Martino and Ellen are half-ancestors.

Step 3 - FreeBMD and marriage search

A quick check in FreeBMD produced the following:

© Crown copyright. Published by permission of the Controller of HMSO and the Office for National Statistics.
You must not copy on, transfer or reproduce records without the prior permission of ONS.
Search engine, layout and database Copyright © 1998-2005 The Trustees of FreeBMD (Ben Laurie, Graham Hart, Camilla von Massenbach and David Mayall), a charity registered in England and Wales, Number 1096940.
We make no warranty whatsoever as to the accuracy or completeness of the FreeBMD data.
Use of the FreeBMD website is conditional upon acceptance of the Terms and Conditions

New Query   Save Search   Download

Key   Births Marriages Deaths   An entry in **Bold** means it has been double keyed   A district in *Italic* means it is suspect (click on it for details)   Information available:
Change of shade means a possible gap in the data   Scan   ? Comment   ✉ Postem

Revise Query

Search for *Type:* Marriages *Surname:* Marelli *First name(s):* Martino

Whilst FreeBMD makes every effort to ensure accurate transcription, errors exist in both the original index and the transcription. You are advised to verify the reference given from a copy of the index before ordering a certificate. If an entry has the symbol next to it you can view the scan of the GRO index page from which the transcription was made in order to verify the reference. Click on the symbol to view the scan.

If you are SURE that our transcription(s) below differs from the GRO index, you can submit a correction request by clicking on the Info button to the right of the entry in question.

Surname	First name(s)	District	Vol	Page
Marriages Mar 1875				
MARELLI	Martino	Holborn	1b	877	Info
Marriages Dec 1891				
Marelli	Martino	St. Saviour	1d	505	Info

Dates of marriages for Martino Marelli

As you can see, there are two marriages listed for Martino; one in 1875 and one in 1891. I already have Lilian Chappell and Albert Marelli. For the purpose of this exercise please see below both marriage certificates for Martino (see also Chapter 1, Step 4).

Martino's first marriage to Ellen McDonald

The surname McDonald tells me that the George McDonald found on the 1891 Census is a relative/nephew of Martino's by marriage. What is odd is that Martino lists his father's name as Martino and gives him the same profession as himself, although he was an orphan and supposedly could not have this knowledge. But it is the second marriage that interests me because it follows the direct family line.

Marriage between Martino Marelli and Amy Alice Plummer

This certificate shows us that Martino records his father as Angelo Marelli, a farmer. The witnesses at this marriage appear to be William Plummer, Amy's father and Ellen Marelli, Martino's daughter. It also shows us that Amy's father is William Plummer as we discovered on the 1901 Census and confirms that Amy was born in about 1867. I can now add this information to the family tree, listing sources, and look for a birth certificate for Amy Plummer.

Step 4 - Birth certificate and the Census

Out of several possibilities using FreeBMD, I found the following record for Alice Amy Plummer:

Births Dec 1867

| Plummer | Alice Amy | | Lambeth | 1d | 281 | [Info] |

Details for Amy Alice Plummer

This was the only result that seemed possible even with the first names reversed, but before purchasing this birth certificate, I decided to verify the information via the 1871 Census since Amy or Alice was alive in 1871. I tried several variations of the name Plummer using both Alice and Amy and her father's name of William. I could find no records of this family on the 1871 Census – very frustrating. I moved to the 1881 Census.

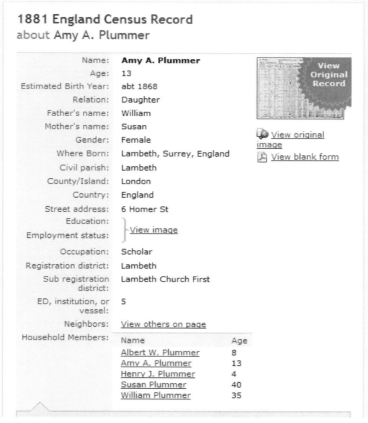

1881 England Census Record
about Amy A. Plummer

Name:	**Amy A. Plummer**
Age:	13
Estimated Birth Year:	abt 1868
Relation:	Daughter
Father's name:	William
Mother's name:	Susan
Gender:	Female
Where Born:	Lambeth, Surrey, England
Civil parish:	Lambeth
County/Island:	London
Country:	England
Street address:	6 Homer St
Education:	
Employment status:	View image
Occupation:	Scholar
Registration district:	Lambeth
Sub registration district:	Lambeth Church First
ED, institution, or vessel:	5
Neighbors:	View others on page

Household Members:	Name	Age
	Albert W. Plummer	8
	Amy A. Plummer	13
	Henry J. Plummer	4
	Susan Plummer	40
	William Plummer	35

View original image
View blank form

Census record for Amy Alice Plummer

The information also gives me details of Amy's siblings and the name of her mother plus approximate birth-dates and locations for each concerned. Although pleased to have found Amy in the 1881 Census, I felt irritated that I hadn't found her on the 1871 Census, so I went back and, based on the above information, I was a little more creative.

Previous searches for both William and Amy/Alice Plummer produced nothing, so this time I keyed in Susan Plummer – still nothing! In frustration, I put in the following information:

1871 England Census

☑ Exact matches only   Search tips

First name   **Last name**   **Spelling**
Susan   Exact ▼

Residence
County or island   **Civil Parish or Township**   **Town**
All available counties ▼

Personal
Gender   **Relationship to head of household**   **Birth Year**
Any ▼   +/- 0 ▼

Birthplace
Country   **County or island**   **Parish or place**
england   Wiltshire   Melksham

Family Members
Father's Given Name(s)

Mother's Given Name(s)

Spouse's Given Name(s)

Census
        Piece   Folio   Page #   Keyword(s)
RG10/

▲ **Hide Advanced Search Options**   **Search**

Searching by Christian name and location of birth

The search produced the following:

| View Record | **Susan Plumlee** | William | abt 1841 | Melksham, Wiltshire, England | Wife | Lambeth | London | |

Out of 16 possible Susans born in Melksham, the most likely was the above record. I clicked on 'View Record' and then 'View Others in Household' and I knew I had my Plummers! The original record confirmed this, listing William's occupation as railway porter (on Amy's marriage certificate dated 1891 William is a railway signalman), and of course Amy as a child.

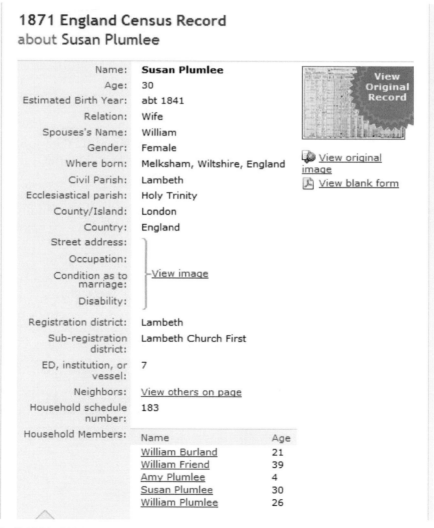

1871 England Census Record
about Susan Plumlee

Name:	**Susan Plumlee**
Age:	30
Estimated Birth Year:	abt 1841
Relation:	Wife
Spouses's Name:	William
Gender:	Female
Where born:	Melksham, Wiltshire, England
Civil Parish:	Lambeth
Ecclesiastical parish:	Holy Trinity
County/Island:	London
Country:	England
Street address:	
Occupation:	
Condition as to marriage:	View image
Disability:	
Registration district:	Lambeth
Sub-registration district:	Lambeth Church First
ED, institution, or vessel:	7
Neighbors:	View others on page
Household schedule number:	183

View Original Record

View original image

View blank form

Household Members:

Name	Age
William Burland	21
William Friend	39
Amy Plumlee	4
Susan Plumlee	30
William Plumlee	26

Census record for Susan Plumlee

As I now have information about Martino's second wife Amy, a direct ancestor, and her parents, my next step is to source her birth certificate which will provide me with the maiden name of her mother before moving to Albert's in-laws, the Chappells.

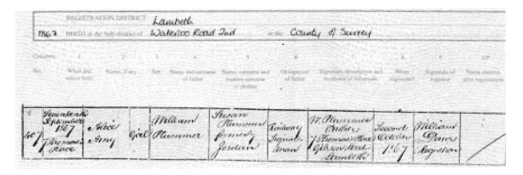

Birth certificate for Alice Amy Plummer

As you can see, Amy's mother was formerly a Jordan and further confirmation that I have the correct certificate is William's occupation. The next obvious step is to locate the marriage certificate for William and Susan.

FreeBMD produced the following marriage search on William Plummer and, by viewing others on the same page, the name Susan Jordan also appears, confirming I had the right information.

Surname	First name(s)	District	Vol	Page
Marriages Dec 1865				
Jordan	Susan	Lambeth	1d	719
Plummer	William	Lambeth	1d	719

Details of Susan and William

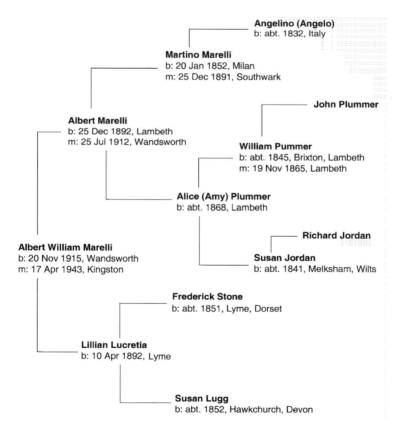

Marriage certificate for William Plummer and Susan Jordan

I now have details of William's and Susan's fathers, plus their occupations and therefore another generation. This certificate also tells me that William's father was deceased by 1865. I can now add this information to the family tree.

Angelino (Angelo)
b: abt. 1832, Italy

Martino Marelli
b: 20 Jan 1852, Milan
m: 25 Dec 1891, Southwark

Albert Marelli
b: 25 Dec 1892, Lambeth
m: 25 Jul 1912, Wandsworth

John Plummer

William Pummer
b: abt. 1845, Brixton, Lambeth
m: 19 Nov 1865, Lambeth

Alice (Amy) Plummer
b: abt. 1868, Lambeth

Albert William Marelli
b: 20 Nov 1915, Wandsworth
m: 17 Apr 1943, Kingston

Richard Jordan

Susan Jordan
b: abt. 1841, Melksham, Wilts

Frederick Stone
b: abt. 1851, Lyme, Dorset

Lillian Lucretia
b: 10 Apr 1892, Lyme

Susan Lugg
b: abt. 1852, Hawkchurch, Devon

The tree so far with the additional information and approximate information taken from Census records

Recap

1. Analyse Census data.

2. Decide if your next step would be better served by reviewing other Census data or by searching BMD certificates.

3. If choosing the Census for further clues it is almost guaranteed that you will have problems with misspellings. Be creative, study the information you have and think of other search options if you can't find what you are looking for.

4. Reading original data can sometimes be difficult. Find examples of 19th century writing to help decipher original documents.

5. Use the Census to provide you with approximate birth-dates to source birth certificates.

6. Use the Census to provide clues for finding marriage certificates.

7. The total cost so far is:

Annual UK Deluxe Membership with Ancestry.co.uk	£ 69.95
Cost of eight certificates	£ 56.00
Total	**£125.95**

Tips

1. A marriage certificate provides information about the births of both parties concerned and gives the names of the father of both parties.

2. A birth certificate provides clues to a marriage date and will give you the maiden name of the mother.

3. Always check as many variations of a spelling as possible before going through laborious searches of districts – although this does produce results, it is time consuming.

4. Even when you have a rare surname it does not mean searching will be straightforward.

5. Look for information pertaining to your family that makes them stand out from the crowd when having difficulty searching, e.g. first name or location of birth, etc.

6. The information found on the Census can vary from Census to Census, so treat the contents as approximate in terms of age, place of birth and so on, until you have other evidence to back it up.

4

Death certificates and the Census

Looking at our family tree, for those for whom I have birth and marriage certificates, I now need to source death certificates. As you can see below, I already have Albert (Bert) Marelli's death certificate as he died only recently, so I am going to look for the death certificates initially for Albert Marelli and then Martino Marelli who both died during the 20th Century.

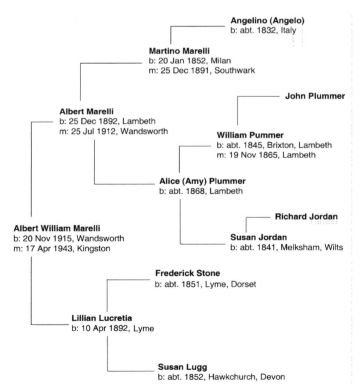

Angelino (Angelo)
b: abt. 1832, Italy

Martino Marelli
b: 20 Jan 1852, Milan
m: 25 Dec 1891, Southwark

Albert Marelli
b: 25 Dec 1892, Lambeth
m: 25 Jul 1912, Wandsworth

John Plummer

William Pummer
b: abt. 1845, Brixton, Lambeth
m: 19 Nov 1865, Lambeth

Alice (Amy) Plummer
b: abt. 1868, Lambeth

Albert William Marelli
b: 20 Nov 1915, Wandsworth
m: 17 Apr 1943, Kingston

Richard Jordan

Susan Jordan
b: abt. 1841, Melksham, Wilts

Frederick Stone
b: abt. 1851, Lyme, Dorset

Lillian Lucretia
b: 10 Apr 1892, Lyme

Susan Lugg
b: abt. 1852, Hawkchurch, Devon

Ancestors of Albert William

For part of this exercise I am going to use findmypast.com to help source death certificates subsequent to the 1901 Census.

Step 1 - Sourcing death certificates

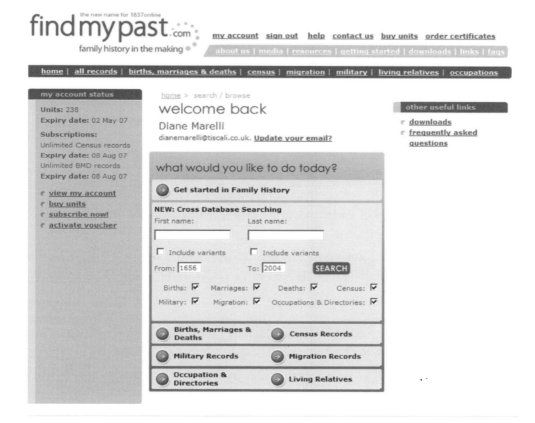

Once you have logged in you will be taken to the above screen.

The first death certificate I am going to look for is that of Albert Marelli, father of Albert William and grandfather of Brian Marelli, my husband. As Albert William is no longer with us, I asked Brian if he could remember his grandfather. After giving the question some thought, he believed his grandfather was still living during the 1970s but couldn't give an exact date.

My search years, to begin with, will be the decade of the 1970s and if I don't find a record of his death during this decade, I will search five years prior to

1970 and five years subsequent to 1980, and keep following this process until I achieve a result.

Looking at the login page of findmypast.com, select Deaths 1837 to 1983.

As you can see above, I have typed in the criteria for my search: event, date range from/to, and the name of the person I am searching for. Then I clicked on 'Search'.

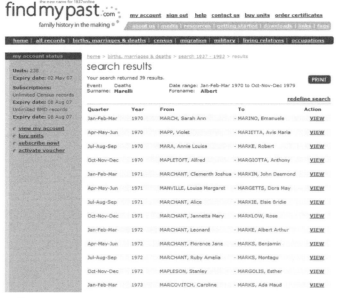

The search results.

The above is a part-view of the result of my search. Each year is split into quarters, i.e. Jan-Feb-Mar (March Quarter), Apr-May-Jun (June Quarter) and so on. It also lists alphabetically, from and to, the pages that house your ancestor by surname spelling, i.e. the surname March to Marino for the January quarter of 1970.

We can now start viewing our search pages as we would if we were to visit the FRC. After a reasonably short time, I found the Civil Registration details of Albert Marelli who died in the third quarter of 1974. Below is a copy of the detail at the top of the page and the registration of death for Albert. In later registers you will find the date of birth, which, in this case, I know to be correct, giving me further confirmation that I now have the correct death certificate.

Detail of the registration of death for Albert Marelli.

If you now go back to Chapter 1, Step 4, you can order a copy of the certificate you have just sourced, if you want to, or leave it until placing a larger order.

My next search is for Martino. Brian has no recollection of his great grandfather in living memory, so I can presume that he died prior to 1943, but I need a start date to commence my search. I know he was alive in 1901 but I do have a further clue. The marriage certificate of Albert to Lilian Chappell, dated July 1912, does not state that Martino is deceased (see Chapter 2, page 25).

If searching for a death certificate during the 20th Century, check if the person was still living in 1901 via the Census.

So my search years for Martino were September 1912 until at least December 1943, but first I checked FreeBMD – unfortunately Martino was not as yet listed. Using findmypast.com I put in my search criteria and checked each quarter for each year since September 1912 and was very despondent when my search reached the beginning of the Second World War. He would be in his late eighties by then. Finally, in the March quarter of 1940, I found the registration details for Martino's death. If I had started at 1943 and worked backwards I could have reduced my search time. Never mind, these things happen all the time.

345

DEATHS REGISTERED IN JANUARY, FEBRUARY AND MARCH, 1940.

Age.	District.		Vol.	Page.			
Marelli, Martino			88	Battersea		1 d	607

Details of the registration of death for Martino Marelli.

Again, you can now go back to Chapter 1, Step 4 and order a copy of the certificate you have just sourced.

I also sourced the death certificate for Amy Plummer who died in 1912 in Wandsworth and Frederick Stone Chappell, who died in Lyme Regis in 1924. I knew from the details of his daughter's marriage to Albert Marelli in 1912 that he was still living at this time, so I took my search from there and found him in 1924. However for his wife, Susan Chappell, née Lugg, I broke the cardinal rule and went off at a tangent before sensibleness took over, eventually! I knew from the 1901 Census that Susan Chappell, née Lugg, was still living at this time. What I couldn't fathom from Frederick's death certificate was if she was still alive when he died in 1924. The reason for this being his daughter from Somerset was the informant on the death certificate, so there is no mention of his wife Susan.

Remember to search for clues on documentation you have already sourced about other family members.

I had no choice but to begin my search from 1901, as she could have died prior to her husband, but as I have no proof that she may have outlived her husband I would also have to search beyond 1924 if necessary.

I created a research form in Excel to keep track of everything I researched, in order not to duplicate my search and waste time. It covers just the years from

1837, when Civil Registration started, and the quarters for each year. I added the names by hand. You could just as easily create such a form by hand and photocopy it, or create something similar in MS Word if you prefer. When I'm going to search specific years for an ancestor, I create a similar grid just for the specific years in which I expect to find an ancestor's record, e.g. Mar, June, Sept, Dec 1860 to 1870. I write out the name, type of certificate and spelling variations of the surname which helps to keep me focused on the job in hand. I have created a free, downloadable PDF of this form on my website, www.dianemarelli.co.uk.

	MAR	JUN	SEPT	DEC		MAR	JUN	SEPT	DEC		MAR	JUN	SEPT	DEC
1901	X	X	X	X	1922	X	X	X	X	1943	X	X	X	X
1902	X	X	X	X	1923	X	X	X	X	1944	X	X	X	X
1903	X	X	X	X	1924	X	X	X	X	1945	X	X	X	X
1904	X	X	X	X	1925	X	X	X	X	1946	X	X	X	X
1905	X	X	X	X	1926	X	X	X	X	1947	X	X	X	X
1906	X	X	X	X	1927	X	X	X	X	1948	X	X	X	X
1907	X	X	X	X	1928	X	X	X	X	1949	X	X	X	X
1908	X	X	X	X	1929	X	X	X	X	1950	X	X	X	X
1909	X	X	X	X	1930	X	X	X	X	1951	X	X	X	X
1910	X	X	X	X	1931	X	X	X	X	1952	X	X	X	X
1911	X	X	X	X	1932	X	X	X	X	1953	X	X	X	X
1912	X	X	X	X	1933	X	X	X	X	1954	X	X	X	X
1913	X	X	X	X	1934	X	X	X	X	1955	X	X	X	X
1914	X	X	X	X	1935	X	X	X	X	1956				
1915	X	X	X	X	1936	X	X	X	X	1957				
1916	X	X	X	X	1937	X	X	X	X	1958				
1917	X	X	X	X	1938	X	X	X	X	1959				
1918	X	X	X	X	1939	X	X	X	X	1960				
1919	X	X	X	X	1940	X	X	X	X	1961				
1920	X	X	X	X	1941	X	X	X	X	1962				
1921	X	X	X	X	1942	X	X	X	X	1963				

Name:	Susan Chappell			Searches Carried Out				Mark
Event:	Death			Spellings:	Chappell			
					Chapple			
					Chapel			

Research form.

You will see above, I spent a great deal of time on this. I was convinced I would find Susan easily enough but my search took me from 1901 to 1955 searching under the name Chappell and then Chapple, and to my horror I still couldn't find her. Next I tried searching Chap (for Chapel, Chapell etc.) but by 1930 I was totally despondent. Something was very wrong. I had found a couple of suspects in other parts of Devon under the correct spelling of her surname, but maybe she went to live with her daughter in Somerset, who was the informant on Frederick's death certificate. The thought of starting again looking in another area did not appeal. This is when I remembered rule number one – try talking to living relatives first, Vic and Bet Marelli.

Sure enough after a conversation with Brian's older cousin, Vic Marelli, the mystery was solved. Apparently Susan Chappell went to live with relatives in the Torquay area of Devon. A quick check of the couple of register pages I had printed off, luckily, and there she was. Susan Chappell lived until she was 94 years of age.

Death certificate for Susan Chappell.

When carrying out larger searches, keep a record of what you have done as you go, otherwise if you get distracted or have to leave your research in a hurry you will forget where you left off.

Always talk to relatives first.

Always print off or record details of all suspects that you find, otherwise you might have to go through a whole search again.

Remember, because someone has lived in one place all their life it doesn't mean they died there. My own mother lived on the Wirral for forty years but for the last year of her life she lived with me in Surrey.

What else should we know about death certificates?

The top section of a death certificate is the same as that of a birth certificate and, as with births, death certificates also have a GRO reference number in the first column between 1 and 500. And if two members of the same family are recorded on the same page they might have the same reference number.

Column 1: When and where died
This is the actual date and place of death. The place of death could be at home, work, hospital, institution or even in another district, depending upon where the person was at this unfortunate time. So the residential address given here may not be that of the deceased but the address of the place at which they died.

The type of residence is not always shown in the address and although it does not state for example, a workhouse or prison, it is worth checking if the address was residential.

Column 2: Name and surname
The same care should be taken with death certificates as with birth and marriage certificates. If a person dies alone they may be dependant on a neighbour to register the death, who may not be in possession of the true identity of the person. A baby dying at birth may not have any name or just that of the father or, if illegitimate, the mother.

Column 3: Sex
Although rare, some mistakes are made when filling in this information.

Column 4: Age
This is the age of the deceased at the time of death, although the age on death certificates, especially during the 19th century, is more often wrong than right as I have found so many times when comparing birth, marriage and Census records with deaths.

We have to remember that the informant of the death, such as a neighbour or workhouse master, may be of no relation to the deceased and could be guessing their age. Also, the person who is deceased quite possibly may have estimated their age due to lack of legal documentation. Even if a family member is the informant, they do not necessarily know the exact age of the deceased. It could also be that the deceased lied about their age for one reason or another, such as a female who was older than her husband. Even with children, mistakes can be made so it is advisable to seek further evidence for the ages of deceased ancestors.

Column 5: Occupation

Here the word 'occupation' can have a different meaning from what we perceive occupation to mean. If the deceased is male, as with Martino, his occupation is shown as 'fishmonger retired', but the occupation of his wife Ellen was recorded as 'Wife of Martino Marelli Ice Merchant' and his daughter Rosalier as 'Daughter of Martino Marelli Ice Merchant'. Sometimes the working occupation of a female is listed as well as the details of the father, or it might say 'of no occupation' if they were keeping house or ill, or sometimes even when they were actually employed.

A man could have no occupation shown, without explanation, meaning they were out of employment, or retired or perhaps ill. Also, the occupation on a death certificate could be totally different from their actual lifelong trade if, for example, in later years they became a night watchman.

If a child was illegitimate then their occupation would be recorded as 'daughter of the mother'.

Column 6: Cause of death

Cause of death can be recorded as follows:

- ♦ Uncertified death. Early recorded deaths where there is nothing other than the cause of death recorded such as old age or senile decay. If the word 'certified' is written under the cause of death, it usually means a doctor has certified the death.

- ♦ Certification by a doctor. The most commonly recorded and usually with a doctor's name. (You can usually establish if a doctor has certified the death by the medical terms used.)

- ♦ Certification by a post-mortem but without an inquest. Sometimes when a doctor has not certified a death, the cause of death is unknown and the coroner may request a post-mortem.

- ♦ Certification following an inquest. An inquest is requested in suspicious or unusual circumstances, as with Martino's daughter Rosalier, and once satisfied, the death will be certified according to the circumstances. Rosalier's death is recorded as accidental but could have been recorded as natural causes. Sometimes a record could read suicide or murder.

Column 7: Signature, description and residence of informant

The informant of the death would sign the certificate if able to write their name or they would make their mark as with other certificates. The informant could be whoever was present at the death. This could sometimes mean a relative even if the name is unfamiliar to you or it could just be an unrelated neighbour, friend or occupier of the property in which they died, such as a rooming house or workhouse. It is important to remember that earlier death certificates do not usually record the relationship of the informant or if they do, they could record someone as being a daughter when they are really a stepdaughter.

By the last quarter of the 19th century, more information about the informant is given making it easier to identify their relationship to the deceased.

If a partner of the deceased is unmarried, they cannot register the death unless they were in attendance when their loved one died.

When the informant is not related, the information recorded is more likely to have errors, as with one of my ancestors being recorded as the widow of her son Samuel, rather than of her husband William. Reasons for this could be that the informant William's daughter-in-law, never knew her father-in-law as he died many years before when she was a young woman, and that she assumed he had the same Christian name as Samuel, her husband.

The address or residence of the informant will be recorded much the same as for births. Early records will more often record just a village, while later certificates will give a full address.

Column 8: Date of registration
Most deaths are registered within a day or two of the date of death but I found some deaths registered as long as eight days after the date of death. Reasons for delay could be because a person died in suspicious circumstances, as with the death of one of Martino's children who died accidentally in bed, and an inquest delays registration. It is important to remember that the date the death is registered is the date you will find it in the indexes.

Column 9: Registrar's signature
Here we have the registrar's signature but if a death is recorded more than a year after the date of death, the signature of the superintendent registrar is also required.

Step 2 - Ordering death certificates

You are now ready to order your certificate and if you choose findmypast.com they have made this a very simple procedure.

From your search results page click on 'order certificates', top right.

This page gives you information about the various ways you can order certificates from the GRO including the online service.

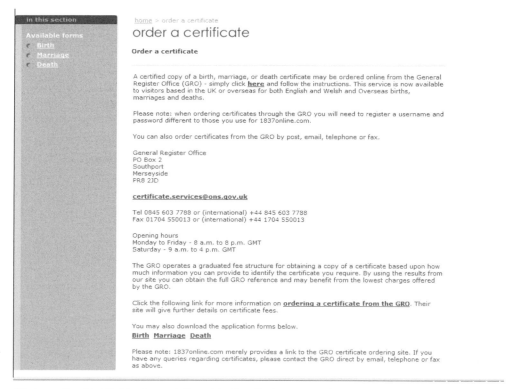

Click on the highlighted word 'here' in the first paragraph.

General Register Office
Official information on births, marriages and deaths

▼Home ▸Births ▸Deaths ▸Stillbirths ▸Marriages ▸Civil Partnerships ▸Adoptions ▸About Us ▸Research ▸Contact Us

| Births | Deaths | Stillbirths | Marriages | Civil Partnerships | Adoptions |

Welcome

These pages give you information about how to register a birth or death in England and Wales, how to go about getting married or form a civil partnership, how to obtain a birth certificate, a marriage certificate, a civil partnership certificate or a death certificate, and how to use the services at the Family Records Centre. Please note that although we can make available to you a great many records that will help you trace your family tree, we do not do everything a genealogist might.

These services are provided or overseen by the General Register Office (GRO) which is part of the Office for National Statistics. Some of these services are provided in partnership with other organisations.

The GRO has a responsibility for England and Wales. There are equivalent offices for Scotland and Northern Ireland.

Many local authorities also offer other celebratory services including: naming ceremonies, renewal of vows, commitment ceremonies and civil funerals. For further information please contact your local register office.

Shortcuts

➥ Modernising Civil Registration: overview
➥ Ordering certificates online
➥ Gender Recognition

News
- Civil partnership registrations
- Legislative proposals to help combat crime
- Registration Modernisation

Research
GRO can often provide guidance and information if you are:

➥ Ordering certificates online
➥ Looking for certificate fees
➥ Investigating your family tree
➥ Looking for overseas records
➥ Traceline - re-establishing contact between family and friends

Search for your local register office
Please enter your full postcode or town in the box below and click GO.

[   ] GO ▸

©2006 Office for National Statistics
Accessibility | Copyright | Terms and Conditions | Privacy Statement | Directgov

Click on 'Ordering certificates online' under the heading 'Research' on the right to order your certificate online.

So although searches can be carried out for recent ancestors, if you don't get information from living relatives it can be a laborious task searching for a death certificate. With births you can estimate from a marriage date, and with a marriage you can estimate from a birth date, but with deaths unless you have a guide to the era of death, then it can be a hard slog after 1901.

Step 3 - Sourcing civil deaths using the Census

The first couple I am going to source is William Plummer and Susan Plummer, née Jordan. William Plummer was born in 1845 and Susan Jordan in 1835, so it is conceivable that they were both living in 1901, so this is where I will start. A search of the 1901 Census in Ancestry.com produced the following record:

Name:	William Plummer
Age:	56
Estimated birth year:	Abt. 1845
Relation:	Father-in-law
Gender:	Male
Where born:	Tooting, London, England
Civil parish:	Battersea
Ecclesiastical parish:	St Barnabas, Clapham Common
County/Island	London
Country:	England

1901 England Census record for William Plummer.

You can select to view the original, as above.

Not only did it tell me that William Plummer was still living and working as a fog signalman for the railway, but it also gave me an insight into his relationship with his daughter Amy and her husband Martino. This also tells me that the families were close, or took responsibility for their elders.

That means that I will have to search for William Plummer from 1901, but as you can see above at this date, William was a widower, meaning Susan Plummer, née Jordan, died pre-1901. So before I go hunting through Civil Registration I really need to establish if Susan Plummer was still living in 1891.

Name:	Susan Plummer
Age:	55
Estimated birth year:	Abt. 1836
Relation:	Wife
Gender:	Female
Where born:	Melksham, Kildare, Ireland
Civil parish:	Wandsworth
Ecclesiastical parish:	St Mary
County/Island:	London
Country:	England

1891 England Census record for Susan Plummer.

The only information that is misleading is the transcription for 'Where born': Melksham, Kildare, Ireland!! Obviously, this was a mistake, and viewing the original Census proved that it was a transcription error and should have read 'Wiltshire'.

Susan Plummer was living in 1891, which meant she died after this date but before 1901, so naturally these are my search years for the Civil Registration record of her death. My first stop, as always is FreeBMD. Luckily I found Susan Plummer listed and was able to order her death certificate online via the GRO.

Death certificate for Susan Plummer. She died in June 1894 at the age of 58.

Finding the Civil Death Registration for William was obviously not going to be as straightforward, although I was hopeful I might be lucky enough to find him on FreeBMD. Sadly, I did not as they seemed to have transcribed only up to 1911. But I can use this information if I can find out how many deaths have been transcribed up until 1911. Look at the bottom of my search page for William in FreeBMD, at the sentence beginning with 'Has our search engine . . .'. I clicked on the word 'here.'

Deaths Dec 1869

Plummer	William	23	Islington	1b	164	Info 𝒢
Plummer	William James	0	Lambeth	1d	272	Info 𝒢
Plummer	William Thomas	0	Holborn	1b	514	Info 𝒢

Has our search engine found the record you are seeking?	Found one partner in a marriage but now looking for the spouse?	Don't understand the results?
Click here to learn what to do now.	Click here for more information.	Perhaps our Frequently Asked Questions could have the answer.

Has our search engine failed to find the record you are seeking? The whole index hasn't yet been transcribed - see here for which years have been transcribed.

Since we haven't yet transcribed the whole index we need more people to help. If you have very basic skills, a computer and half an hour a week, FreeBMD needs you! You don't have to be a good typist - just accurate! Help us and speed up the rate at which free birth, marriage and death indexes become available.

Click here to learn more and volunteer.

FreeBMD Main Page

Search page for William Plummer.

 **Coverage Charts**

FreeBMD is an ongoing project, the aim of which is to transcribe the Civil Registration index of births, marriages and deaths for England and Wales, and as such the whole index has not yet been transcribed.

The FreeBMD Database was last updated on Fri 18 Aug 2006 and currently contains 120,727,211 distinct records (155,289,660 total records).

The records that have been transcribed are not evenly distributed; the graphs for

Births, Marriages and Deaths

show which years, quarters and events are most complete.

However, please note these are based on **estimates** and, in particular, a value of 100% does **not** guarantee that all entries have been transcribed. See below for further information on this.

A count of the number of records transcribed for each event and year *(updated Fri 18 Aug 2006)* is available here

How the percentages are calculated

The percentage coverage given by the above graphs is only an estimate for the following reason:

- The GRO gives the total number of entries for deaths in a year, only to the nearest thousand.
- Where entries have been transcribed twice (for validation) we make an estimate of whether two entries that are different should be counted once or twice.

In view of this the percentages can be up to 3% out, for example a percentage of 60% could in reality be anything between 57% and 63%. However, most of the time the percentages are within 2%.

FreeBMD Main Page

From here select 'births', 'marriages' or 'deaths'; for my purposes I clicked on 'deaths'.

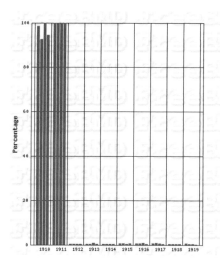

Percentage of deaths held in FreeBMD by year (1910–1919).

As you can see, nearly all civil deaths have been transcribed up until 1911. This is where I made my decision to search not from 1901 but from 1911, in the hope I could save some time. I am pleased to say that my decision paid off and I found William Plummer in the first quarter of 1917 and saved myself ten years of searching.

The next stage using the Census, will take you back another generation. For the purpose of this exercise I will use the parents of William Plummer (who was married to Susan Jordan).

From William's birth certificate below I know the names of both his parents and his father's occupation but nothing else, except of course that his father, John Charitee Plummer was living in 1845. Obviously both parents would have been born pre-Civil Registration, but they may have married post-Civil Registration which means I could find their marriage records and their death records.

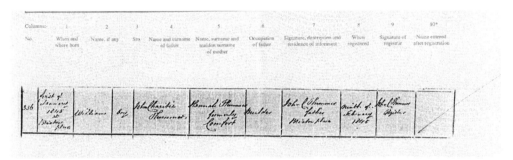

William Plummer's birth certificate.

I also have the marriage certificate for William Plummer and Susan Jordan and this document has provided me with an excellent clue.

Marriage certificate for William Plummer and Susan Jordan.

At the time of this marriage John Plummer was definitely no longer living, which means that he died pre-1865. So my first port of call is the 1861 Census to ascertain if both of William's parents were living at this time.

The 1861 Census.

Looking at the 1861 Census tells me that William's father died pre-1861, but his mother died post-1861. I also have other information about William's siblings and what looks to be a sister of Hannah – Rose Comfort, aged 20. Also, at the point in time the eldest child was born about 1838 meaning it is quite possible I could acquire the marriage details of William Plummer's parents.

My next stop was the 1851 Census.

> The information about Hannah's sister could prove useful when trying to find information about Hannah's birth, as does the place of birth for both sisters which is Dorking.

The 1851 Census.

John was living in 1851, therefore my search criteria for his death record will be the years 1851 to 1861. Sadly, this Census also informs me that there was another child born prior to Civil Registration, meaning I probably will not be able to acquire their marriage certificate. Searches of the 1871 and 1881 Censuses informed me that Hannah Plummer died during this decade. I found the following:

Deaths Jun 1855

Plummer, John Charitee	Wandsworth	1d	278

Deaths Jun 1877

Plummer, Hannah Age 66	Lambeth	1d	336

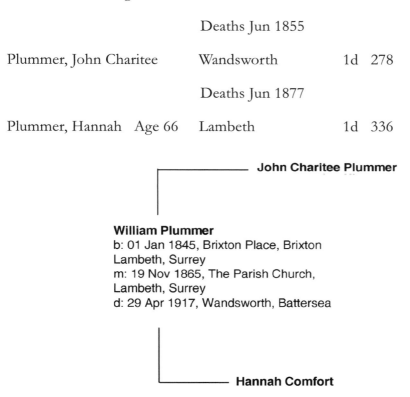

Parents of William Plummer.

Using either findmypast.com or Ancestry.com I can now go directly to the year and quarter to check the information and then order my certificates online via the GRO (see Chapter 1, Step 4). To be certain, I carried out a search of marriages from September 1837 to December 1850 but, as I now suspected, did not find the marriage certificate for John Charitee Plummer and Hannah Comfort.

The death certificate for John Charitee Plummer confirmed that I had the correct one, his occupation is listed as a carpenter and undertaker. As he died in the Surrey County Lunatic Asylum, I have to wonder if his chosen career played on his mind in any way.

Death certificate for John Charitee Plummer.

The cause of his death was apoplexy. I gathered the following information about apoplexy from Wikipedia, an online, free encyclopedia.

Apoplexy is an old-fashioned medical term, generally used interchangeably with cerebrovascular accident (CVA or stroke) but having other meanings as well.

The use of *apoplexy* for the term 'stroke' is derived from the fact that many patients lose consciousness during the acute stage of the vascular compromise (either through bleeding or ischemia). It is not to be confused with cataplexy (an attack of the neurological syndrome narcolepsy).

Occasionally, the term 'apoplexy' is used to describe haemorrhaging within other organs; in such usage, however, it is coupled with an adjective describing the site of the bleeding. For example, bleeding within the kidneys can be called 'renal apoplexy', or bleeding within the pituitary gland can be called 'pituitary apoplexy'.

In non-medical terms it is also used colloquially, particularly in its adjective form *apoplectic*, to mean furious, enraged, or upset to the point of being unable to deal with the situation rationally or diplomatically.

Step 4 - Updated family tree

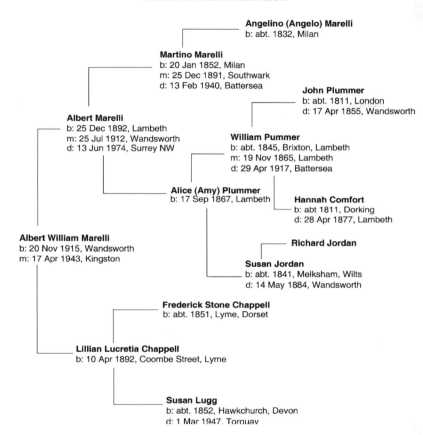

Ancestors of Albert William Marelli

Angelino (Angelo) Marelli
b: abt. 1832, Milan

Martino Marelli
b: 20 Jan 1852, Milan
m: 25 Dec 1891, Southwark
d: 13 Feb 1940, Battersea

John Plummer
b: abt. 1811, London
d: 17 Apr 1855, Wandsworth

Albert Marelli
b: 25 Dec 1892, Lambeth
m: 25 Jul 1912, Wandsworth
d: 13 Jun 1974, Surrey NW

William Pummer
b: abt. 1845, Brixton, Lambeth
m: 19 Nov 1865, Lambeth
d: 29 Apr 1917, Battersea

Alice (Amy) Plummer
b: 17 Sep 1867, Lambeth

Hannah Comfort
b: abt 1811, Dorking
d: 28 Apr 1877, Lambeth

Albert William Marelli
b: 20 Nov 1915, Wandsworth
m: 17 Apr 1943, Kingston

Richard Jordan

Susan Jordan
b: abt. 1841, Melksham, Wilts
d: 14 May 1884, Wandsworth

Frederick Stone Chappell
b: abt. 1851, Lyme, Dorset

Lillian Lucretia Chappell
b: 10 Apr 1892, Coombe Street, Lyme

Susan Lugg
b: abt. 1852, Hawkchurch, Devon
d: 1 Mar 1947, Torquay

Family tree – further updated.

Recap

1. Using findmyfamily.com to research.

2. Searching for deaths post-1901.

3. Keeping a track of your searches.

4. Ordering certificates straight from findmyfamily.com.

5. Sourcing Civil Registration records pre-1901 using the Census.

6. Total cost so far is:

Annual UK Deluxe Membership with findmyfamily.com	£ 69.95
Cost of 14 certificates	£ 98.00
Total	**£167.95**

Optional cost if choosing to utilise another source:

Subscription to findmyfamily.com Census/BMD	£ 65.00
(You could choose either or both Ancestry and findmyfamily.com)	
Total	**£232.95**

 Tips

1. If searching for a death certificate during the 20th century, check via the Census if the person was still living in 1901 via the Census.

2. Always talk to relatives before going off on a tangent to research your ancestors.

3. Always print off details of all suspects that you find, otherwise you might find yourself having to go through the whole painful process again.

4. Remember, just because someone has lived in the same place all their life, it does not necessarily mean that is where they died.

5. When using FreeBMD don't forget to check coverage charts of what records have been transcribed.

6. Always allow for transcription errors in resource sites.

7. Always allow for transcription errors in the original Census.

8. Don't forget to note names of other persons living at the same address even if their name means nothing to you now. They might turn out to be relatives giving you clues to other generations, such as Rose Comfort, sister of Hannah Plummer.

9. Don't forget to be inventive in surname spellings when searching.

10. Don't forget you can search by Christian names, date of birth and locations, including whole districts.

5

Beyond 1837 and the Census

To take us to the next generation you will find other records sourced below:

♦ The death of Amy Plummer and Lilian Chappell
♦ The marriage of Frederick Chappell and Susan Lugg
♦ Frederick Chappell's death

The marriage details of Frederick and Susan gave me the names of their fathers.

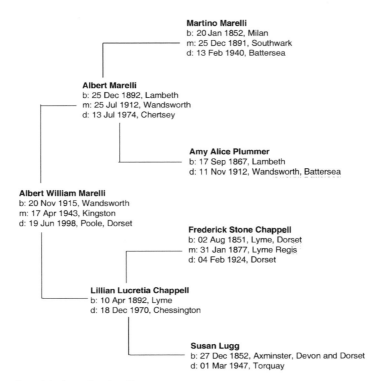

Martino Marelli
b: 20 Jan 1852, Milan
m: 25 Dec 1891, Southwark
d: 13 Feb 1940, Battersea

Albert Marelli
b: 25 Dec 1892, Lambeth
m: 25 Jul 1912, Wandsworth
d: 13 Jul 1974, Chertsey

Amy Alice Plummer
b: 17 Sep 1867, Lambeth
d: 11 Nov 1912, Wandsworth, Battersea

Albert William Marelli
b: 20 Nov 1915, Wandsworth
m: 17 Apr 1943, Kingston
d: 19 Jun 1998, Poole, Dorset

Frederick Stone Chappell
b: 02 Aug 1851, Lyme, Dorset
m: 31 Jan 1877, Lyme Regis
d: 04 Feb 1924, Dorset

Lillian Lucretia Chappell
b: 10 Apr 1892, Lyme
d: 18 Dec 1970, Chessington

Susan Lugg
b: 27 Dec 1852, Axminster, Devon and Dorset
d: 01 Mar 1947, Torquay

Further details added to the family tree.

Step 1 - How long do they live?

To keep things clear we are going to follow Frederick Stone Chappell. Thanks to Frederick's birth certificate I know that his father was called Samuel Chappell, occupation shoemaker, that it is possible he was still living in 1877, as the marriage certificate does not say 'Deceased', and that his mother was called Mary Ann Sampson.

There is a number of things I could do here. Try to trace the death of Samuel Chappell by using the Census to reduce my search years, or start with the 1861 Census when Frederick would have been about 10 years old, which could provide me with further clues to a marriage date of his parents.

My first search for Frederick Chappell did not produce the result I required, so I chose a Soundex search on his name and found him under the spelling of Chappel.

Add	Name			Age	Rank	Where born
Pickle Sq, Lyme	Samuel Chappel	Head	Married	65	Navy Pensioner/ Cordwainer	Colyton, Devon
	Mary Ann	Wife	Married	55	Charwoman	Axmouth
	Henry	Son	Unmarried	24	Painter/Glazier	Axmouth
	Frederick Stone	Son	Unmarried	9	Scholar	Lyme

Information from the 1861 Census

From the above I now know that Frederick had an older brother called Henry, who was 15 years his senior. I also have the ages of his parents and places of birth. What is interesting is that Samuel was once in the navy, although apparently retired and his occupation is listed as cordwainer. By typing in old occupations on the address line of my browser several sites produced the following definition:

Cordwainer – shoemaker, originally any leather-worker using leather from Cordova/Cordoba in Spain

I was very confident that I had the correct family and based on the above information I searched the 1851 Census.

Add	Name			Age	Rank	Where born
Mill Green, Lyme	Samuel Chappel	Head	Married	48	Shoemaker	Colyton, Devon
	Mary Ann	Wife	Married	34	Charwoman	Axmouth
	Henry	Son	Unmarried	13	Painter/Glazier	Lyme

Information from the 1851 Census.

Again even though there is a big discrepancy in the ages of Samuel and Mary Ann, between the two Census records I am confident I have the right family. The only irritating piece of information is that the date of birth for Samuel Chappel is now between the years of 1796 and 1803, and the date of birth for Mary Ann between 1806 and 1817.

Naturally I wanted to source the 1841 Census. Given the above information, I thought this would be fairly easy and to my delight it was, as they were living in Lyme at that time. The 1841 Census gave the birth-date for Samuel as about 1814, and for Mary Ann about 1816, and Henry, their eldest, about 1837.

Before I try to source the marriage details for Samuel and Mary Ann, I am going to source their death details. Although Frederick's marriage certificate does not state that his father Samuel was deceased, I am going to check the 1871 Census for Frederick who at this time might still have been living at home with Samuel and Mary Ann.

Unfortunately, I could not find Frederick or his father even using Soundex, so I looked under his mother's name, Mary Ann Chappell, and found Frederick and her both living in Pickle Square, Lyme. Mary Ann was recorded as 'Widow of Mariner'. What is worth noting is that Frederick was recorded as Fred S., and this did not come up on a Soundex search. I now know that Samuel Chappell died pre-1871 but post-1861, and Mary Ann Chappell post-1871. Searching FreeBMD under the spelling of Chappell, Chappel and finally Chapple, I found him:

Deaths Mar 1870

Chapple Samuel   72   Axminster   5b   4

The death certificate proved to be the correct one. Samuel Chapple died aged 72 in Pickle Square, Lyme – occupation pensioner in the Coast Guard Service.

In the 1881 Census, I found Frederick under Fred T. Chappell, living with his wife Susan and his widowed mother Mary Ann, aged 68. Getting wise as to how Frederick was recorded, I searched the 1891 Census under the name Fred and sure enough he wasn't there! Typical, I found him as Frederick S. Chappel still living in Lyme, but in Coombe Street with his wife, four children and his widowed mother Mary Ann, now aged 78.

Mary Ann was not recorded as living in the 1901 Census, so my search years for her death index are from 1891 to 1901. I found her in 1893, making her 80 years of age from the information on the 1881 and 1891 Census records, but to my dismay her age recorded is 72 years:

Deaths Mar 1893

Chappell Mary Ann   72   Axminster   5b   2

Again, this proved to be the right certificate, if not the right age, or maybe it was the right age! Mary Ann is recorded as widow of Samuel Chappell, shoemaker, living at Coombe Street, Lyme, and Frederick Chappell was present at her death.

Step 2 - Marriage records beyond 1837

To complete this family unit, I now need to source the marriage record for Samuel Chappell and Mary Ann Sampson.

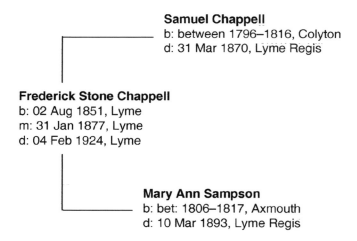

Samuel Chappell
b: between 1796–1816, Colyton
d: 31 Mar 1870, Lyme Regis

Frederick Stone Chappell
b: 02 Aug 1851, Lyme
m: 31 Jan 1877, Lyme
d: 04 Feb 1924, Lyme

Mary Ann Sampson
b: bet: 1806–1817, Axmouth
d: 10 Mar 1893, Lyme Regis

Samuel Chappell and Mary Ann Sampson are added to the family tree.

As their first child, Henry, was born about 1837, I am presuming that Samuel and Mary Ann married pre-Civil Registration, so I am going to utilise FamilySearch, a free site providing genealogical information worldwide. Please note this site is great as a guide to give clues for finding church records but never rely on the information found without locating original source documentation.

Home page, http://www.familysearch.org

I put in the name Samuel Chappell, selected Marriage as the event, put in the year 1837 with a range of 10 years and selected England. This is what the search produced:

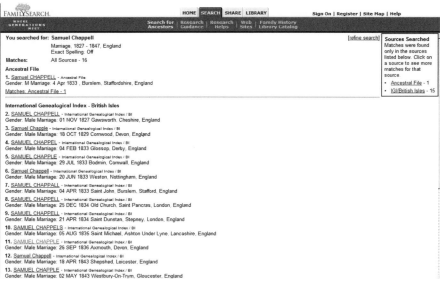

Search results for Samuel Chappell.

To the right of the screen you will see there are only 16 possible matches; 1 ancestral and 15 IGI (International Genealogical Index). Looking down the page, the most positive is number 11. Samuel Chapple, 1836, Axmouth; where Mary Ann Sampson was born. I clicked on number 11 and found the following.

IGI record for Samuel Chapple

Step 3 - Original sources beyond 1837

The source information at the bottom of the above page is important should you wish to obtain the original record. Although I have not as yet found this particular record I do have one for an ancestor from my family – William Podevin.

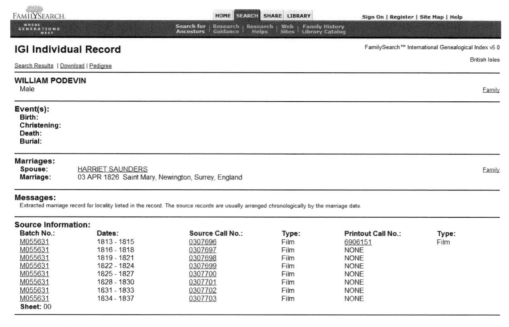

IGI record for William Podevin.

The above record is that of my five times great grandfather's and mother's marriage record. I decided to trace the information to the original source. I went back to the home page for FamilySearch and looked up a Family History Centre related to this site near where I live.

Family History Centers are branch facilities of the Family History Library in Salt Lake City. Centers provide access to most of the microfilms and microfiche in the Family History Library to help patrons identify their ancestors. Everyone is welcome to come to the centers and use Family History Center resources.

I found one in Aldershot and took a copy of the record I had sourced to them and placed an order to view the microfilm. Within one week I had a call to say the film was in. I went to view the original record only to find they did not have facilities for me to make a copy of the information. I transcribed the details and later that day I searched the Internet for Saint Mary's Church in Newington.

Website for Saint Mary's Church in Newington.

Besides giving me lots of information about the church for my family file it also provided a link to record offices (see the index on left).

Diocesan record offices

I emailed the link for the London Metropolitan Archives and they emailed back with an enquiry form which I posted off, for a fee, and within a short time I received the following:

Marriage record for William Podevin and Harriet Saunders.

So again, with the help of the Internet it is possible to access records without having to go to the source location. Remember to source original records as above.

Back to Samuel Chappell and Mary Ann Sampson – I can now add their marriage details to my tree and utilise the same method as above to find the original details.

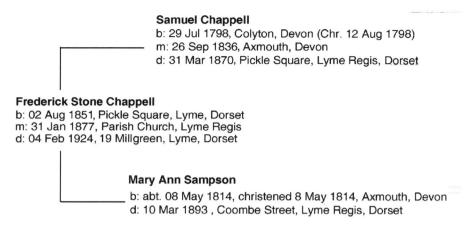

Samuel Chappell
b: 29 Jul 1798, Colyton, Devon (Chr. 12 Aug 1798)
m: 26 Sep 1836, Axmouth, Devon
d: 31 Mar 1870, Pickle Square, Lyme Regis, Dorset

Frederick Stone Chappell
b: 02 Aug 1851, Pickle Square, Lyme, Dorset
m: 31 Jan 1877, Parish Church, Lyme Regis
d: 04 Feb 1924, 19 Millgreen, Lyme, Dorset

Mary Ann Sampson
b: abt. 08 May 1814, christened 8 May 1814, Axmouth, Devon
d: 10 Mar 1893 , Coombe Street, Lyme Regis, Dorset

Updated family tree.

Step 4 - Birth records beyond 1837

The next step will be to try to source church records of the births for
Samuel and Mary Ann. The main problem here is that I have such a range of
possible birth-years owing to the information received from the Census and
death certificates. I go back to FamilySearch and key in the name Mary Ann
Sampson, date 1810 with a range of 10 years either side.

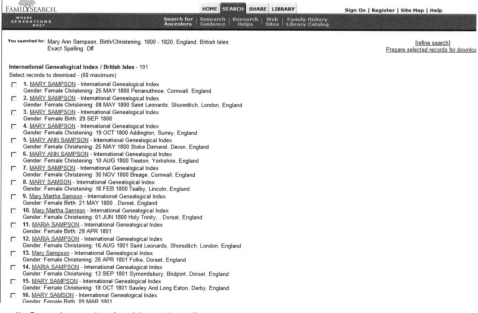

FamilySearch results for Mary Ann Sampson.

This search brought up 191 possible records, but by clicking on 'refine search' to the right, I can reduce this search by adding further information.

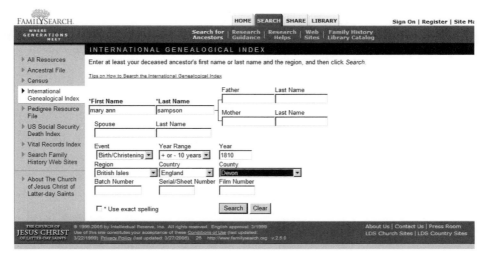

Search narrowed down by geographical location

This search produced the following:

Refined search results for Mary Ann Sampson.

Looking down the list, number 17 seemed the most likely.

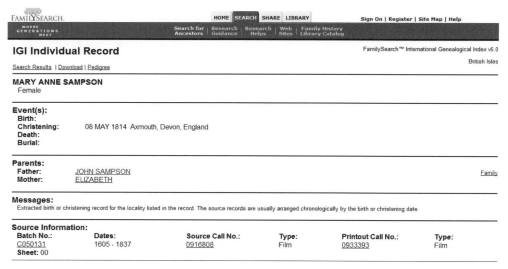

IGI record for Mary Ann Sampson.

I believe this to be the correct record. If Mary Anne Sampson was born in 1814 it would make her about 79 at the time of her death; this ties in with the 1891 Census, the 1881 Census and the 1871 Census. Additionally, all the Census records show her as being born in Axmouth. I now also have the name of her father and the Christian name of her mother.

Before I obtain original records I will try and source Samuel Chappell. I know from the Census records that he was born in Colyton, Devon but again I have a range of years in which he could have been born. Using the same screen in FamilySearch as I did with Mary Anne Sampson, I clicked on 'search results' and then 'refine search' but changed the details for my next search.

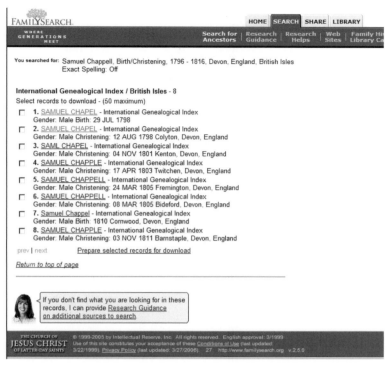

FamilySearch results for Samuel Chappell.

The most obvious is number 2 for a Samuel Chapel born in Colyton in Devon.

IGI record for Samuel Chapel.

Again looking at the information I already have, this birth-date matched the information on his death certificate and the age I have on the 1861 Census.

Step 5 - The search for siblings beyond 1837

I decided to look for further clues by carrying out a search of other children of William Chappell and Honor. By clicking on search results from my last search page and refining the results again, I can alter the search criteria to find siblings of Samuel Chappell.

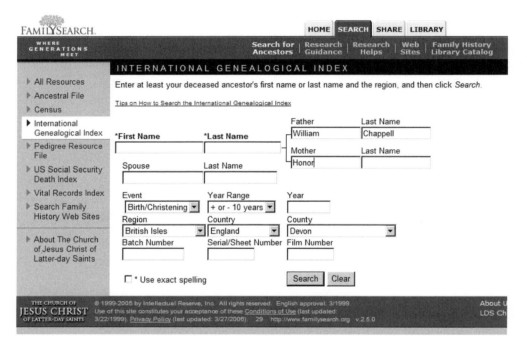

By taking out the 'first name' and 'last name' and putting in the names of parents, then removing all other criteria except event, region, country and county you can source children of couples and siblings of ancestors

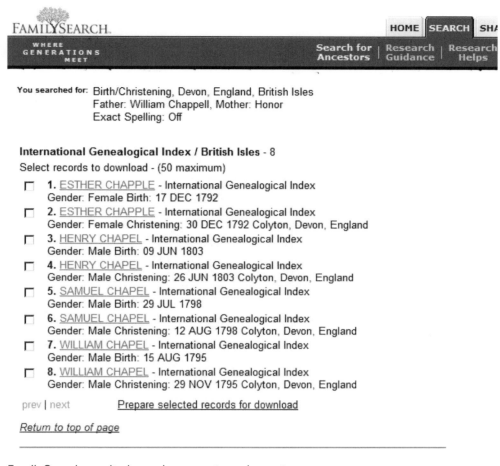

FamilySearch results by region, county and country.

This search brought up details of the birth and christening dates of four children for a William and Honor Chappell in Colyton, Devon.

Step 6 - Ancestors born in the 18th century but still living in 1841

I couldn't look for these ancestors previously as I did not know of their existence until I started investigating FamilySearch, but I could now establish whether Samuel's parents and siblings were still alive in 1841 by looking at the Census.

In Ancestry.co.uk I put in my search criteria for Honor and William Chappell. I tried several permutations of both the surname and Christian names for Honor, William and children, but without success. Trying Christian names gave me lots of individuals named Honor and William, but none related to the family I was researching. I continued without success and eventually decided upon another way of searching, rather than face searching through the whole of Colyton in Devon and quite possibly again in Lyme, Dorset.

I went back to my 1841 Census search screen in Ancestry.co.uk and unticked 'Exact matches only' in the top left. I put in Hon* (the asterisk means wild card and it will search for all Christian names beginning with Hon). I chose Devon as the place of birth and residence but without a result, so I then chose Dorset.

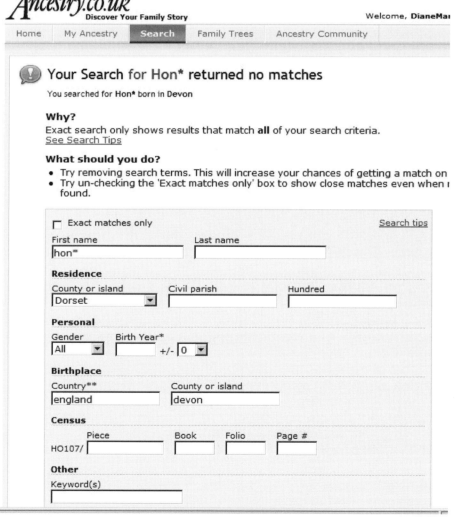

Searching using a wild card option.

It was a large search but before I went through each one I decided to go straight to the letter C. Luckily on the second page, there was Honnor Chappel in Lyme Regis. Could this be her?

		Name	Estimated Birth Year	BirthPlace	Civil Parish	County/Island	View Image
★☆☆☆☆	View Record	**Honour Channing**	abt 1791	Devon, England	Shute	Devon	📷
★☆☆☆☆	View Record	**Honour Channing**	abt 1826	Devon, England	Shute	Devon	📷
★☆☆☆☆	View Record	**Honour Chappa**	abt 1821	Devon, England	Bampton	Devon	📷
★★★★☆	View Record	**Honnor Chappel**	abt 1757		Lyme Regis	Dorset	📷
★☆☆☆☆	View Record	**Honor Chapple**	abt 1821	Devon, England	Bishops Nympton	Devon	📷
★☆☆☆☆	View Record	**Honor Chapple**	abt 1815	Devon, England	North Molton	Devon	📷
★☆☆☆☆	View Record	**Honour Chapple**	abt 1781	Devon, England	Newton Ferrers	Devon	📷

Copyright © 1998–2006, MyFamily.com Inc. and its subsidiaries.
Searches using wild card will give several results.

Yes, I think it is!

> Out of curiosity, I tried searching for Honnor Chappel in the normal way but without luck! So I tried again with just the birth year and in various other ways but could still not create the above result!

The address was the same as that for Samuel and Mary Ann. On the very next page I found Honor Chappell aged 84 and a William Chappell aged 45. I believed William to be the brother of Samuel because his birth-year is the same as that of William Chappell born to Honor and William Chappell, see below:

Copyright © 1998–2006, MyFamily.com Inc. and its subsidiaries.
1841 Census records for Honnor Chappel and William Chappel.

IGI Individual Record

Search Results | Download | Pedigree

WILLIAM CHAPEL
  Male

Event(s):
  Birth: 15 AUG 1795
  Christening: 29 NOV 1795 Colyton, Devon, England
  Death:
  Burial:

Parents:
  Father: WILLIAM CHAPEL
  Mother: HONOR

IGI record for William Chapel.

I am now about 90% certain I have the right records for Samuel's birth, those of his siblings and the names of his parents, but what would make me happier would be to find the death records for Honor and what appears to be her son William, as per the 1841 Census.

Oddly, I could find neither of them on the 1851 Census, so my search took me to the decade between 1841 and 1851. I found a couple of death records for a William Chappell and one proved to be correct and what was even more exciting was the informant of the death.

Death certificate for William Chappell.

Mary Ann Chappell was present at the death – Now I am confident I'm on the right track. Also, another clue is William Chappell, brother of Samuel, who is recorded to be a cordwainer!

I found the death record for Honor Chappell dated 1849 and as I now have the original documentation, I could now add these details to the main tree (see the end of this chapter).

Using the same method as above, I wanted further evidence that I have the right information about Mary Ann Sampson's birth but the Census records for 1861, 1871, 1881 and 1891 put her at about the right age. Although her death certificate records her as 72 years in 1893 making her birth date 1821, I think I'm about 75% convinced I have the right details.

To be more certain I found two possible marriages in Axmouth for John Sampson – one was dated 1813 to an Elizabeth, and the other to a Betty Hake in 1798. Both couples had several children, and John and Elizabeth had a daughter called Mary Ann Sampson born in 1814, the year following their marriage. Although John and Betty had a daughter called Mary born in 1798, she died in 1799. I am now 90% certain that I have the right Mary Ann Sampson born to John and Elizabeth Sampson in 1814, Axmouth.

I also went on to find an Elizabeth Sampson in the 1841 Census, working as a Maid Servant at Hawksdown Farm in Colyton, aged 68. My Elizabeth died in 1850 aged 80 on the death certificate, so there is only a discrepancy of 2 years. The death certificate for Elizabeth Sampson records her as the widow of John Sampson, with an Ann Hamer present at death.

As yet I cannot find a link between Ann Hamer and Elizabeth Sampson, but in the 1851 Census I found Ann Hamer (under the transcribed spelling of Harne) aged 47, living with her husband and children in Colyton. Maybe she is related through marriage, because the other John Sampson who married Betty Hake had a daughter called Ann born in 1803, which fits with the age of Ann Hamer. However, I cannot find a record of Ann Sampson's marriage to a Hamer, so this could be a cold trail, but not until I can confidently eliminate her from my research.

> **Never discount the names of persons detailed on BMD certificates, there could be a connection that might provide further clues to discovering your ancestors.**

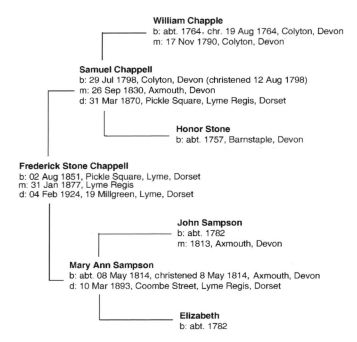

William Chapple
b: abt. 1764, chr. 19 Aug 1764, Colyton, Devon
m: 17 Nov 1790, Colyton, Devon

Samuel Chappell
b: 29 Jul 1798, Colyton, Devon (christened 12 Aug 1798)
m: 26 Sep 1830, Axmouth, Devon
d: 31 Mar 1870, Pickle Square, Lyme Regis, Dorset

Honor Stone
b: abt. 1757, Barnstaple, Devon

Frederick Stone Chappell
b: 02 Aug 1851, Pickle Square, Lyme, Dorset
m: 31 Jan 1877, Lyme Regis
d: 04 Feb 1924, 19 Millgreen, Lyme, Dorset

John Sampson
b: abt. 1782
m: 1813, Axmouth, Devon

Mary Ann Sampson
b: abt. 08 May 1814, christened 8 May 1814, Axmouth, Devon
d: 10 Mar 1893, Coombe Street, Lyme Regis, Dorset

Elizabeth
b: abt. 1782

Honor Stone, John Sampson and Elizabeth can now be added to the family tree.

Recap

1. Church records will take you beyond Civil Registration.

2. You may find ancestors who, although born and married prior to 1837, actually died post-1837.

3. You can search for birth, marriage and death certificates pre-1837 online via church records.

4. Once you have found an entry for an ancestor, you can source the original document using research services.

5. The total cost so far is:

Annual UK Deluxe Membership with Ancestry.co.uk	£ 69.95
Cost of 17 certificates	£119.00
London Met	£ 35.00
Total	**£223.95**

Optional cost if choosing to utilise another source:

Subscription to findmyfamily.com Census/BMD   £ 65.00
(You could choose either or both Ancestry and findmyfamily.com)

                           Total   **£288.95**

➤ Tips

1. When searching on the Census, shortened names such as Fred for Frederick will not always come up even when carrying out a Soundex search. (Soundex is not foolproof).

2. When searching using FamilySearch, it is easy to get carried away and keep searching and printing. Try to keep your searches to a generation until you have finished researching, documenting and recording your sources otherwise you will just end up with a mass of paperwork that won't make sense.

3. Remember to investigate ways to manipulate research sites such as FamilySearch to get quick results, such as finding siblings. But only use this site as a guide to finding original sources.

4. You can book research services at most history/archive centres but it will cost you, although if you weigh up time and transport, the cost could be less.

5. You will more often than not find discrepancies in the ages of your ancestors. This does not necessarily mean you have the wrong person, you just need to look for other sources to confirm your findings.

6. Do obtain original sources pre-1837 to prove your findings.

7. Remember if someone was born and married prior to 1837, it does not mean you can't trace them via the Census or death certificates. Although the average age at death was a great deal lower than it is today, you will find that some of your ancestors lived to grand old ages.

8. Never discount the names of persons detailed on BMD certificates, there could be a connection that might provide further clues to discovering your ancestors.

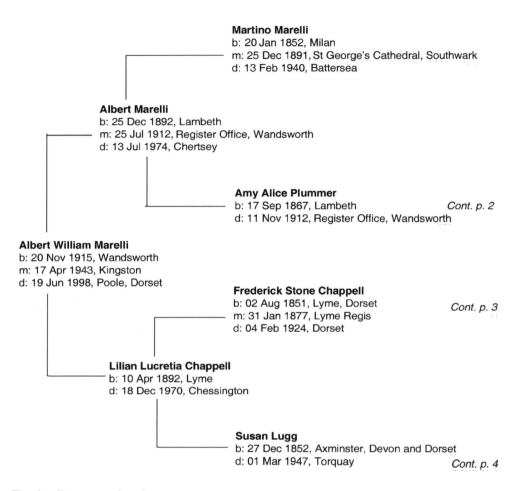

Martino Marelli
b: 20 Jan 1852, Milan
m: 25 Dec 1891, St George's Cathedral, Southwark
d: 13 Feb 1940, Battersea

Albert Marelli
b: 25 Dec 1892, Lambeth
m: 25 Jul 1912, Register Office, Wandsworth
d: 13 Jul 1974, Chertsey

Amy Alice Plummer
b: 17 Sep 1867, Lambeth   *Cont. p. 2*
d: 11 Nov 1912, Register Office, Wandsworth

Albert William Marelli
b: 20 Nov 1915, Wandsworth
m: 17 Apr 1943, Kingston
d: 19 Jun 1998, Poole, Dorset

Frederick Stone Chappell
b: 02 Aug 1851, Lyme, Dorset   *Cont. p. 3*
m: 31 Jan 1877, Lyme Regis
d: 04 Feb 1924, Dorset

Lilian Lucretia Chappell
b: 10 Apr 1892, Lyme
d: 18 Dec 1970, Chessington

Susan Lugg
b: 27 Dec 1852, Axminster, Devon and Dorset
d: 01 Mar 1947, Torquay   *Cont. p. 4*

The family tree updated.

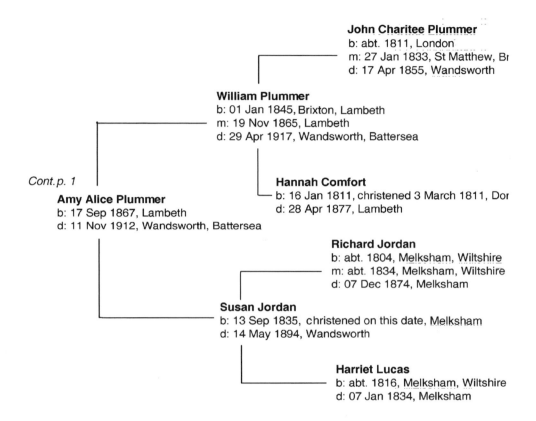

John Charitee Plummer
b: abt. 1811, London
m: 27 Jan 1833, St Matthew, Br
d: 17 Apr 1855, Wandsworth

William Plummer
b: 01 Jan 1845, Brixton, Lambeth
m: 19 Nov 1865, Lambeth
d: 29 Apr 1917, Wandsworth, Battersea

Hannah Comfort
b: 16 Jan 1811, christened 3 March 1811, Dor
d: 28 Apr 1877, Lambeth

Cont. p. 1
Amy Alice Plummer
b: 17 Sep 1867, Lambeth
d: 11 Nov 1912, Wandsworth, Battersea

Richard Jordan
b: abt. 1804, Melksham, Wiltshire
m: abt. 1834, Melksham, Wiltshire
d: 07 Dec 1874, Melksham

Susan Jordan
b: 13 Sep 1835, christened on this date, Melksham
d: 14 May 1894, Wandsworth

Harriet Lucas
b: abt. 1816, Melksham, Wiltshire
d: 07 Jan 1834, Melksham

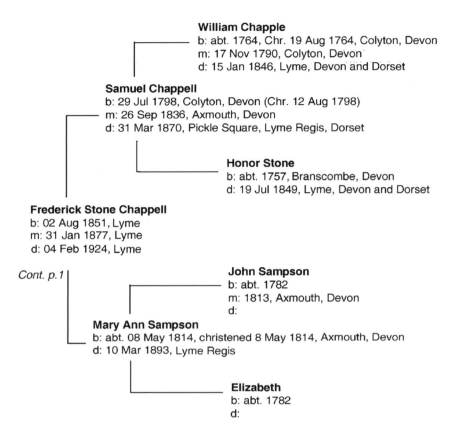

William Chapple
b: abt. 1764, Chr. 19 Aug 1764, Colyton, Devon
m: 17 Nov 1790, Colyton, Devon
d: 15 Jan 1846, Lyme, Devon and Dorset

Samuel Chappell
b: 29 Jul 1798, Colyton, Devon (Chr. 12 Aug 1798)
m: 26 Sep 1836, Axmouth, Devon
d: 31 Mar 1870, Pickle Square, Lyme Regis, Dorset

Honor Stone
b: abt. 1757, Branscombe, Devon
d: 19 Jul 1849, Lyme, Devon and Dorset

Frederick Stone Chappell
b: 02 Aug 1851, Lyme
m: 31 Jan 1877, Lyme
d: 04 Feb 1924, Lyme

Cont. p.1

John Sampson
b: abt. 1782
m: 1813, Axmouth, Devon
d:

Mary Ann Sampson
b: abt. 08 May 1814, christened 8 May 1814, Axmouth, Devon
d: 10 Mar 1893, Lyme Regis

Elizabeth
b: abt. 1782
d:

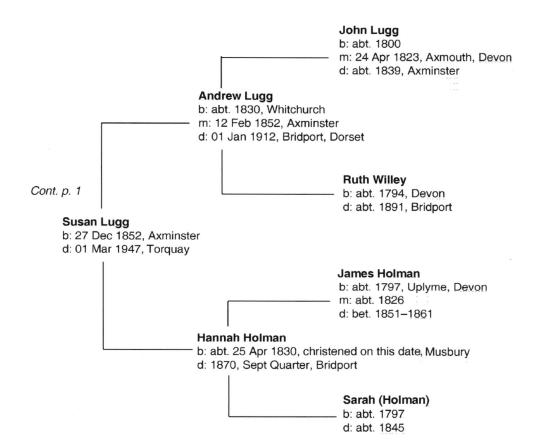

John Lugg
b: abt. 1800
m: 24 Apr 1823, Axmouth, Devon
d: abt. 1839, Axminster

Andrew Lugg
b: abt. 1830, Whitchurch
m: 12 Feb 1852, Axminster
d: 01 Jan 1912, Bridport, Dorset

Ruth Willey
b: abt. 1794, Devon
d: abt. 1891, Bridport

Cont. p. 1

Susan Lugg
b: 27 Dec 1852, Axminster
d: 01 Mar 1947, Torquay

James Holman
b: abt. 1797, Uplyme, Devon
m: abt. 1826
d: bet. 1851–1861

Hannah Holman
b: abt. 25 Apr 1830, christened on this date, Musbury
d: 1870, Sept Quarter, Bridport

Sarah (Holman)
b: abt. 1797
d: abt. 1845

6

Search tips

How to search the Census when you can't find an ancestor

It is not always possible to find an ancestor by surname search but you can
search by Christian name, location, place of birth, age, etc.

For the purpose of this exercise we are going to use Ancestry.co.uk. (Please
note that the following example is a random selection of research I have
recently carried out on behalf of a client, Nicole Sheard.)

I was trying to locate a family by the name of Warhurst in the 1841 Census
in Cheshire. I tried searching for one particular member of the family but the
one shown below is the wrong person. I tried again and chose to search using
Soundex but still got the same result.

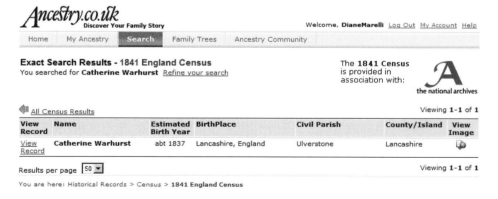

I altered my search criteria, took out the surname of my subject but added
place and estimated date of birth.

Refine your search of the 1841 England Census

☑ Exact matches only   Search tips

First name   Last name   Spelling
catherine   Exact ▼

Residence

County or island   Civil parish   Hundred
Any   ▼

Personal

Gender   Birth Year*
All   ▼   1828   +/- 10 ▼

Birthplace

Country**   County or island
England   Cheshire

Census

        Piece   Book   Folio   Page #
HO107/

Other

Keyword(s)

e.g. Foreign Parts

▲ **Hide Advanced Search Options**   Search

Copyright © 1998–2006, MyFamily.com Inc. and its subsidiaries.
Searching using only date and place of birth.

This search came up with 484 possible candidates to check through, so I
decided that, as the surname began with W, I would start at the last page and
work forward. It worked, and on the penultimate page I found the Catherine I
was looking for transcribed as Catherine Whartursh.

View Record	Catherine Wainwright	abt 1826	Cheshire, England	Doddleston	Cheshire	
View Record	Catherine Walker	abt 1829	Cheshire, England	Christleton	Cheshire	
View Record	Catherine Walker	abt 1826	Cheshire, England	Delamere	Cheshire	
View Record	Catherine Wallace	abt 1834	Cheshire, England	Wybunbury	Cheshire	
View Record	Catherine Walsh	abt 1821	Cheshire, England	St John the Baptist	Cheshire	
View Record	Catherine Walton	abt 1829	Cheshire, England	Tarporley	Cheshire	
View Record	Catherine Wamby	abt 1821	Cheshire, England	Prestbury	Cheshire	
View Record	Catherine Warrington	abt 1825	Cheshire, England	Prestbury	Cheshire	
View Record	Catherine Webb	abt 1837	Cheshire, England	Astbury	Cheshire	
View Record	Catherine Webb	abt 1823	Cheshire, England	Great Budworth	Cheshire	
View Record	Catherine Welsh	abt 1826	Cheshire, England	Chorley	Cheshire	
View Record	Catherine Wharton	abt 1837	Cheshire, England	Birkenhead	Cheshire	
View Record	Catherine Whartursh	abt 1828	Cheshire, England	Mottram in Longden Dale	Cheshire	
View Record	Catherine White	abt 1836	Cheshire, England	Stockport	Cheshire	
View Record	Catherine Whitehead	abt 1821	Cheshire, England	Prestbury	Cheshire	
View Record	Catherine Wilcock	abt 1831	Cheshire, England	Bowden	Cheshire	

Results per page 50 ▼

Viewing **401-450** of **484**
‹ Prev | 1 2 3 4 5 6 7 8 **9** 10 | Next ›

You are here: Historical Records > Census > **1841 England Census**

🖶 View printer-friendly

Refine your search of the 1841 England Census

Results revealed over several pages of records.

So, as you can see, there is great flexibility when searching for that elusive ancestor. I have searched many times using the above method and have had a great deal of success.

There is another way I could have located Catherine Warhurst. I knew from previous Census records that she came from Mottram in Longden Dale and had I not been successful finding her, I would have chosen this next method. I did not choose this method originally as it can be quite time consuming.

From the home page in Ancestry.co.uk I selected the 1841 Census for England.

Birthplace

Country**

County or island

Census

	Piece	Book	Folio	Page #
HO107/				

Other

Keyword(s)

e.g. Foreign Parts

▲ **Hide Advanced Search Options**

Search

To browse census images, click on a county link below. Subsequent screens will allov to choose a civil parish and an enumeration district.

Please choose a county:

Bedfordshire	Hampshire	Oxfordshire
Berkshire	Herefordshire	Rutland
Buckinghamshire	Hertfordshire	Shropshire
Cambridgeshire	Huntingdonshire	Somerset
Cheshire	Kent	Staffordshire
Cornwall	Lancashire	Suffolk
Cumberland	Leicestershire	Surrey
Derbyshire	Lincolnshire	Sussex
Devon	Middlesex	Warwickshire
Dorset	Norfolk	Westmorland
Durham	Northamptonshire	Wiltshire
Essex	Northumberland	Worcestershire
Gloucestershire	Nottinghamshire	Yorkshire

If you scroll down this page you will find that you can pinpoint a county. In this case I selected Cheshire and this is what I found.

Welcome, DianeM

| Home | My Ancestry | Search | Family Trees | Ancestry Community |

You are here: Search > Census > UK Census Collection > 1841 England Census > **Cheshire**

1841 England Census

Please choose a civil parish in Cheshire:

Acton	Guilden Sutton	St John the Baptist
Alderley	Halton	St Martin
Aldford	Handley	St Mary on the Hill
Ashton upon Mersey	Hardhill	St Michael
Astbury	Henbury	St Olave
Audlem	Heswall	St Oswald
Backford	Hilbre Island	St Peter
Baddiley	Holy and Undivided Trinity	Stockport
Barrow	Ince	Stoke
Barthomley	Kingsmarsh	Sutton
Basford	Knutsford	Swettenham
Bebington	Leighton	Tarporley
Bidstone	Little Budworth	Tarvin
Birkenhead	Lymm	Tattenhall
Bowden	Malpas	Taxall
Brereton cum Smethwick	Marbury	Thornton le Moors
Bromborrow	Marton	Thurstaston
Bunbury	Mere	Tilston
Burton	Middlewich	Toft
Butley	Millington	Tytherington
Cheadle	Mobberley	Upton
Chorley	Mottram in Longden Dale	Wallasey
Christleton	Nantwich	Warburton

Selecting the county will break it down into civil parishes.

Ancestry.co.uk
Discover Your Family Story   Welcome, DianeMa

| Home | My Ancestry | **Search** | Family Trees | Ancestry Community |

You are here: Search > Census > UK Census Collection > 1841 England Census > Cheshire > **Mottram i**

1841 England Census

Please choose a sub-registration district in Mottram in Longden Dale:

Mottram

Newton and Godley

Stayley

Census Records - Sub-Registration Districts

Occasionally, counties will contain parishes with the same name or a large parish might include multiple instances of an Enumeration District number. Sub-registration districts, which are a related to civil registration districts, are then used to distinguish which parish or part of a parish is referenced.

Copyright © 1998–2006, MyFamily.com Inc. and its subsidiaries.
Selecting Mottram in Longden Dale gave 3 more options.

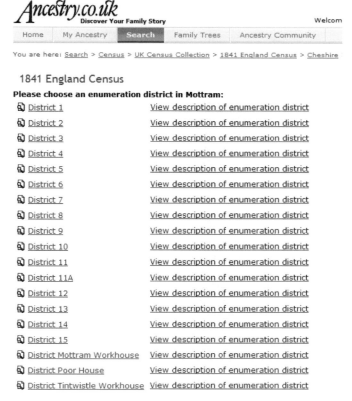

Ancestry.co.uk
Discover Your Family Story   Welcom

| Home | My Ancestry | **Search** | Family Trees | Ancestry Community |

You are here: Search > Census > UK Census Collection > 1841 England Census > Cheshire

1841 England Census

Please choose an enumeration district in Mottram:

District 1	View description of enumeration district
District 2	View description of enumeration district
District 3	View description of enumeration district
District 4	View description of enumeration district
District 5	View description of enumeration district
District 6	View description of enumeration district
District 7	View description of enumeration district
District 8	View description of enumeration district
District 9	View description of enumeration district
District 10	View description of enumeration district
District 11	View description of enumeration district
District 11A	View description of enumeration district
District 12	View description of enumeration district
District 13	View description of enumeration district
District 14	View description of enumeration district
District 15	View description of enumeration district
District Mottram Workhouse	View description of enumeration district
District Poor House	View description of enumeration district
District Tintwistle Workhouse	View description of enumeration district

Census Records - Enumeration Districts

Copyright © 1998–2006, MyFamily.com Inc. and its subsidiaries.
Selecting Mottram gave a list of the enumeration districts.

If I had an address, I could look at the descriptions of the enumeration districts. Failing that I could search through each district, but upon closer inspection District 1 and 2 were for Hattersley which didn't mean anything to me, but District 3 was headed Mottram in Longdale. Luckily, I found my Warhurst in District 4.

Estimating death search years post-1901

There is another way to help estimate a death during the 20th century. We are currently concentrating on creating a four- or five-generation pedigree tree, but you naturally collect other family names from the Census as you go. Let's go back to the 1901 Census for Martino and family:

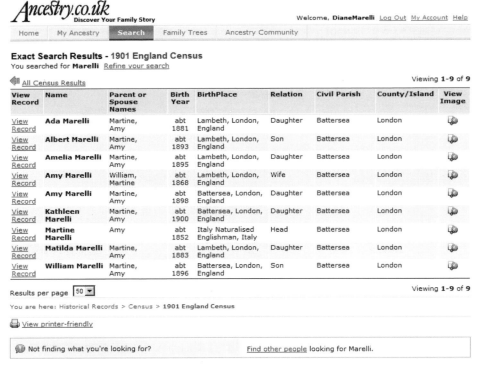

The 1901 Census for the Marelli family.

In 1901, Martino and Amy had seven children living with them. It would be safe to assume that some if not all went on to marry at some stage during the early part of the 20th century. Their marriage certificates will provide information as to whether Martino was still living at the time of their marriage. I sourced marriage certificates for Amy Marelli in 1921, which recorded that Martino was still living and working as a restaurant proprietor.

Other marriages gave me further clues. William Marelli in 1924, Kathleen Marelli in 1925, Philomena Marelli in 1926, Winifred Marelli in 1931 and Henry Marelli in 1932, all recorded Martino as still living at the time of their marriages. Previously without this information, I had to search from 1911 to 1940 to find the death details for Martino, but with the clues provided by the marriages of his children, my search years shrink to 1932–1940.

Searching with limited information: a live exercise

There will be occasions when funds just don't permit the purchase of certificates to begin your research, but there is still a lot you can achieve

Besides writing about family history, I also provide a research and gift service www.dianemarelli.co.uk. For my good friend Lisa Castle's 50th birthday, I decided to research her family history and obtain old family photographs with the help of her children Danielle and Lewis, to present to her in a bound landscape book. Cleverly, her daughter Danielle said she needed to have all the old family photographs scanned for a college project and persuaded Lisa to allow me to remove all her pictures and take them away for scanning. I returned the photographs and she was none the wiser as to the real reason I required the photographs.

A few days later I phoned Lisa and said I was currently without a client and needed to keep my hand in with research and would she mind if I did a bit for her. She was happy to allow me to do this but couldn't find her parents' birth or marriage certificates. Several phone calls later I managed to acquire the following information:

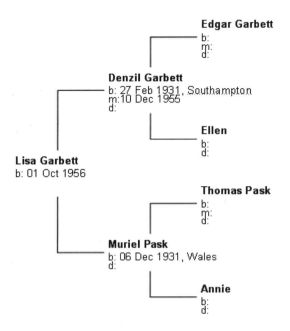

Standard pedigree tree for Lisa Castle.

Lisa also mentioned a surname of Bonfield but wasn't sure which side of the family or where she'd heard the name before. Although I desperately wanted copies of the birth and marriage details it was getting to the point of being obvious, so there was nothing left to do but order the certificates myself.

Using findmyfamily.com I found the Civil Registration birth records for both parents, then, rather than wait for these certificates to arrive, I looked for the marriage records for Thomas Pask and Edgar Garbett. Having no idea about when they married or where Denzil and Muriel fell in the pecking order of possible siblings, I decided to search from 1925–1931 and further back if necessary. (I was dreading the Wales connection with possible surnames of Jones or Davies to contend with.) I looked for Edgar Garbett's marriage and found one in the December quarter for 1930, to someone with the surname of Cousins. If I could find the mirrored marriage details for an Ellen Cousins to Garbett then I was onto a winner. This got me thinking, how far could I realistically get without purchasing certificates?

I am now going to take you through a research exercise from scratch. Together we will see how far we could get with limited information before ordering certificates. Still using findmyfamily.com I revised my search criteria and entered Ellen Cousins.

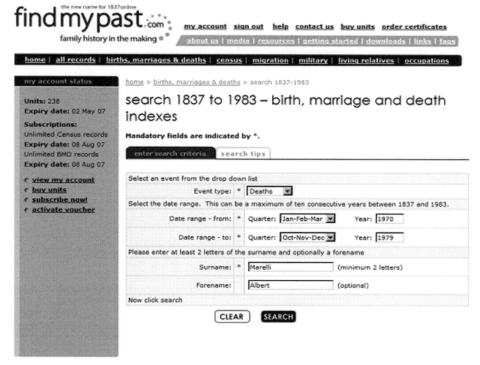

Searching for Ellen Cousins.

Detailed record for Ellen Cousins.

Yes, I had the right details. I could now add Ellen's surname and marriage details to my tree.

I carried out the same procedure for the Pask marriage to Annie and was beginning to think my luck had run out when I found their details in the September quarter of 1920. Thomas Pask had married Annie Meskill in Newport, Monmouthshire, meaning I could now add her surname and marriage details to the tree.

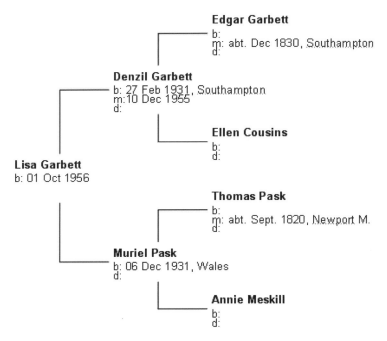

Standard pedigree tree for Lisa Castle.

With this result, I thought I would now purchase marriage certificates for Denzil, Edgar and Thomas but before I did that I wondered if it might be possible to trace at least birth records for one set of grandparents enabling me to search further on the 1901 Census. I checked first to see if there was an Edgar Garbutt and Ellen Cousins on FreeBMD.

And I found them. Thank you so much FreeBMD!

Births Mar 1907

Surname	First name(s)	Mother	District	Vol	Page
GARBETT	**Edgar**		**Pontypool**	**11a**	**190**

Births Dec 1911

Cousins	Ellen E G	Bonfield	S.Stoneham	2c	189

Birth records for Edgar Garbett and Ellen Cousins.

The location of birth and surname of the mother, Bonfield, was so exciting and it confirmed that I had the correct Ellen Cousins, as Lisa had remembered the name Bonfield. A quick phone call confirmed that Edgar was indeed born in Wales. I wondered if I could find a marriage for Cousins and Bonfield and did a quick check on FreeBMD.

Surname	First name(s)	District	Vol	Page
Marriages Mar 1895				
Bonfield	Alice	Wareham	5a	397
Cousins	William	Wareham	5a	397

Marriage records for Alice Bonfield and William Cousins.

I had no idea where Wareham was so I clicked on Wareham, as underlined in the above image, and found district information.

District Information

Surname	Given Name	District	Volume	Page
Marriages Mar 1895				
Bonfield	Alice	Wareham	5a	397

The district **Wareham** is in the county of **Dorset** and information about it can be found here.

District information on FreeBMD.

Then by clicking on the word 'here' I was led to registration districts in Dorset.

 GENUKI Contents  List of Counties

REGISTRATION DISTRICTS IN DORSET

The list below shows the civil registration districts in the county of Dorset betw the years 1851, 1861, 1871, 1881, 1891 and 1901.

Click on a district name to see the places and dates covered, or see the Index

- Axminster
- Beaminster
- Blandford
- Bridport
- Cerne
- Chard
- Dorchester
- Mere
- Poole
- Shaftesbury
- Sherborne
- Sturminster
- Wareham
- Weymouth
- Wimborne
- Wincanton

List of registration districts in Dorset.

I selected Wareham and found the following:

 GENUKI Contents List of Districts

WAREHAM REGISTRATION DISTRICT

Registration County : Dorset.
Created : 1.7.1837.
Sub-districts : Bere Regis; Corfe Castle; Swanage; Wareham
GRO volumes : VIII (1837-51); 5a (1852-1930).

Parishes in Dorset (1837-1930):

Affpuddle, Arne, Bere Regis, Bloxworth, Chaldon Herring, Church Knowle, Coombe Keynes, Corfe Castle, East Holme, East Lulworth, East Stoke, Kimmeridge, Langton Matravers, Moreton, Morden, St. Martin, Steeple, Studland, Swanage, Turners Puddle, Tyneham, Wareham, West Lulworth, Winfrith Newburgh, Wool, Worth Matravers.

Registers now in South & West Dorset *district.*

Detailed information on Wareham and its parishes.

This marriage took place in a sub-district of Dorset as listed above. Even though I had the marriage record, I was unhappy with Dorset.

There was only one thing for it and that was to check the 1901 Census to see if there were any clues I could pick up there, even without hard evidence that I was on the right track. I tried Alice Cousins born in Dorset, first hoping to find her married to William and couldn't believe it when Alice Cousins popped up at the top of my search. With only four to choose from and only one married to a William, it would be safe to assume this is the correct record.

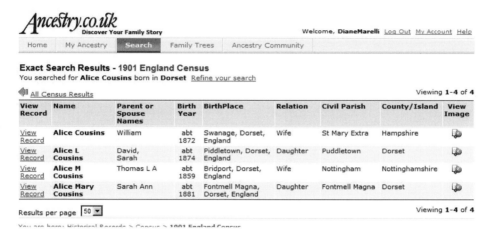

Exact Search Results - 1901 England Census
You searched for **Alice Cousins** born in **Dorset** Refine your search

All Census Results   Viewing **1-4 of 4**

View Record	Name	Parent or Spouse Names	Birth Year	BirthPlace	Relation	Civil Parish	County/Island	View Image
View Record	**Alice Cousins**	William	abt 1872	Swanage, Dorset, England	Wife	St Mary Extra	Hampshire	
View Record	**Alice L Cousins**	David, Sarah	abt 1874	Piddletown, Dorset, England	Daughter	Puddletown	Dorset	
View Record	**Alice M Cousins**	Thomas L A	abt 1859	Bridport, Dorset, England	Wife	Nottingham	Nottinghamshire	
View Record	**Alice Mary Cousins**	Sarah Ann	abt 1881	Fontmell Magna, Dorset, England	Daughter	Fontmell Magna	Dorset	

Results per page 50   Viewing **1-4 of 4**

You are here: Historical Records > Census > **1901 England Census**

Copyright © 1998–2006, MyFamily.com Inc. and its subsidiaries.
1901 Census records for Alice Cousins.

1901 England Census Record
about Alice Cousins

Name:	**Alice Cousins**
Age:	29
Estimated Birth Year:	abt 1872
Relation:	Wife
Spouses's Name:	William
Gender:	Female
Where born:	Swanage, Dorset, England
Civil parish:	St Mary Extra
Ecclesiastical parish:	Woolston St Marks
County/Island:	Hampshire
Country:	England
Street address:	
Occupation:	
Condition as to marriage:	View image
Education:	
Employment status:	
Registration district:	South Stoneham
Sub-registration district:	St Mary Extra
ED, institution, or vessel:	5
Neighbors:	View others on page
Household schedule number:	40

View Original Record

View original image
View blank form

Household Members:	Name	Age
	Alice Cousins	29
	Kate Alice Cousins	3
	William Cousins	36
	William C Cousins	4

The original document also informed me that William Cousins was born in Portsmouth, Hants. I knew I should be ordering at least a couple of certificates at this stage to confirm what I had found so far, but with the ages of the Cousins family I couldn't resist looking at the 1891 Census.

The 1891 Census told me that Alice Bonfield was working in Bournemouth as a servant, but living away from home, so I had no other information about her parentage. The 1881 Census provided me with a very different picture.

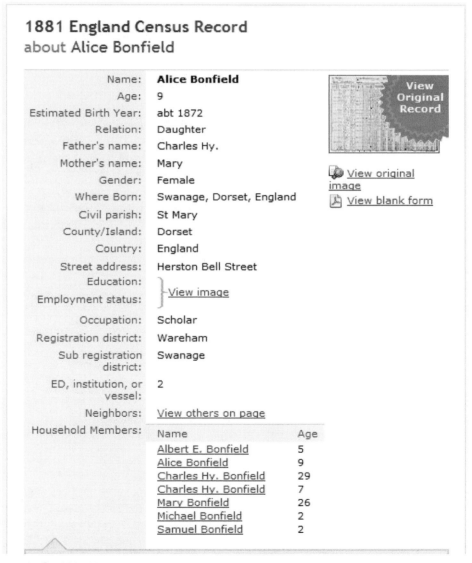

1881 England Census Record
about Alice Bonfield

Name:	**Alice Bonfield**
Age:	9
Estimated Birth Year:	abt 1872
Relation:	Daughter
Father's name:	Charles Hy.
Mother's name:	Mary
Gender:	Female
Where Born:	Swanage, Dorset, England
Civil parish:	St Mary
County/Island:	Dorset
Country:	England
Street address:	Herston Bell Street
Education:	}View image
Employment status:	
Occupation:	Scholar
Registration district:	Wareham
Sub registration district:	Swanage
ED, institution, or vessel:	2
Neighbors:	View others on page

View Original Record

View original image
View blank form

Household Members:	Name	Age
	Albert E. Bonfield	5
	Alice Bonfield	9
	Charles Hy. Bonfield	29
	Charles Hy. Bonfield	7
	Mary Bonfield	26
	Michael Bonfield	2
	Samuel Bonfield	2

1881 Census record for Alice Bonfield.

I would get round to verifying this current vein of research but first I just wanted to check if I could find a marriage of a Charles Henry Bonfield to a Mary. Taking the age of the eldest child from 1881 gave me about 1872 as the year I needed to search from.

Surname	First name(s)	District	Vol	Page	
Marriages Dec 1871					
Bonfield	Charles Henry	Wareham	5a	695	Info
COOPER	Mary	Wareham	5a	695	Info

Marriage details for Charles Henry Bonfield to Mary Cooper.

I really ought to be ordering certificates because the above finds could easily be incorrect, but my instincts tell me to continue. As Charles Bonfield and Mary Cooper were married in December 1871, then I was hoping to find them both living with their respective parents in the 1871 Census.

I found Charles in the 1871 Census aged 19 along with the names of his siblings and his parents. I found Mary Cooper in the 1861 Census living with her family.

1871 England Census Record
about Charles H Bonfield

Name:	**Charles H Bonfield**
Age:	19
Estimated Birth Year:	abt 1852
Relation:	Son
Father's name:	Samuel
Mother's name:	Judith
Gender:	Male
Where born:	Swanage, Dorset, England
Civil Parish:	Swanage
Ecclesiastical parish:	Salisbury
Town:	Swanage
County/Island:	Dorset
Country:	England
Street address:	
Occupation:	
Condition as to marriage:	View image
Disability:	
Registration district:	Wareham
Sub-registration district:	Swanage
ED, institution, or vessel:	2
Neighbors:	View others on page
Household schedule number:	60

View Original Record

View original image

View blank form

Household Members:	Name	Age
	Albert Bonfield	17
	Angelina Bonfield	14
	Charles H Bonfield	19
	Ellin Bonfield	7
	Frederich T Bonfield	11
	Judith Bonfield	51
	Samuel Bonfield	52
	Elizabeth Kernan	24
	Fanny Kernan	4 months

1871 Census record for Charles Henry Bonfield.

1861 England Census Record
about Mary Cooper

Name:	**Mary Cooper**
Age:	6
Estimated Birth Year:	abt 1855
Relation:	Daughter
Father's name:	Michael
Mother's name:	Georgena
Gender:	Female
Where born:	Swanage, Dorset, England
Civil parish:	Swanage
County/Island:	Dorset
Country:	England
Street address:	
Occupation:	View image
Condition as to marriage:	
Registration district:	Wareham
Sub-registration district:	Swanage
ED, institution, or vessel:	1
Neighbors:	View others on page
Household schedule number:	32

View Original Record

View original image
View blank form

Household Members:	Name	Age
	Ann Cooper	2
	Georgena Cooper	25
	Mary Cooper	6
	Michael Cooper	26

1861 Census record for Mary Cooper.

I looked for William Cousins and found him living with his brother Charles in the 1881 census.

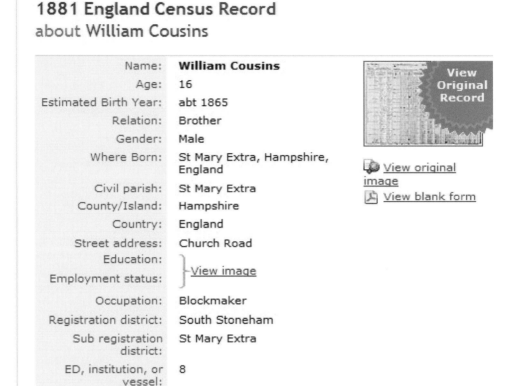

1881 England Census Record
about William Cousins

Name:	**William Cousins**
Age:	16
Estimated Birth Year:	abt 1865
Relation:	Brother
Gender:	Male
Where Born:	St Mary Extra, Hampshire, England
Civil parish:	St Mary Extra
County/Island:	Hampshire
Country:	England
Street address:	Church Road
Education:	⎫
Employment status:	⎬ View image
Occupation:	⎭ Blockmaker
Registration district:	South Stoneham
Sub registration district:	St Mary Extra
ED, institution, or vessel:	8
Neighbors:	View others on page

View Original Record

View original image
View blank form

Household Members:	Name	Age
	Chs. Cousins	24
	Chs. Cousins	2
	Itta Cousins	22
	William Cousins	16

1881 Census record for William Cousins.

Looking for William Cousins in the 1871 Census caused me a little concern as the one I found that appears to be correct but has place of birth as Havant, rather than Portsmouth even though closely linked.

1871 England Census Record
about William Cousins

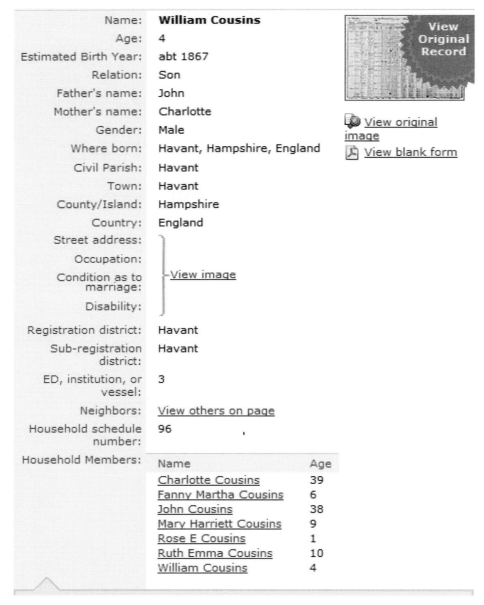

Name:	**William Cousins**
Age:	4
Estimated Birth Year:	abt 1867
Relation:	Son
Father's name:	John
Mother's name:	Charlotte
Gender:	Male
Where born:	Havant, Hampshire, England
Civil Parish:	Havant
Town:	Havant
County/Island:	Hampshire
Country:	England
Street address:	
Occupation:	
Condition as to marriage:	View image
Disability:	
Registration district:	Havant
Sub-registration district:	Havant
ED, institution, or vessel:	3
Neighbors:	View others on page
Household schedule number:	96

View original image
View blank form

Household Members:

Name	Age
Charlotte Cousins	39
Fanny Martha Cousins	6
John Cousins	38
Mary Harriett Cousins	9
Rose E Cousins	1
Ruth Emma Cousins	10
William Cousins	4

At this stage I go only by instinct.

If all the unproved research above is correct, this is what Lisa's family tree will look like this so far:

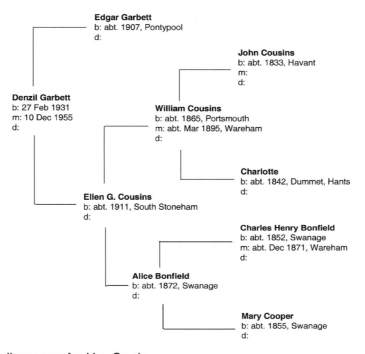

Edgar Garbett
b: abt. 1907, Pontypool
d:

John Cousins
b: abt. 1833, Havant
m:
d:

Denzil Garbett
b: 27 Feb 1931
m: 10 Dec 1955
d:

William Cousins
b: abt. 1865, Portsmouth
m: abt. Mar 1895, Wareham
d:

Charlotte
b: abt. 1842, Dummet, Hants
d:

Ellen G. Cousins
b: abt. 1911, South Stoneham
d:

Charles Henry Bonfield
b: abt. 1852, Swanage
m: abt. Dec 1871, Wareham
d:

Alice Bonfield
b: abt. 1872, Swanage
d:

Mary Cooper
b: abt. 1855, Swanage
d:

Standard pedigree tree for Lisa Castle.

I am now going to send for some certificates to help me prove the above and will provide the results at the end of this book (see page 243). The certificates I will order first are:

♦ Denzil Garbett's birth certificate

♦ Certificate of Edgar Garbett's marriage to Ellen Cousins

♦ Edgar Garbett's birth certificate

♦ Ellen Cousins's birth certificate

Things you should know about the Census

1841 Census

For those under 15, ages were given exactly (if known). For people over 15, ages were rounded down to the nearest five years. For example, someone of 64 would appear as 60, another of 29 as 25. However, this was not always the case. When viewing the 1841 Census for two of my husband's ancestors, Richard and Harriet Jordon, Richard's age is recorded as 36 and Harriet's as 26. So do be aware and cross-refer where possible.

Some information relating to the place of birth was also given, but was restricted to whether or not a person was born in the county of residence ('Y' for Yes, 'N' for No), and, if not, whether in Scotland (S), Ireland (I), or foreign parts (F).

Census dates
A census was taken to record those living in a household at midnight on a Sunday. The dates of the Census varied from year to year.

- Sun/Mon 6/7 June 1841
- Sun/Mon 30/31 March 1851
- Sun/Mon 7/8 April 1861
- Sun/Mon 2/3 April 1871
- Sun/Mon 3/4 April 1881
- Sun/Mon 5/6 April 1891
- Sun/Mon 31 March/1 April 1901

Knowing when the Census was taken is useful when trying to assess dates of birth.

Public Record Office Census references

The Census records at the PRO are classified under the following:

1841	HO107
1851	HO107
1861	RG9
1871	RG10
1881	RG11
1891	RG12
1901	RG13

These references prove extremely useful when making copies of the Census but forgetting to note which year it is.

Although 1841 and 1851 have the same Census reference it is easy to spot the difference between the two, as the 1841 Census had two pages per sheet (the information recorded is considerably less than you will find with later Census years).

Finding other related sources on the Internet

How other researchers on the Internet can help you

There are many people researching their ancestors who post their findings on the Internet. There are also one-name study groups that are compiling lists worldwide of a variety of differing surnames, some obscure and some common. Posting your research information on the Internet will help you if you are searching for a family member by a particular name. Others looking for ancestors will also contact you, enabling your research to expand more quickly and efficiently. There is more about family history forums in Chapter 7, and how to launch a web page using Family Tree Maker in Chapter 8.

I have two examples to show you now. The first is one I sourced while searching the Internet. I decided to look for various family names in different areas, keying in similar information to below:

Google search by varying surnames.

☆ ✛ | G | chapple chappell family history devon - Google Search | |

Did you mean: ***chappell*** chappell family history devon

Chappel **Family** Genealogy Forum
Re: James **Chappell** 1838-1899 **Devon** - Anne Slocomb 11/03/02 ? Chappel m. Edward
West abt 1800 in Nova Scotia - Betty Storey 6/26/02. **Chapple Family** of ...
genforum.genealogy.com/chappel/ - 42k - Cached - Similar pages

Chapple Family Genealogy Forum
Re: Charles **Chapple**/Chappel/**Chappell** married in Alabama 1892 - Melissa Hogan 12/29/03.
Chapple line, Hugh 1704 to John 1807, **Devon** - Laura McMahan 8/24/03 ...
genforum.genealogy.com/**chapple**/ - 16k - Cached - Similar pages

GENUKI/**Devon**: Plymouth - Genealogy
MMC The King's 'Catholick **Chappell**' 1687. **Devon** & Cornwall Notes ... Plymouth Marriage
Index: Volume 1:, Exeter, **Devon Family History** Society (2001). ...
genuki.cs.ncl.ac.uk/DEV/Plymouth/ - 66k - Cached - Similar pages

GENUKI/**Devon**: Even More North **Devon History**
Even More North **Devon History**. by Peter Christie. (Edward Gaskell, **Devon**, 1998) ...
Chapman, Michael 147 **Chappell**, Mr 62 **Chapple**, Eliza 104 Charles I 75 ...
genuki.cs.ncl.ac.uk/DEV/**Devon**Indexes/EvenMoreNorthDevonHist.html - 20k -
Cached - Similar pages

Cyndi's List - Surnames, **Family** Associations & **Family** Newsletters ...
Welcome to the Clan CLEARY **Family History** and Genealogy Web Site ... Chapell, Chappel,
Chappell, Chappelle, Chapele, Capwell, **Chapple**), CAPLENA (includes ...
www.cyndislist.com/surn-c.htm - Similar pages

Cyndi's List - Personal Home Pages - "F"
A **Family History**: CHAPPELL'S/NAHRSTADTs and Related Families ... GRIFFITHS from
Montgomeryshire, Wales, CHAPPLE from **Devon**, England, DRAKE from **Devon**, ...
www.cyndislist.com/home-f.htm - Similar pages

Chapple page 3 1800-1854
Chapple Family History. Use the numbered child links eg [53] to navigate the CHAPPLE ...
Henry **Chappell** (son) age under 4 months, born Axminster **Devon**. ...
www.stevenjones.me.uk/html/**chapple**_3.html - 73k - Cached - Similar pages

Chapple page 6 1855-1878
Chapple Family History. Use the numbered child links eg [102] to navigate the CHAPPLE ...
Charles **Chapple** (head) age 37, born Beer **Devon** occ Boat Builder. ...
www.stevenjones.me.uk/html/**chapple**_51.html - 84k - Cached - Similar pages

This particular enquiry brought up the above information.

This search brought up lots of possibilities, but the most thrilling was finding
the last two entries from the same website http://www.stevenjones.me.uk

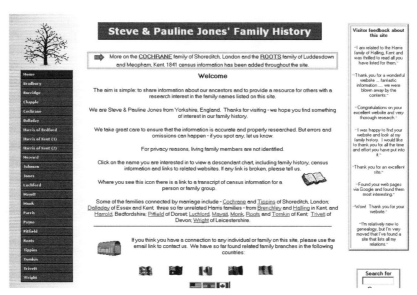

Home page of http://www.stevenjones.me.uk

Down the left hand side of the page is a list of surnames, including Chapple, so I clicked it and the most amazing information came up.

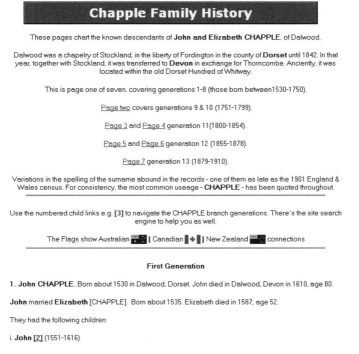

Chapple family information on http://www.stevenjones.me.uk

To say I was flabbergasted was an understatement and although I knew it was going to be interesting viewing, I really couldn't quite believe that I would be lucky enough to have a family link. I checked my records for what Chapple or Chappell family members I had against those recorded on the website.

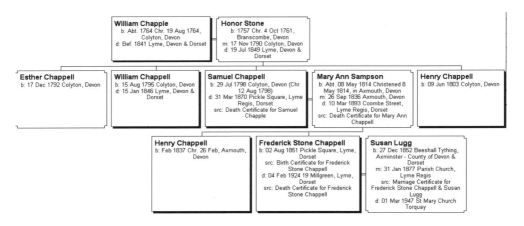

Descendants of William Chapple.

The eldest known ancestor I have on this branch of the family is William Chapple (Chappell) who was married to Honor Stone. The William Chapple on my tree I believed was born in Colyton where he married Honor Stone. I had also found information relating to the births of both Honor Stone and William Chapple.

IGI Individual Record

Search Results | Download | Pedigree

HONOR STONE
Female

Event(s):
Birth:
Christening:
Death:
Burial:

Marriages:
Spouse: WILLIAM CHAPPLE
Marriage: 17 NOV 1790 Colyton, Devon, England

IGI record for Honor Stone married to William Chapple.

IGI Individual Record

Search Results | Download | Pedigree

WILLIAM CHAPEL
Male

Event(s):
Birth:
Christening: 19 AUG 1764 Colyton, Devon, England
Death:
Burial:

Parents:
Father: HENRY CHAPEL
Mother: ELIZABETH

IGI Individual Record

Search Results | Download | Pedigree

HONOUR STONE
Female

Event(s):
Birth:
Christening: 04 OCT 1761 Branscombe, Devon, England
Death:
Burial:

Parents:
Mother: ELIZA STONE

IGI records for William Chapel and Honour Stone.

Everything connected well except for the fact that Honour (Honor) Stone, who looks illegitimate as there is no mention of the father, was born in Branscombe. I wasn't sure how far Branscombe was from Colyton, and even if a great distance, it didn't really prove anything as she could have been born anywhere and travelled to find work. I located Branscombe in Devon via Genuki.

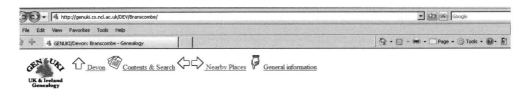

GENUKI/Devon: Branscombe - Genealogy

⬆ Devon   📄 Contents & Search   ⇐⇒ Nearby Places   🖐 General information

GENUKI
UK & Ireland
Genealogy

BRANSCOMBE

"BRANSCOMBE, a pleasant village, on the coast of the English channel, at the mouth of a rivulet, 5 miles E. by N. of Sidmouth, and S.W. of Colyton, has in its parish 956 souls, and 3422A. 3R. 18P. of land, including *Dean* and *Weston* hamlets, and many scattered houses. The Dean and Chapter of Exeter are lords of the manor, owners of most of the soil, appropriators of the great tithes, and patrons of the *vicarage*, valued in K.B. at £18. 15s. 10d., and in 1831 at £190, and now enjoyed by the Rev. S.H. Peppin, B.A., who has 10A. of glebe, and an ancient residence, mantled with ivy and vines. The great tithes were commuted in 1843, for £242, and the vicarial for £225 per annum. The *Church* (St. Winifred,) is a cruciform Gothic structure, with a tower and five bells. The Stuckey and Bartlett families were long seated at *Weston Barton*, as lessees of the manor; and *Edge Barton* was anciently the seat of the Branscombes, one of whom was sheriff of the county for five years, in the reign of Edward III. Many women and girls in this neighbourhood are employed in making lace, and here are quarries of excellent freestone. The *Wesleyans* have a small chapel in the village." [From White's *Devonshire Directory* (1850)]

A parish under the Peculiar jurisdiction of the Dean and Chapter of Exeter.

- Biography
- Cemeteries
- Census
- Church History
- Church Records
- Description and Travel
- Directories

- Gazetteers
- Genealogy
- History
- Land and Property
- Occupations
- Schools

Select map to view parish boundaries in detail.

Information on Branscombe using GENUKI.

I selected 'Nearby Places' at the top of the screen and, as you will see, Colyton is only 4 miles from Branscombe.

~ 1 miles SW SY190880 Branscombe, Devon
~ 3 miles N SY200930 Southleigh, Devon
~ 3 miles ENE SY240900 Seaton, Devon
~ 4 miles W SY140880 Salcombe Regis, Devon
~ 4 miles ENE SY250910 Axmouth, Devon
~ 4 miles NE SY240930 Colyton, Devon
~ 5 miles NNW SY180950 Farway, Devon
~ 5 miles N SY190950 Northleigh, Devon
~ 5 miles WNW SY130910 Sidbury, Devon
~ 5 miles W SY120870 Sidmouth, Devon

Places within 5 miles of Branscombe, OS Gridref SY195884.

I went back to the Chapple family history site to see if I could find my William Chapple born in 1764 in Colyton.

Eighth Generation

27. Henry CHAPPLE. Henry died 1805.

On 18/2/1764 Henry married **Elizabeth JOY**, in Colyton, Devon. Elizabeth died 1809.

They had the following children:

i. **William**, born 1764. William was baptized in Colyton, Devon on 19/8/1764.

ii. **Mary**, born 6/12/1766.

iii. **Ann**, born 7/8/1767.

iv. **Betty**, born 1/4/1769.

v. **Esther**, born 7/12/1770.

vi. **Henry**, born on 1/3/1773 in Colyton, Devon. Henry was baptized in Colyton, Devon on 11/3/1773. Henry died as infant on 1/4/1773 in Colyton, Devon.

vii. **Samuel**, born on 29/5/1779. Samuel died on 28/2/1798, age 18.

viii. **Richard [37]**, born 1780.

Detailed information on the Chapple family from http://www.stevenjones.me.uk

I cannot describe my excitement at this find. If this connection could be verified, then the Chappell/Chapple family tree would have another nine generations.

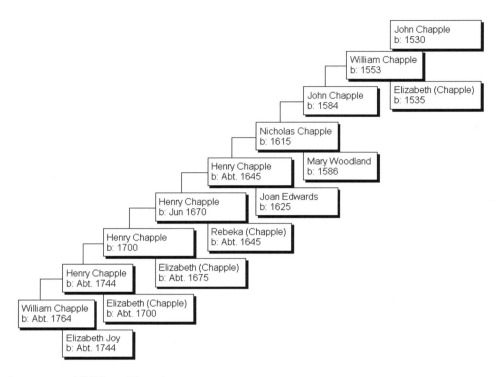

Ancestors of William Chapple.

I had to find out more. I took the plunge and emailed Steve Jones, the owner of the website, and sent him what information I had, and asked if he thought there might be a link. This is a copy of the reply:

Hi Diane

Thanks for your message.

I have looked at the tree you supplied and there is certainly a link, insofar as the ancestors you have for William Chapple b. 1764 match the ones I have. It is who William married that has always presented me with a difficulty.

It is this. William was born in Colyton so it is a reasonable assumption that he was married there too; my early Chapples did not stray far. But there are 2 marriages for a William Chapple in Colyton. One on 17 Nov 1790 to Honor Stone (the link you've made), and another on 21 Nov 1789 to Jenny Stoford. I've never been able to prove which one's 'my' William.

Now, if you have the evidence to resolve this it would be very helpful to say the least. Please let me know what your source is.

I was thrilled to hear from Steve and remembered some confusion over the marriage of William Chapple. The marriage Steve is talking about is detailed below:

IGI Individual Record

Search Results | Download | Pedigree

WILLIAM CHAPPLE
Male

Event(s):
Birth:
Christening:
Death:
Burial:

Marriages:
Spouse: JENNY STOFORD
Marriage: 21 NOV 1789 Colyton, Devon, England

IGI record for marriage of William Chapple to Jenny Stoford.

How irritating! Not only had I completely forgotten about this marriage, I could not remember why I discounted this record because I had not made any notes, or if I had, they were now lost to me.

I sent Steve all the Census and civil records pertaining to my William Chapple and descendants, to prove my connection and he agreed; but his concern, quite naturally, was how we could verify that my William Chapple married to Honor Stone was the correct descendant of William Chapple and Elizabeth Joy. He wrote:

I have no doubt that your research from William C and Honor Stone is sound. The only remaining niggle in the back of my mind is whether the William who married Honor Stone was the son of Henry C and Elizabeth Joy. As I mentioned before, there were 2 William Chapples from Colyton who married in 1789 (to Jenny Stoford) and 1790 (to Honor Stone). We need to sort out which of them had the Henry/Elizabeth parentage to be sure of the link.

I am in touch with Chapple descendants in Canada, NZ, Australia and here in UK so I will email them to see if they can help. (It also means, of course, that if we can prove the link, your husband will have gained instant global cousins.)

If you have any info on this tricky point please let me know.

Somehow we had to eliminate the marriage of a William Chapple to a Jenny Stoford as neither was connected to me, but they could be the rightful link to the family tree of Steve Jones.

I searched every avenue – the Census, the NBI (National Burial Index) available on CD-Rom and church records for Devon also available on CD-Rom, but with no luck. I could find nothing else about a William and Jenny Chapple in the Census. Neither could I find a record of Jenny Stoford's birth using a variety of different spellings, or a record of her death. The only information I could find that led me to believe that my William belonged to Steve's family history was by looking at the names of the children:

The children of Henry and Elizabeth:
William
Mary
Ann
Betty
Esther
Henry
Samuel
Richard

The children of William and Honor Stone:
Esther
Henry
Samuel
William

Searching for children of William Chappell and Honor Stone resulted in the following:

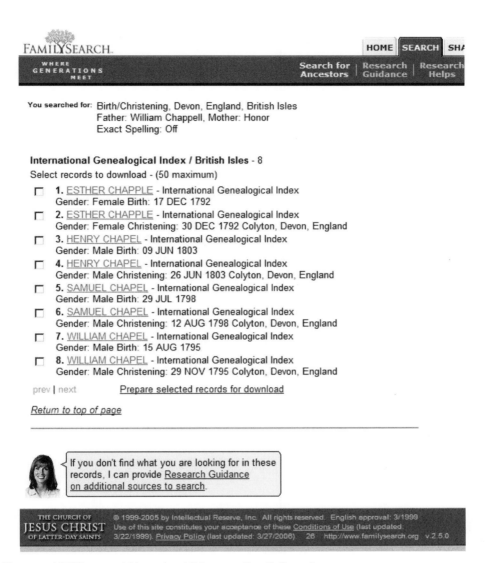

Names of William and Honor's children on FamilySearch.

Is it a coincidence that both families share the same Christian names or is there something in it? The only evidence of Jenny Stoford on FamilySearch is the following:

You searched for: Jenny Stofford, Devon, England, British Isles
Exact Spelling: Off

International Genealogical Index / British Isles - 2

Select records to download - (50 maximum)

☐ **1.** JENNY STAFFORD - International Genealogical Index
Gender: Female Christening: 09 DEC 1772 Paignton, Devon, England

☐ **2.** JENNY STOFORD - International Genealogical Index
Gender: Female Marriage: 21 NOV 1789 Colyton, Devon, England

Information on Jenny Stoford.

Both entries could relate to the same person but there is no record on this site that I can find for a death of a Jenny Stoford or similar, also there are no children recorded under the names of William Chapple and Jenny.

You searched for: Birth/Christening, British Isles
Father: William Chapple, Mother: Jenny
Exact Spelling: Off

International Genealogical Index / British Isles (No Matches)

IGI record for children of William and Jenny.

I hate it when this happens ('No Matches')!

However another thing of interest is the name Lucretia that appears in both my husband's and Steve's family histories. As I have no evidence to contradict my findings, as yet, I am inclined to believe there is a link between my husband's Chapple, Chappells or Chapels and Steve Jones's Chappels. I received this last email from Steve and it looks as though all the Chappell hunters have come to the same conclusion.

Hi Diane

Thanks for your last email. Apologies for the delay in replying but I was awaiting responses from fellow Chapple researchers on the two William Chapple marriages in Colyton.

The consensus seems to be that William married twice – once to Jenny Stofford in Nov 1789 and second to Honor Stone a year later. The conclusion must be that Jenny died very soon after the marriage for William to remarry again a year later. The info has come from Keith Chapple, my first cousin once removed, who derived much of his info from Roy Chapple who still lives in Devon and has done all the leg work looking up original sources. Don Chapple Feist in NZ concurs.

All of which means, to cut a long story short, that your husband Brian is my 6th cousin, once removed.

I have been doing a bit more research and found a family for Henry Chapple b. 1837. He married Charlotte CARNELL in the quarter ending Sept 1869 in Axminster. They had no children of their own that I can find but in the 1881 Census an 'adopted child' appears – John Bowden LUGG who was born in 1879. John appears with them in the 1891 Census but I can find no trace of him in 1901. Charlotte had died by then as well – in 1900. Henry was living on his own.

One thing struck me in the Census records about the spelling of the family name. There's more variation in this branch than I have ever come across before – and you will see from my website that I've come across quite a few! I will update the site with the new info as soon as I can.

Do you know what happened to Frederick Stone Chapple's other children – Reginald and Frederick Jnr in particular? I've located both in the 1901 Census but after that the trail gets more difficult and, I guess, will remain so until 1911 comes along in 2012 unless family memories/records still survive.

Look forward to hearing from you.

Regards

Steve

My instinct is to agree with Steve that William did marry once before to a Jenny Stoford and that she died shortly afterwards, but I will keep looking for more corroborative evidence.

I continue to stay in contact with Steve Jones. It's great when you can share research and help one another. Heaven only knows how long it would have taken me to find all the wonderful information in his website, if ever! It never ceases to amaze me how many family historians are loath to share their information with others. Why?

Another interesting piece of information is that one of the ancestors on Steve's family history, James Chapple b. 1612, could be Brian's second cousin 10 times removed. Nothing interesting in that you might think, except when you look at his death in detail in 1635. The cause of death was hanging! James, baptised in Colyton, Devon 15/11/1612. James was hanged at Exeter for the murder of Alice Bragg. An abstract from the Chancery Warrants:

> 24th May. II Charles I. (A.D. 1635) . . . at the Assize held at Exeter on the 18th March 8 Charles I (A.D. 1632) James Chapel and Thomas Whitmore, husbandmen, both of Colliton, in the county of Devon, were convicted of the murder of Alice Bragg, on the previous 2nd of February, by inflicting a mortal wound in her throat, and that John Sampson, of Colliton, gentleman, was also convicted for having aided and abetted the said James and Thomas before the murder, namely on the 31st January before the said 2nd of February, &c. The lands &c of all are therefore forfeited &c. It was found by Inquisition taken at Exeter the 15th January 10 Charles I (A.D. 1635), that the said John Sampson was seized in his demesne as of fee of and in all that late dissolved Chantry of St. John the Baptist in Colcombe within the parish of Colliton and of and in &c. Here follows the description of other property of the said John Sampson: Know ye that we by these presents &c do give &c, to Peter Newton, John Chase of Membury, Henry Godsall of Taunton, merchant, Philip Lissant of Taunton, the younger, mercer, and Robert Carswell of Lyme Regis, mercer, all the said Chantry &c. Delivered to the keeper of the Great Seal to execute on the 4th June, 1635.

Another interesting point above is the name Sampson. The Chappell family would marry into the Sampson family some generations later. Again, thank you, Steve, for this wonderful piece of history. I was beginning to think that my husband's family were saints and mine sinners. I would appreciate hearing from anyone who has information about the Chappell family.

In the meantime, should I claim all those extra generations on behalf of my husband? I think it would be rude not to!

How you can help other researchers on the Internet

If you are searching the Internet for family history connections then I can guarantee that something in your research will be of interest to someone else. Since my first book was published I've have no end of letters and emails from people who believe we share common ancestors, some of which are still open to question but some with very definite links.

Obviously, we are not all lucky enough to have a published book about our findings but you can donate your research to history centres or places such as The Society of Genealogists who have their own website (http://www.sog.org.uk) and promote their findings in their Library Update Magazine online.

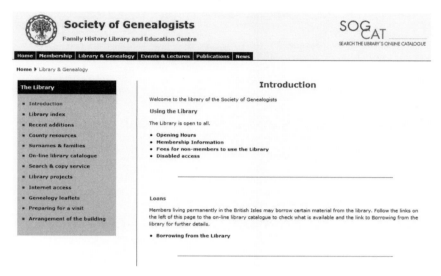

SOG home page.

On the menu to the left click on 'Recent additions'.

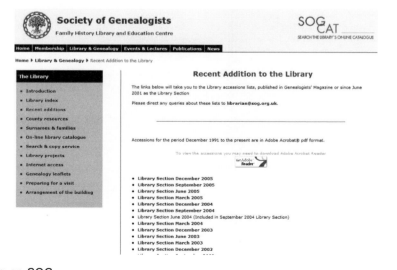

Searching on SOG.

Once transcribed, you can view the SOG progress, select one from the list and scroll down to the family history section.

LIBRARY SECTION

Library update Genealogists' Magazine December 2005 vol 28 no 8

Accessions

The accessions list this quarter is smaller than usual due to the need to re-index our catalogue database. So large is it that the job took four weeks to complete, during which time no cataloguing could be done.

All of the notable items in this list are, unusually these days, in book form. You may have read in the last magazine, the obituary of my predecessor at the Society, Lawson Edwards. He left his book collection to the Society and a few of the hundreds of volumes appear below (some of the Oxford history of England series etc.). More will appear in due course as we catalogue them. In the same month, we also received a donation of five boxes of books withdrawn from the House of Lords library.

Two of the items which I have singled out for your notice are the Royal Navy lieutenants' passing certificates 1691-1902 which form volumes 289-290 of the List and Index Society. From about 1789 these certificates are usually accompanied by notices of baptism. Berkshire Family History Society is to be congratulated on the completion of its mammoth twelve year project to make abstracts from all the Overseers of the Poor documents at Berkshire Record Office. In 2004 they completed the project by the issue of a composite index to all 26 volumes of the abstracts. Other items include the Victoria County History volume covering the city of Chester, the Harleian Society publication of the visitation of London 1678, an almost complete set of indexes to the 1841 census of Caithness and the latest Passenger and immigration lists index. Lastly I would like to commend to you a London Topographical Society volume of maps which cover a later period than is usually noted here: they are the London County Council bomb damage maps 1939-45. Each one is detailed enough to show individual buildings and those which have been coloured in indicate houses etc which were destroyed or damaged by bombs - black for total destruction, purple for damaged beyond repair and so on. This has confirmed my suspicions about my own house which is shown black on the map and explains why my roof is a different colour tile from the neighbours and why I am always digging up burnt brick fragments in the garden!

Library Wants

The Bourne Society local history records, nos. 1, 8, 12, 20, 28 and 30 to date; also any issues of their bulletin.

Bugle annual [best of the *Black Country Bugle*] 1980, 1990 and 1995 onwards.

Fareham past and present, vol. 1, nos. 1-8, vol. 3, nos. 9-11, vol. 4, nos. 2, 10 and 12-13.

The Great War, nos. 1-20, 2001-2005, plus special editions, vols. 1-2.

A history of the Baptist Church at Colwell, Isle of Wight 1834-1964, by Basil T. Cheverton.

Leicestershire historian, vol. 1, no. 3, 1968, vol. 2, no. 4, 1973, vol. 3, no. 1, 1982/83.

Royalty digest, vol. 1 - vol. 9, no. 8 inclusive.

Dial stone: news sheet of the Walton and Weybridge Local History Society. Any issues prior to no. 175, Jan. 2002 and indexes to issues 1-150.

Walton and Weybridge Local History Society monographs. Any except nos. 64-67 inclusive.

Sue Gibbons, Librarian

SOG library section online.

3. FAMILY HISTORY

Adams. See Cheney. Adamson/Aitchison/Allward. See Wallace. Alp/Alpe/Alps. See Ulph. Amos. See McElligott. Andrews. See Schlamp. Arden. See Kingsbury. Ashley. See Mountbatten - Edwina Mountbatten. Atkinson. See Lloyd. Aulph. See Ulph. Austen. Jane Austen: her life, her work, her

Brunton. See Noverre. Budd/Bulhead/Bullied. See Lyne. Burchall. See Lloyd. Burdon. See Cheney. Busfield. See Lloyd. Butt. The state of mind of Mrs. Sherwood, by Smith, Naomi Royde. 1946. D: R Morgan. [FH/BUT] Butterworth. See Brook. Cadle. Genealogy of the Cadle family including the English descent, by Cadle, Henry. 1915. D: M Bristow. [FH/CAD] Campbell. See McElligott. Capper. See Kent. Carus-Wilson. See Wallace.

9

Genealogists' Magazine

Library Section

Anon. [FH/HIC] Hill. See Hart. Hindley. Behind my Hindleys 1692-1944, by Sheppard, Phyl (donor). 2005. [FH/HIN] Hoare. Conversations, by Hoare, William. 2005. D: A Laycock. [FH/HOA] Hoatson. See McElligott. Hobbs. See Shone. Hobson/Hodgson. See Lloyd. Holf. See Ulph. Holland. A history of the family of Holland of Mobberley & Knutsford in the county of Chester with some account of the family of Holland of Upholland & Denton in the county of Lancaster, from materials collected by the late Edgar Swinton Holland, by Irvine, William Fergusson ed. 1902. D: J Gibson & M Twiss. [FH/HOL] Honeyfield. Honeyfield 400 years: 1600-2000, by Honeyfield, Harold R (donor). 2nd edn. 2005. [FH/HON] Hopkin(s). Hopkins & Kitchin descendants trees, by Church, Judith M (donor). 1999. [FH tracts, vol. 218] Horne. See Lister. Hosking. See McElligott. House. From Rockbourne to Portsea Island: a history of the House family, by Kingston, Eleanor R (donor). 1984. [FH tracts, vol. 243] Huckle. See McElligott. Huffman. See Wilson - A supplement to "Dear John". Hull. See McElligott. Hutchings. See Williams - The descendants of George Williams. Hutchinson/Hyde/Ingham. See McElligott. Irvine. See Williams - The Williamses of Penycoed. Jenkins. See Lloyd. Johnston. See Wallace. Johnstone. See Cheney. Jones. See Bagnold & McElligott. Joscelyne. See Kent. Joseph. See Phillips. Junger. Storm of steel, by Junger, Ernst. 2004. D: C Bullen. [FH/JUN] Kendal(l). A year at Killington Hall: the 1876 diary of Agnes Ann Kendal - life in Victorian England through the eyes of a farmer's daughter, by Robinson, Judith M S. 2004. D: N Newington-Irving. [FH/KEN] Kent. The descendants of Thomas Kent of Mendham, Suffolk born about 1700 & thoughts on his antecedents, by Joscelyne, Ben (donor). Rev. edn. 2004. [FH/KEN] King. Letters from Luxor: life in Poland before

Lishman, tallow chandler & his wife Sarah Snowball of Houghton-le-Spring in the county of Durham, by Wright, Jean D (comp. & donor). 2004. [FH tracts, vol. 243] Lister. A story of four families: the Lister families of the East Riding of Yorkshire & Kent; the Moreton families of Winchester & Hampshire; the Horne families of Northamptonshire, the Romney Marsh & Tasmania; the Maclean families of Bualnaluib, Loch Ewe & London: also including the Young families of Somerset, Wiltshire, Hampshire, Australia & the USA; the Lippiatt families of Somerset; the Taylor families of Hampshire & the USA; the Talbot families of Northamptonshire & New Zealand; the Goodman families of New Zealand, by Lister, Paul (donor). 2004. [FH/LIS] Littlebury. See Blaxill. Lloyd. Extracts from "The Lloyds of Harley Street, associated family & friends", by Lloyd, C R S (donor). 2005. [FH/LLO] Lock. See Williams - The Williamses of Penycoed. Lord. See Lloyd. Lovering/Lowe. See Cheney. Lyne. The Lyne family of Winkleigh, Roborough & Dolton, Devonshire: tree researched from original parish registers, census returns during 1965-2004, by Lyne, Peter (donor). 2005. [FH/LYN] Macaulay. Rose Macaulay, by Babington Smith, Constance. 1972. D: R Morgan. [FH/MAC] MacKenzie. See Wallace. Mackereth. See Cheney. Maclean. See Lister. MacNab. See Wallace. Macnaughton. See Williams - The descendants of George Williams. MacQueen. See Williams - The Williamses of Penycoed. MacRobert. See Wallace. Mallet. See Williams - The Williamses of Penycoed. Marillier. Those jollier days: some memories of things which have gone for ever, by Marillier, Harry Currie. 1942. D: C G Marillier. [FH/MAR] Mayhead. Mayhead family history. Nd. D: J Smith. [FH/MAY] McCarthy. Notes on the story of one family of the McCarthys of Clann Diarmaide of MacCarthaigh Mor, by MacCarthaigh, Desmumhan. 1979. D: A

Here is what you can expect to find in the family history section.

Another way would be to list the names of ancestors for which you have a particular interest on family history forums, such as GenForum, (more about forums in Chapter 7). By far the best way is to launch your own family history website or page. You can launch a page through the Family Tree Maker software, more about this in Chapter 8.

7

Behind the names and dates

By now you should have an impressive pedigree of your ancestors and will have probably added other ancestors taken from the Census. You will:

♦ Know when they were born, married and died

♦ Have addresses taken from the Census and Certificates

♦ Have details of occupations

♦ Have details about cause of death, providing medical histories of your ancestors

♦ Have details of surrounding neighbourhoods etc.

What you won't have is detailed information about their lives. But you can learn what their lives were like by researching further. Here are some questions to consider:

♦ What was happening in the country at the time of their birth, marriage or death? How might these events have affected their lives and those of their extended families?

♦ What were their occupations and what did those occupations involve?

♦ Did they spend time as a family in a workhouse? If they did, what circumstances beyond their control put them there? Perhaps they were workers on the land but it was a bad year for crops. Perhaps the death of a breadwinner shattered their lives.

♦ What caused their death? If it was a fever such as typhus, was there an epidemic locally? Did such occurrences affect their status in life?

Widespread deaths, as awful as it seems, can provide opportunities for those left behind as well as misfortune.

♦ Did they live in lodgings? Did they have a house to themselves? Did they have lodgers? Did they move around the country? What caused them to move – was it work, death or to be with family? Perhaps they had a military background. You can chart the progress of a family by tracking their occupations and types of lodgings through researching old maps or studying the Census and certificates to find out if they improved their lot through time, or if they declined.

♦ Are there any books about a town, village or city in which they lived?

♦ Do other family members have any memorabilia such as photographs, postcards or letters?

♦ Did religion play a big part in their lives? If a family was of a certain religious denomination until a point in time then changed to another religion, what could have been the cause of this?

♦ Many Victorian districts survive today; do some of the homes of your ancestors still exist?

♦ Do graves where your ancestors were buried survive today? Do churches where they were christened or married exist today?

The list could go on and on.

By putting certificates and Census information into chronological order by family and researching history surrounding key events, their occupations, illnesses, causes of death, where they lived, their religious beliefs, by collecting old photographs and reading about the towns or villages in which your ancestors lived, you can build a picture of their lives and get to understand them, if not know them personally.

There are so many avenues available to you to learn more about the lives of your forebears that it impossible for me to record them all, but I hope the following will guide you further into finding out who your ancestors were.

Newspapers

In my first book *Meet Your Ancestors*, I discovered newspaper articles concerning two of my ancestors, my five times great aunt and uncle, Henry and Emily Pudwine on the Newspaper Detectives website (www.newspaperdetectives.co.uk).

The Newspaper Detectives is transcribing an index of articles printed in the *Surrey Advertiser* during the 19th century and to date have transcribed 1864–1867 and 1872. You can search alphabetically for your subject or surname and you will be given an exact date, names of persons involved, if applicable, and the story's headline.

This information enables you to go straight to the newspaper source, at the Surrey History Centre in Woking where back copies of the *Surrey Advertiser* can be viewed on microfilm, and print a copy of the relevant stories.

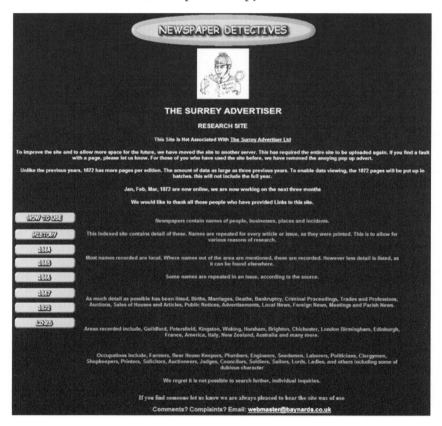

Home page of the Newspaper Detective

Although I haven't yet scanned every article in the last two additions, I did search in 1866 records for family names and found the information below.

21/04/1866	Emily	Pudwine	Guildford, A Wife And A Policeman, Assault, Fined 20s
10/11/1866	*	Pudwine	Guildford, Drunk, 14 Days Prison

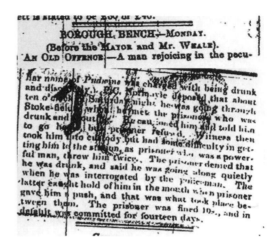

Information on Emily Pudwine and husband from Newspaper Detectives.

These stories are very entertaining to my family but what is also of great interest is reading a local newspaper written at the time that my ancestors were living. Although it is important to remember that, just as today, newspaper reporters of yesterday used their creative skills to create reader interest and also had their own views, beliefs and prejudices. However, I have no reason to doubt that the above is true, although the reporter definitely had a sense of humour. Both of these articles most certainly built a picture in my mind of an attractive young couple full of life and fun. I visualised Emily as trim, in a pretty, although not expensive, calico dress, with sparkling eyes and a mischievous grin – how wrong could I be! More a little later.

Another great newspaper resource is the British Library Online: www.uk.ol ivesoftware.com. By accessing newspaper archives of the same period, you can find local, national and world history during the time your forebears were living.

The British Library

THE BRITISH LIBRARY

Welcome to the British Library Online Newspaper Archive

Please note: presently, the Online Archive browser minimum requirements are: Internet Explorer 5, Netscape 4.79 or 6.2. The minimum screen resolution is 800 X 600.

When using Internet Explorer for Windows, make sure that the security setting "Run ActiveX controls and Plug-ins" is enabled in the browser.

For questions related to the British Library or the Online Newspaper Archive content, please click here.

For technical support regarding the operation of the Online Newspaper Archive, please click here.

Click here to enter

Produced in partnership with

The British Library home page.

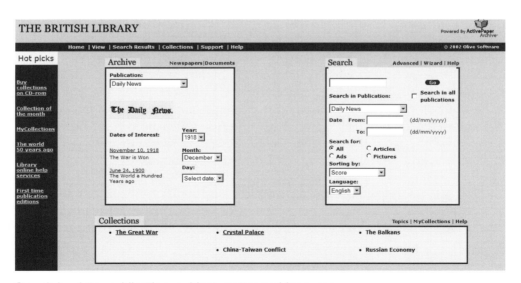

Search by date, publication, subject matter and language.

Besides hoping to find interesting news about your ancestors, you could also find information that will help you understand particular environments in which they were sometimes forced to live, such as I did with my grandmother. She was placed in a workhouse aged just 10 weeks until she was 16 years of age. The articles below helped my mother understand why my grandmother was the way she was.

THE POOR LAW GIRL.

To the Editor of *The Daily News*.

Sir,—You have given space in your columns for a discussion on the Poor Law—whether or not it shall live. I have read some outside opinions and the Guardians' defence. May I give a few whispers from within, as I was brought up in a Poor Law home?

Poor Law children are terribly mixed in rank, character, and appearance. Some have gentle feelings and kind dispositions; others show bad breeding. Some are backward scholars and others have great talents. "The workhouse nursery is the least objectionable to visit," so I am told by one who knows. The children look upon the Guardians as men to be revered and referred to in a whisper. If one is seen coming towards the dayroom the girls are told to smile—not an easy thing to do to order—and if they are unable to do so they get into serious trouble afterwards. Has the Guardian any idea of how the children live, of the low atmosphere they breathe, or of the degrading punishments given them for very small misdeeds and mistakes?

What becomes of us? When we are fifteen we are sent into the world, of which we are ignorant, to become general servants, as if we were responsible working girls who should know what is required of us. We are not; we feel helpless and alone, besides being strangers to life's simplest ways and habits. We have never entered a shop or handled money; at every turn we find ourselves lost, in the street, kitchen, dining-room, drawing-room or bedroom; everywhere things are new and strange, and we lack the speech, manners, knowledge and courage which are so badly needed to cope with life. Our minds are, as it were, chained up through rule and discipline; individuality is unknown to us, our capabilities have no standard, and we have no sense of self or of our importance as human beings.

In consequence of this, "Home" Girls are backward, shy, thoughtless and slow. Many of them have no taste for housework, yet all are catalogued for domestic service. These are England's special girls. What do your readers think of the Poor Law system now?

GRACE BUMPSTEED.

Daily News, 16 December 1918.

"THE POOR LAW GIRL."

To the Editor of *The Daily News*.

Sir,—Your correspondent is, no doubt, relating her own particular experience; but what would she have been if the Poor Law had not stepped in and helped her?

Experience teaches us that no child is sent to the workhouse unless the conditions of life are such that she is unable to obtain sufficient nourishment and care in the home from which she comes.

A child is taken into the workhouse, cared for, washed, clothed, and fed from infancy until it is about five years old. Then it is transferred to a cottage home, where it is located with other 30 to 25 children, and sent to the county school. The cottage homes are in the country (most of the children come from the slums). The children are not dressed in uniform; they sit side by side with other children, and have an equal chance of obtaining scholarships.

When they are about 14 two of the girls are appointed to assist the foster mother in cleaning the home, and are taught to bake, sew, knit, and darn. For further domestic training two of the eldest girls take duty in the superintendent's house, and help in all kinds of work, including waiting at the table.

When one thinks of all that is being done for these children, one cannot but wonder what would have become of them if they had not received the care and attention of the Poor Law.

A GUARDIAN.

Daily News, 19th December 1918.

The newspapers available on the site from 1851.

The National Archives

Whilst looking at the new entries on the National Archives website, I came across a live archive called Victorian prisoners. On the right-hand side of this screen under 'popular content', out of nothing more than curiosity, I decided to search through some of the pictures. Imagine my surprise when I came across this page, in particular the bottom listing shown below:

The National Archives, www.nationalarchives.gov.uk

page 1 2 3 4 5 6 7 8 9 10 〉 〉〉

Description ⌄		Date ⌄	Catalogue ref	Details
Name (and alias if used) of prisoner	Turner , Elizabeth	1873 May 31	PCOM 2/291/146	See details ›
Age on discharge:	61			
Place of Birth:	Kent ...			
Name (and alias if used) of prisoner	Vernon , Joshua	1873 Apr 26	PCOM 2/291/10	See details ›
Age on discharge:	30			
Place of Birth:	Clapham ...			
Name (and alias if used) of prisoner	Harrigan , Mary	1872 December 21	PCOM 2/290/9	See details ›
Age on discharge:	24			
Place of Birth:	Surrey ...			
Name (and alias if used) of prisoner	Goldsmith , Henry	1873 February 1	PCOM 2/290/165	See details ›
Age on discharge:	18			
Place of Birth:	Bath ...			
Name (and alias if used) of prisoner	Sherwood , James	1873 January 25	PCOM 2/290/161	See details ›
Age on discharge:	14			
Place of Birth:	Guildford ...			
Name (and alias if used) of prisoner	Trimmer , William	1873 January 25	PCOM 2/290/162	See details ›
Age on discharge:	14			
Place of Birth:	Hampshire ...			
Name (and alias if used) of prisoner	Redwine (Emily Noller?) , Emily	1873 January 25	PCOM 2/290/150	See details ›
Age on discharge:	32			
Place of Birth:	Surrey ...			

Search results under 'popular content'.

Emily Redwine (Pudwine) née Noller (Voller) had to be my ancestor. From previous experience I knew to expect many transcription errors or variations in the spelling of both surnames. I clicked on 'See details'.

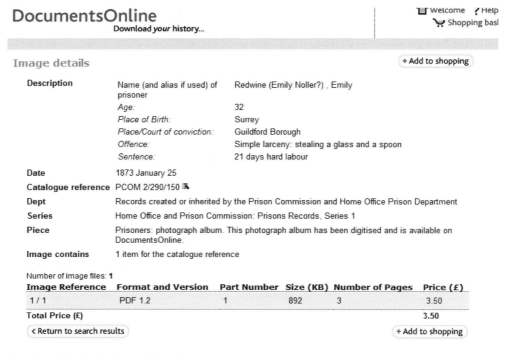

Details of Emily Pudwine/Redwine.

The place of conviction is Guildford, where Emily Pudwine, née Voller was living at this time. I decided to purchase a copy of the image and was able to download it immediately.

Form X.

$\frac{416}{3}$ 597

Wandsworth Gaol,

County of Surrey

25 Jany 1873.

PARTICULARS of a Person convicted of a Crime specified in the 20th Section of the Prevention of Crimes Act, 1871.

Name .... Emily Redwine 2191

and

Aliases... Emily boller

Description when liberated.	Age (on discharge)	32	Photograph of Prisoner.
	Height..	5ft 2	
	Hair..	Dk Brown	
	Eyes...	Dk Blue	
	Complexion................................	Fresh	
	Where born................................	Surrey	
	Married or single	Married	
	Trade or occupation	Laundress	
	Any other distinguishing mark	None	

[17 08]   E. & S.—20,000.—2.72.

Conviction record for Emily Pudwine/Redwine.

My goodness, what a sour puss! But she was in prison and obviously not thrilled by her predicament and I'm glad to say she bears no family resemblance.

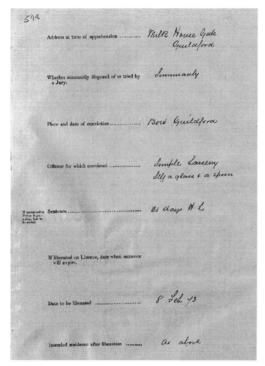
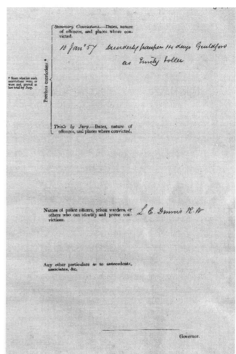

Conviction record continued.

The above lists a previous crime for being a disorderly pauper when she was aged just 17. So what with the above image and the previous newspaper cutting, it was obvious that my five times great aunt Emily Pudwine was no saint.

I never thought I would wish this, but I searched through the other 619 records of Victorian prisoners hoping to find more family members, but sadly Emily was it! I'm not really disappointed because what are the odds that I would even find one ancestor? What a wonderful resource!

DocumentsOnline

Download *your* history...

Browse

Click on a category to view images

Family History

- WW1 Campaign Medals (5459710) ›
- WW2 Seamen's Medals (108390) ›
- Famous Wills (103) ›
- Wills (1016127) ›
- Death Duty Registers (71757) ›
- Victorian Prisoners Photograph Albums (626) ›
- Registers of Seamen's Services (581413) ›
- Women's Army Auxiliary Corps (WAAC) (7006) ›
- French Muster Rolls (5902) ›
- Royal Naval Division (50109) ›
- Victoria Cross Registers (1237) ›
- Domesday Book (23045) ›

Other Records

- New Releases (293) ›
  - FOI Releases (77) ›
  - Cabinet minutes & memoranda from 1975 (202) ›
  - Cabinet Secretary's Notebooks (3) ›
  - Security Service (11) ›
- Society & Law (1642) ›
- Home & Foreign Affairs (1920) ›
- Military & Defence (12035) ›
- Arts, Recreation & Travel (73) ›
- Science & Environment (85) ›

Other documents and records available online at the National Archives.

Out of curiosity, I searched Wills and was amazed to find the Will of John Charitee Plummer, my husband's four times great grandfather.

Will of John Charitee Plummer.
Documents above are reproduced by kind permission of the National Archives.

Again, for £3.50, I was able to purchase a copy of the above document. It is the likes of sites such as the Newspaper Detectives that I have to thank for leading me to the newspaper cutting that led me to this wonderful historical source.

The Old Bailey

Another great resource of the many waiting to be discovered on the Internet is the one below for The Proceedings of The Old Bailey, London 1674 to 1834.

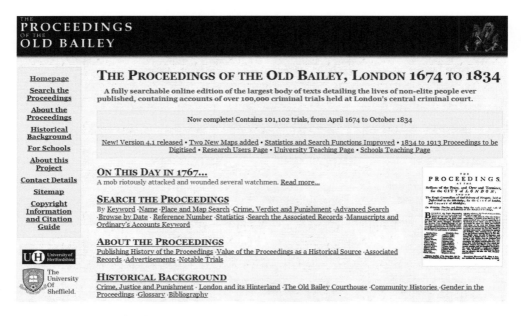

Home page of the Old Baily, http://www.oldbaileyonline.org

The Commonwealth War Graves Commission

Home page of CWGC, http://www.cwgc.org

By searching under the name of my half-brother I found the following information:

In Memory of
Ordinary Seaman CHARLES PATRICK MOLONEY

D/MD/X 2966, H.M.S. Rawalpindi., Royal Naval Volunteer Reserve
who died age 23
on 23 November 1939
Son of Charles and Ellen Moloney, of Liverpool.
Remembered with honour
PLYMOUTH NAVAL MEMORIAL

Commemorated in perpetuity by
the Commonwealth War Graves Commission

Search for Charles Patrick Moloney revealed the above details.

I keyed 'HMS Rawlpindi' on the address line of my Internet Page and found many sites providing information about this ship, including this one, http://en.wikipedia.org/wiki/HMS_Rawalpindi.

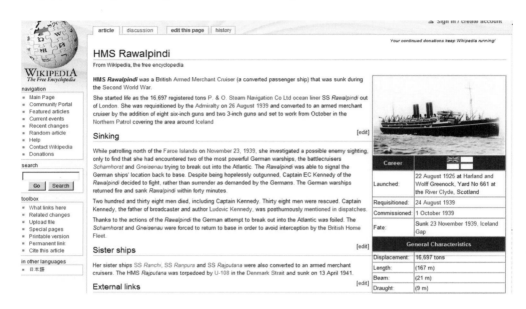

Information from Wikipedia, Copyright © 2000, 2001, 2002 Free Software Foundation, Inc.

Family history forums

Genforum

Genforum is an information site and also a wonderful resource to post questions asking for help or advice about your family research. You can search by country and surname.

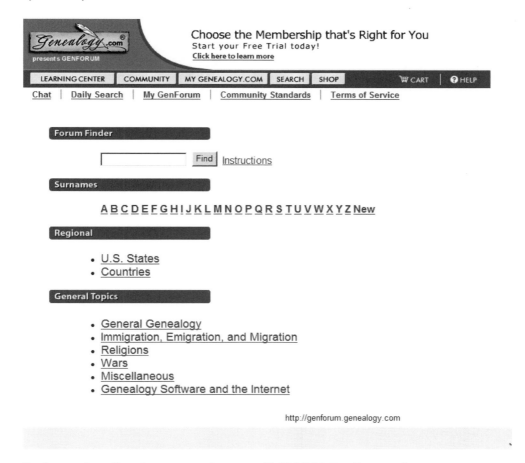

Genforum, http://genforum.genealogy.com/© 2005 MyFamily.com, Inc.

By selecting 'Countries' you can see the extent of possibilities available to you.

- Albania
- Argentina
- Armenia
- Australia
- Austria
- Bahamas
- Bangledesh
- Barbados
- Belarus
- Belgium
- Belize
- Bermuda
- Bolivia
- Bosnia/Herzegovina
- Brazil
- Bulgaria
- Cambodia
- Canada
- Chile
- China
- Colombia
- Costa Rica
- Croatia
- Cuba
- Cyprus
- Czech Republic
- Denmark
- Dominican Republic
- Ecuador
- Egypt
- El Salvador
- England
- Estonia
- Finland
- France
- Georgia
- Germany/Prussia
- Greece

- Greenland
- Grenada
- Guatemala
- Haiti
- Holland
- Honduras
- Hong Kong
- Hungary
- Iceland
- India
- Indonesia
- Iran
- Iraq
- Ireland
- Isle of Man
- Israel
- Italy
- Jamaica
- Japan
- Kenya
- Korea
- Kuwait
- Latvia
- Lebanon
- Lithuania
- Luxembourg
- Macedonian Republic
- Malawi
- Malaysia
- Malta
- Mexico
- Monaco
- Montenegro
- Morocco
- Namibia
- Nepal
- Netherlands
- New Zealand

- Nicaragua
- Nigeria
- Northern Ireland
- Norway
- Pakistan
- Panama
- Peru
- Philippines
- Poland
- Portugal
- Puerto Rico
- Romania
- Russia
- Sardinia
- Saudi Arabia
- Scotland
- Serbia
- Singapore
- Slovak Republic
- Slovenia
- South Africa
- Spain
- Sri Lanka
- Sudan
- Sweden
- Switzerland
- Taiwan
- Thailand
- Turkey
- Ukraine
- United Arab Emirates
- United Kingdom
- United States
- Uruguay
- Venezuela
- Virgin Islands
- Wales

Options available if searching by country.

Home: Surnames: Surname Forums Beginning with M

A B C D E F G H I J K L M N O P Q R S T U V W X Y Z New

Jump To: Ma Mc Me Mh Mi Mk Ml Mo Mr Ms Mu My

- Maack
- Maag
- Maas
- Mab
- Mabb
- Mabbit
- Mabbs
- Mabe
- Mabee
- Maben
- Maber
- Maberley
- Maberry
- Mabes
- Mabey
- Mabie
- Mabin
- Mabini
- Mable

Web page if searching by surname.

This forum serves all obvious variations

Moloney Family Genealogy Forum

Search this forum:

| Go |

Find all of the words ▼

179 Messages Posted

Jump to # | Go |

Post New Message | **Latest Messages** | **Today's Messages** | **Last Seven Days**

If you select a name, you are given the option to post messages and also contact other contributors

To the right of the above it tells us that there are 179 messages posted about the Moloney family name and below is a sample of those messages:

- MOLONEY DANAHER IN LIMERICK ·
- Moloneys Ireland/Canada/Michigan 1800's forward
- malony/keogh clare/kyneton 1811-
- Moloney's from Kilballyowen(Hospital), Limerick, Ir
- Martin Moloney - One Hundred Years before Me -
- Thomas F. Moloney 1860 Philadelphia Asbury Park
  - Re: Thomas F. Moloney 1860 Philadelphia A
- Michael MOloney/MAloney born abt. 1839 Tippera
  - Re: Michael MOloney/MAloney born abt. 18

Messages posted regarding the surname Moloney.

Genes Reunited

Most of us by now have heard of Friends Reunited, but there is also Genes Reunited, which is becoming a fast favourite with researchers looking for both living relatives and ancestors. The home page below will give you an idea of how easy it is to use for searching, reading and replying to messages etc. (messages will be forwarded to you!).

Website of Genes Reunited, http://www.genesreunited.co.uk

I have posted several queries on this site and never failed to get a response such as this one:

Example of a query.

Genealogy Quest

This is another information site that has provided me with various bits and pieces including old medical terms.

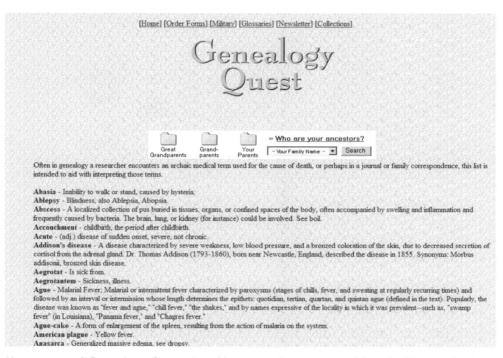

Home page of Genealogy Quest, http://www.genealogy-quest.com/glossaries/diseases1.html

The Hall Genealogy Website

This site directed me to various military and marine links besides offering information about the Hall family and a list of old occupations.

Home page of Hall Genealogy website, http://www.rmhh.co.uk

I selected marine and military and up came a huge list of military links, and occupations shown below:

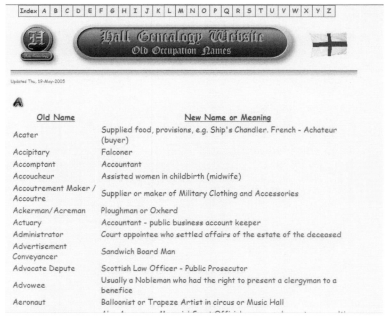

Links can be found to other resources and websites.

The website also provides a list of occupation names.

The Victorian Dictionary

When I want to learn anything about Victorian social history, this site is my first choice. It provides detailed information about 19th century life.

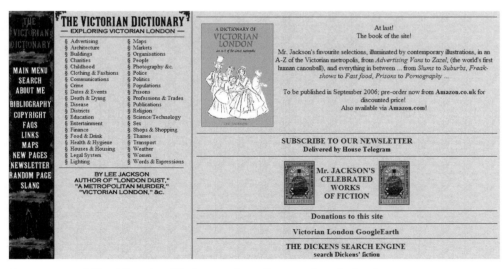

Home page of The Victorian Dictionary, http://www.victorianlondon.org

I came across this site trying to find out information about the trade of an ice man and fishmonger but more than that, I wanted to know how they managed to store and cultivate ice before the invention of the refrigerator.

Victorian professions and trades

By selecting professions and trades I found the following:

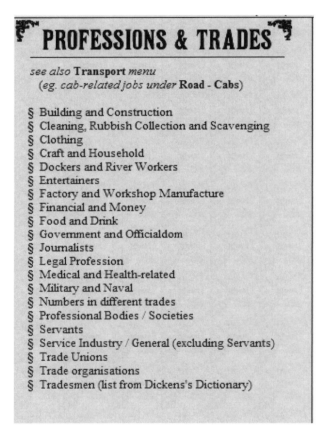

PROFESSIONS & TRADES

see also **Transport** *menu*
   (eg. cab-related jobs under **Road - Cabs**)

§ Building and Construction
§ Cleaning, Rubbish Collection and Scavenging
§ Clothing
§ Craft and Household
§ Dockers and River Workers
§ Entertainers
§ Factory and Workshop Manufacture
§ Financial and Money
§ Food and Drink
§ Government and Officialdom
§ Journalists
§ Legal Profession
§ Medical and Health-related
§ Military and Naval
§ Numbers in different trades
§ Professional Bodies / Societies
§ Servants
§ Service Industry / General (excluding Servants)
§ Trade Unions
§ Trade organisations
§ Tradesmen (list from Dickens's Dictionary)

List of trades available on the site.

Selecting food and drink brings up another extensive list.

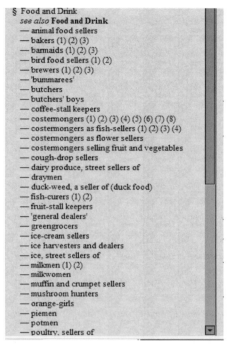

§ Food and Drink
see also **Food and Drink**
— animal food sellers
— bakers (1) (2) (3)
— barmaids (1) (2) (3)
— bird food sellers (1) (2)
— brewers (1) (2) (3)
— 'bummarees'
— butchers
— butchers' boys
— coffee-stall keepers
— costermongers (1) (2) (3) (4) (5) (6) (7) (8)
— costermongers as fish-sellers (1) (2) (3) (4)
— costermongers as flower sellers
— costermongers selling fruit and vegetables
— cough-drop sellers
— dairy produce, street sellers of
— draymen
— duck-weed, a seller of (duck food)
— fish-curers (1) (2)
— fruit-stall keepers
— 'general dealers'
— greengrocers
— ice-cream sellers
— ice harvesters and dealers
— ice, street sellers of
— milkmen (1) (2)
— milkwomen
— muffin and crumpet sellers
— mushroom hunters
— orange-girls
— piemen
— potmen
— poultry, sellers of

Sublist below 'food and drink'.

After narrowing down to fish-curers, up pops a long article about the fish industry.

without a fire, and putting the candle out to save it, a planning how to raise money. 'Can we borrow there?' 'Can we manage to sell if we can borrow?' 'Shall we get from very bad to the parish?' Then, perhaps, there's a day lost, and without a bite in our mouths trying to borrow. Let alone a little drop to give a body courage, which perhaps is the only good use of spirit after all. That's the pinch, sir. When the rain you hear outside puts you in mind of drownding!"

Subjoined is the amount (in round numbers) of wet fish annually disposed of in the metropolis by the street-sellers:

	No. of Fish.	lbs. weight.
Salmon	20,000	175,000
Live-cod	100,000	1,000,000
Soles	6,500,000	1,650,000
Whiting	4,440,000	1,680,000
Haddock	250,000	500,000
Plaice	29,400,000	29,400,000
Mackarel	15,700,000	15,700,000
Herrings	875,000,000	210,000,000
Sprats	"	3,000,000
Eels, from Holland	400,000	65,000
Flounders	260,000	43,000
Dabs	270,000	48,000
Total quantity of wet fish sold in the streets of London	932,340,000	263,281,000

From the above Table we perceive that the fish, of which the greatest quantity is eaten by the poor, is herrings; of this, compared with plaice there is upwards of thirty times the number consumed. After plaice rank mackerel, and of these the consumption is about one-half less in number than plaice, while the number of soles vended in the streets, is again half of that of mackerel. Then come whiting, which are about two-thirds the number of the soles, while the consumption to the poor of haddock, cod, eels, and salmon, is comparatively insignificant. Of sprats, which are estimated by weight, only one-fifth of the number of pounds are consumed compared with the weight of mackerel. The pounds' weight of herrings sold in the streets, in the course of a year, is upwards of seven times that of plaice, and fourteen times that of mackerel. Altogether more than 260,000,000 pounds, or 116,000 tons weight of wet fish are yearly purchased in the streets of London, for the consumption of the humbler classes. Of this aggregate amount, no less than five-sixths consists of herrings; which, indeed, constitute the great slop diet of the metropolis.

An extract from the article on the fish industry.

The Canal Museum

Another fabulous site is the Canal Museum providing me with everything I needed to know about ice and ice men during the 19th century. It gave me more insight into the life of Martino Marelli. The point of this exercise is to show you how surfing the net can help put flesh on the bones of your ancestors; bringing the names and dates to life. Always search for information about trades; you might be lucky enough to find detailed information like I did.

You may wonder if The Canal Museum or ice and ice merchants related to your family history. If your ancestors worked in London with fresh food, such as fish and meat, or perhaps you have Italian ancestors who sold cream or ice cream, or ancestors that worked on the canals of London or in the docks, then this site will help you start to build a picture of their lives. My husband remembers an ice wagon coming around his locality when he was a child before his parents owned a fridge, so in some way ice men did play a part in the lives of your ancestors.

The London Canal Museum also provides information about the history of London's canals, the cargoes carried, the people who lived and worked on the waterways, and the horses that pulled their boats. The museum is located in a former ice warehouse built in about 1862–63 for Carlo Gatti, the famous ice cream maker, and features the history of the ice trade and ice cream as well as the canals.

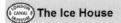 **The Ice House**

The ice well, ice trade, ice cream, and related history

Norway's Ice to London

History of Ice Cream

Carlo Gatti, Ice Entrepreneur

Mrs. A.B. Marshall, the Queen of Ice Cream

The Building at 12-13 New Wharf Road

Ragazzo, online e-book - a novel by Felicity Kinross

Before the early years of the 19th century ice was gathered from ponds, rivers, and indeed from the canals and was stored in underground ice stores. Ice began to be imported from Norway in the 1820's and it was necessary to dig large ice wells in London in order to store it to meet the growing demand. Luxury items like ice cream had to be made fresh and eaten straight away, there was no mechanical refrigeration until around the turn of the century. Carlo Gatti (1817-78) was a Swiss Italian who came to England in the 1840's. He started a cafe at Charing Cross which was then an innovation. It was a great success and he soon expanded his business to include cafes and restaurants. The Swiss were amongst the first to offer the British public comfortable, safe and welcoming restaurants at moderate prices with some continental cuisine.

Ice was sold to restaurants and to fishmongers and others to keep food chilled. The mass import of ice reduced its price to a level where the manufacture of ice cream and its sale to the general public became an economic possibility. The ice wells at 12/13 New Wharf Road (Now the Museum) were in use until at least 1902. After then, the first floor of the building was constructed as stables for the horses which were needed to pull the ice delivery carts. A floor was built over the top of the ice wells which were later used for rubbish dumping. The last import of any ice from Scandinavia was in 1921 by which time mechanical ice production was well established.

The Canal Museum website, http://www.canalmuseum.org.uk/ice/index.html

Norway's Ice to London

19th Century London wanted ice in far greater quantities than the British climate provided. Whilst ice was gathered from lakes, and indeed from the Regent's Canal, and was stored, the amount of ice available was small and its quality often poor. Ice started to be imported from the United States in the 1840's, with the Wenham Lake Ice Company as one of the most famous names in the business. Carlo Gatti brought his first consignment of ice from Norway to London in 1857, of 400 tons, and one of the two ice wells at 12-13 New Wharf Road was almost certainly dug to receive it and store it until it was wanted by customers. Customers wanted ice for food preservation, for making ice cream, and for medical use. In the last 40 years of the century Norwegian ice dominated the market in London. In this page we tell how ice was supplied to London in the years between the middle and end of the 19th Century, after which ice manufactured in factories began to compete with the natural product.

Ploughing the Harvest

Horse drawn ploughs were used on the mountain lakes of southern Norway which had the merit of accessibility as well as providing supplies of good quality clean ice.

Sawing the Ice

Individual block of ice had to be cut by hand, using metal saws

Loading the ship

The ships were loaded at a number of points along the Norwegian coast. Most of the cargoes were loaded along the coast south of Oslo. In the 1890's Norway was exporting 340,000 tons of ice each year.

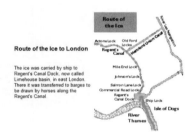

Route of the Ice to London

The ice was carried by ship to Regent's Canal Dock, now called Limehouse basin, in east London. There it was transferred to barges to be drawn by horses along the Regent's Canal.

Unloading in London

We cannot be sure whether this picture is loading or unloading, however it shows how the ice dogs were used to lift blocks of ice to or from the hold of a ship, and indeed the same method must have been used when the ice arrived at the ice store which is now the museum. Unfortunately the museum does not have any photographs of ice traffic on the Regent's Canal. The traffic ceased in the early years of the 20th Century and, if any photographs were ever taken, they have probably not survived.

Delivery to the Customer

Although there are few records of the operation of the wells, we do know about the delivery of ice to customers, which, using factory made ice, continued well into the twentieth century with relatively little change. Ice was delivered in carts like these - a model made in the late 19th Century is in the museum. The "ice man" would chip off a block of ice of the size you wanted.

Copyright

So far as is known, all the images reproduced on this page are either out of copyright, or taken from the collection of the London Canal Museum. Graphics are © Canal Museum Trust

The above three illustrations help me to visualise Martino Marelli's life.

County Record Offices

Surrey History Centre

Your area may have a local history centre and will definitely be worth visiting. My local history centre based in Woking, Surrey is a very good example, which I visit personally and via their online resources. The Surrey History Centre has proved to be a very good friend throughout my research and has provided me with invaluable information about my Surrey ancestors.

To discover what is available online, go to Surrey County Council, http://www.surreycc.gov.uk/surreyhistorycentre.

The Surrey History Centre is a resource of printed materials (archives, books and collections) relating to Surrey's past and present. At step 1 choose 'Archives or books' and then 'Collections'.

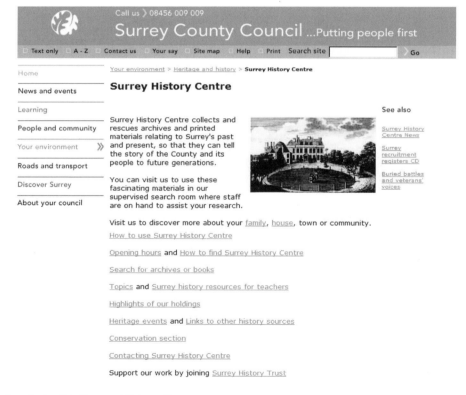

2. Leads to the Surrey History Centre.

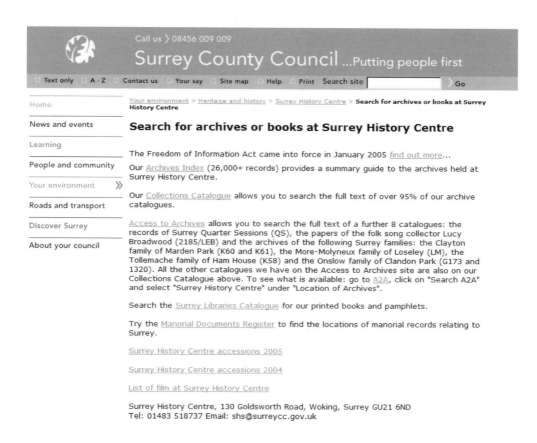

3. I chose to search the 'Collections Catalogue'.

Surrey History Centre Collections Catalogue

For a Basic Search, enter your search below and click on the SEARCH button.

Search Terms: Tickner   and ▼

Search   Clear

An Advanced Search is also available, or you can Browse the Table of Contents.

If your search does not find what you want, please contact us for advice.

Surrey History Centre Website

130 Goldsworth Road Woking Surrey GU21 6ND Tel: 01483 518737 Email: shs@surreycc.gov.uk

SURREY
COUNTY COUNCIL

4. I have ancestors in Surrey by the surname of Tickner, so I simply keyed in the surname and hit 'Search'.

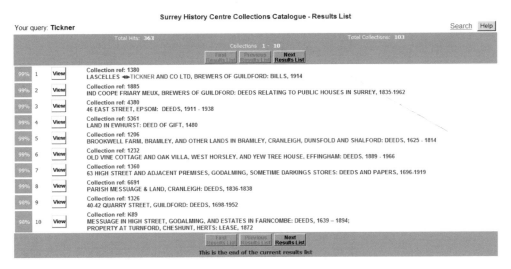

5. A list of collections with the name Tickner.

The above images are reproduced with kind permission of Surrey County Council.

I searched through the extremely interesting collection and eventually came across the names of two possible ancestors:

Item ref: 892/5/15
Grant of annuity by StephenTickner of Bramley in Shalford, husbandman, to John Balchin of Thorncombe Street, Shalford, yeoman, and Richard Punter of Bramley, yeoman.

Close or croft of land and pasture called The Heather Bonners (6a), through which a footway leads from Hascombe towards Bramley; and parcel of pasture and woodground called Bonners Brooke (10a).

The premises lie together in Bramley abutting E on a close of Stephen Tickner called The Upper Bonners, W on the highway between Hascombe and Guildford, N on a close called The Further Bridges, parcel of Burtley Farm, and S on two other closes of Stephen Tickner called The Barne Field and The Plottes.

A £5 annuity out of the premises is to be paid jointly to Balchin and Punter and their heirs as a dower for Margaret, now wife of Stephen Tickner, for her life time, should she survive her husband; the first payment to be made at the first quarterly festival after Tickner's death. Steward's memorandum, nd [?c.1700], is endorsed that a quit rent to the manor of Bramley is payable on Bonners and that this deed is of use in identifying where the premises are.

Date(s): 26 Feb 1625

Item ref: 892/5/23
Grant by John Caryll of Tangley, esq, lord of the manor of Bramley, to William Tickner of Bramley, esq.

Cottage, garden and orchard (½a) at Palmers Cross in Bramley.

The lord grants the premises, which are already in Tickner's occupation, to be held of the manor of Bramley on a 1000 year lease at 12d rent pa and two fat hens, payable at the manor house at Tangley, suit of court, heriot 5s and relief 5s.

Date(s): 28 Sep 1652

What was most interesting about this find was the fact that two other possible family names were also included, Balchin and Punter, and to me this meant I was on the right track and would now start obtaining sources from church and manorial records to prove this branch of my family history.

A visit to the Surrey History Centre produced the original source documents enabling me to have photocopies taken for my family file (see the example showing Stephen Tickner's marriage to Margaret Punter). This is only one example of what I found. Original sources are often not easy to read so it is worth obtaining a copy to study at your convenience.

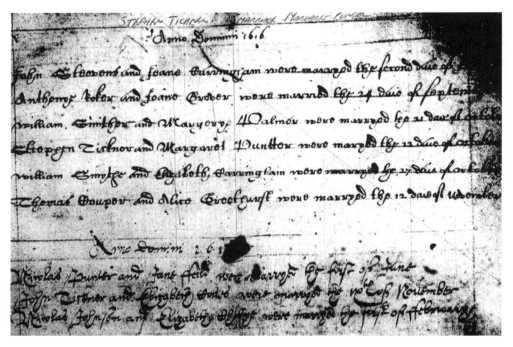

Church record for marriage of Stephen Tickner to Margaret Punter, 1616, see 4th line.
Reproduced by kind permission of Surrey History Centre. Copyright of Surrey History Centre.

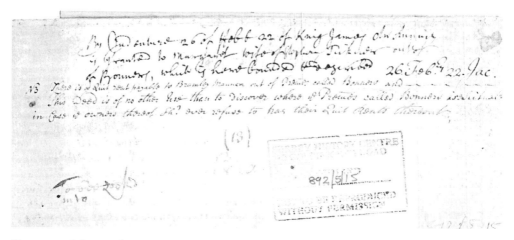

The manorial record.
Reproduced by kind permission of Surrey History Centre. Copyright of Surrey History Centre.

Although I could see the original manorial document, obtaining a copy was difficult which is why I have only this small piece above. The document dated 26 February 1624 was on beautiful thick waxy paper, but was quite fragile. I could have ordered copies via their website as the Surrey History Centre offers a Digitisation Service that provides copies of documents that are not suitable for photocopying. For those unable to visit the Surrey History Centre they also offer a paid research facility.

If you go back to the main page and select 'How to use Surrey History Centre' you will be given the following information:

At Surrey History Centre you can . . .

♦ visit our search room to consult documents and local studies materials
♦ get advice on sources relevant to your research
♦ attend events and view special exhibitions
♦ watch archive films
♦ use your portable computer
♦ use our refreshment room
♦ use the Internet and CD-ROMs for research
♦ buy books, cards, maps and gifts in person in our foyer or by post from Surrey County Council's Online Shop.

When you visit . . .

♦ it is advisable to book: please telephone us on 01483 518737
♦ bring a Surrey County Libraries ticket or a County Archive Research Network (CARN) card to use our collections. If you do not have either of these, bring something official as proof of ID and address, such as a driving licence or bank statement
♦ bring pencils ro write with (no pens)
♦ bring a 20p piece for a locker to store your belongings, including handbags. For coats there are secure hangers for which you will need a £1 coin. Both coins are returnable.

Surrey History Centre can also . . .

♦ offer, free of charge, advice and information about our archives and local studies collections
♦ provide brief answers to telephone enquiries
♦ supply copies from our catalogues and finding aids
♦ provide digital copies of documents
♦ provide fiche copies and film copies of many Surrey parish registers
♦ provide photocopies of documents – see Surrey History Centre table of fees
♦ provide a research service at a reasonable hourly charge
♦ help educational users of all ages to make the most of original sources – see our Surrey history resources for teachers
♦ give guided tours of our facilities to groups by appointment
♦ visit your local group or society to give talks
♦ offer advice on donating and loaning to Surrey History Centre
♦ offer advice from our Conservation Section on caring for your records
♦ encourage use of sources in local areas through our outreach programme.

Surrey History Centre, 130 Goldsworth Road, Woking, Surrey GU21 6ND
Tel: 01483 518737 Email: shs@surreycc.gov.uk

In the last section above, whilst on their websites, if you click on the fourth bullet point down 'provide digital copies of documents' you will be tkaken to the Digitisation of archive and library material page and here you can look at the service provided and the list of costs for this service:

Surrey History Centre services and table of fees

Certified copies
Photocopies
Microform copies
Digital imaging service
Reproductions of historic maps of Surrey
Books
Paid research service (See table below).
Publication fees

Below are the costs for the Digital imaging and paid research services:

Digital imaging service

	Fee at SHC	Handling fee for postal orders within UK and EU	Handling fee for postal order from rest of world
A4 basic paper	£3.50 (£2.98+52p VAT)	£2.00 per order (£1.71+29p VAT)	£2.00 per order
A4 photo quality paper	£7.00 (£5.96+££1.04 VAT)	£2.00 per order (£1.71+29p VAT)	£2.00 per order
A3 basic paper	£7.00 (£5.96+£1.04 VAT)	£2.00 per order (£1.71+29p VAT)	£2.00 per order
A3 photo quality paper	£14.00 (£11.92+£2.08 VAT)	£2.00 per order (£1.71+29p VAT)	£2.00 per order
Images on CD	£6.00 (£5.11+89p VAT) for first image £3.00 (2.56+44p VAT) for subsequent ones	£2.00 per order (£1.71+29p VAT)	£2.00 per order

| Copies of Dennis photographs | No public photography permitted of these items. Copies provided by SHC digital imaging service with additional charge of £5.00 (£4.25+75p VAT) per item for conservation of Dennis Archive | £2.00 per order (£1.71+29p VAT) | £2.00 per order |

Paid research service

	VAT is shown for UK and EU orders	Fee for orders from rest of world
½ hour	£11.00 (9.36+£1.64 VAT)	£.11.00
1 hour	£22.00 (18.72+£3.28 VAT)	£22.00
1½ hours	£33.00 (£28.09+£4.91 VAT)	£33.00
2 hours	£44.00 (£37.45+£6.55 VAT)	£44.00
2½ hours	£55.00 (£46.81+£8.19 VAT)	£55.00
3 hours	£66.00 (£56.17+£9.98 VAT)	£66.00

You can order a wide variety of documentation. The costs are listed on their website.

Local History Services

The Weald of Kent, Surrey & Sussex

I came across this site while carrying out research for another project and was thrilled with the amount of information it provides on family history. The following images show some of the material available on this website.

Home page of The Weald of Kent, Surrey and Sussex, http://thesussexweald.org/

Lists of family records as well as individual records.

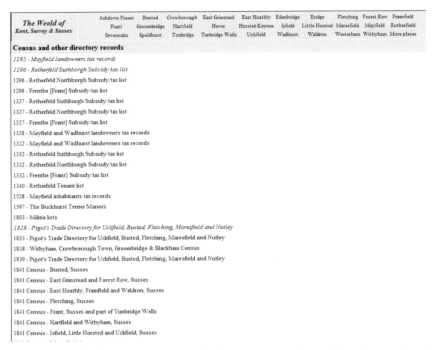

The Weald of Kent, Surrey & Sussex	Ashdown Forest	Buxted	Crowborough	East Grinstead	East Hoathly	Edenbridge	Exridge	Fletching	Forest Row	Framfield
	Frant	Groombridge	Hartfield	Hever	Horsted Keynes	Isfield	Little Horsted	Maresfield	Mayfield	Rotherfield
	Sevenoaks	Speldhurst	Tonbridge	Tunbridge Wells	Uckfield	Wadhurst	Waldron	Westerham	Withyham	More places

Census and other directory records

1295 - Mayfield landowners tax records

1296 - Retherfeld Suthborgh Subsidy/tax list

1296 - Retherfeld Northborgh Subsidy/tax list

1296 - Frenthe [Frant] Subsidy/tax list

1327 - Retherfeld Suthborgh Subsidy/tax list

1327 - Retherfeld Northborgh Subsidy/tax list

1327 - Frenthe [Frant] Subsidy/tax list

1328 - Mayfield and Wadhurst landowners tax records

1332 - Mayfield and Wadhurst landowners tax records

1332 - Retherfeld Suthborgh Subsidy/tax list

1332 - Retherfeld Northborgh Subsidy/tax list

1332 - Frenthe [Frant} Subsidy/tax list

1340 - Retherfeld Tenant list

1528 - Mayfield inhabitants tax records

1597 - The Buckhurst Terrier Manors

1803 - Militia lists

1828 - Pigot's Trade Directory for Uckfield, Buxted, Fletching, Maresfield and Nutley

1833 - Pigot's Trade Directory for Uckfield, Buxted, Fletching, Maresfield and Nutley

1838 - Withyham, Crowbrorough Town, Groombridge & Blackham Census

1839 - Pigot's Trade Directory for Uckfield, Buxted, Fletching, Maresfield and Nutley

1841 Census - Buxted, Sussex

1841 Census - East Grinstead and Forest Row, Sussex

1841 Census - East Hoathly, Framfield and Waldron, Sussex

1841 Census - Fletching, Sussex

1841 Census - Frant, Sussex and part of Tunbridge Wells

1841 Census - Hartfield and Withyham, Sussex

1841 Census - Isfield, Little Horsted and Uckfield, Sussex

Other records include Census records and directory records, such as tax and trade records, and lists of possible militia men.

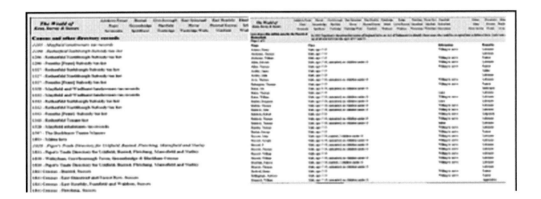

Historical directories

Another way of finding out about the social history of the place your ancestors resided is via a website called Historical Directories.

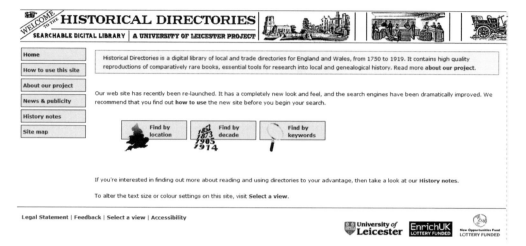

Home page of Historical Directories, http://www.historicaldirectories.org/hd/index.asp

You can search by keyword, such as a family name, decade or location.

If you search by keywords you will be given a choice of default key names to choose from that relate to the publisher, owner or printer at the time the directory was originally compiled. You might be looking for a specific directory, such as Kelly for instance. If none of these defaults relate to you, leave them as 'all' and choose your own keyword as I did. I typed in the surname Marelli and was given a variety of directories which housed that name and provided both business and private addresses at the time of publication.

'Find by location'; I chose the county of Devon.

HISTORICAL DIRECTORIES

Directories 1 to 10 of 35 found for Location=Devon

Previous Page | Next Page

Title	Location	Decade	Key name	
Slater's Directory of Berks, Corn, Devon ..., 1852-53	Berkshire Cornwall Devon Dorset Gloucestershire Hampshire Somerset Wiltshire Wales	1850s	Slater	Directory | Fact File
Kelly's Directory of Devon & Cornwall, 1914. [Part 2. Devon: Private Resident & Trade Directories]	Devon	1910s	Kelly	Directory | Fact File
Kelly's Directory of Devon & Cornwall, 1914. [Part 1. Devon: County & Localities]	Devon	1910s	Kelly	Directory | Fact File
Kelly's Directory of Devon & Cornwall, 1893. [Part 2. Devon: Court & Trades Directories]	Devon	1890s	Kelly	Directory | Fact File
Kelly's Directory of Devon & Cornwall, 1893. [Part 1. Devon: County & Localities]	Devon	1890s	Kelly	Directory | Fact File
Kelly's Directory of Devon & Cornwall, 1902. [Part 1: Devon]	Devon	1900s	Kelly	Directory | Fact File
History, Gazetteer & Directory of Devon, 1878-79	Devon	1870s	White, W.	Directory | Fact File
History, Gazetteer & Directory of Devon, 1850	Devon	1850s	White, W.	Directory | Fact File
Post Office Directory of Exeter, 1895-96	Devon	1890s	Besley	Directory | Fact File
Pigot & Co.'s Directory of Berks, Bucks ... , 1844. [Part 1: Berks to Glos]	Berkshire Buckinghamshire Cornwall Devon Dorset Gloucestershire	1750-1849	Pigot	Directory | Fact File

Home
How to use this site
Find by location
Find by decade
Find by keywords
About our project
News & publicity
History notes
Site Map

An extensive list of the Directories available.

Gravestone inscriptions & cemeteries

Graveyards are often a neglected source by family historians but there are many volunteer projects running on the Internet. By keying 'cemeteries' into a search engine, a variety of sites was resourced including the following two:

Home page of Cemsearch-uk, http://www.cemsearch.co.uk

Home page of Scottish Graveyards, http://www.scottishgraveyards.org.uk

In the menu to the left of the image is a category called 'graveyard projects' and clicking on this page produced a list of graveyard projects outside of Scotland and beyond the UK. When you are having problems locating information about an ancestor or their extended family via the Census or Civil Registration, a cemetery might provide you with some clues. My brother, Kevin, went hunting for the grave of our grandparents believed to be in a cemetery in Liverpool. He phoned the Liverpool Cemeteries Office and was given a plot number, but when he got there a family by another name was buried in the plot. He called me to say it was a wild goose chase but I recognised the name and it turned out to be the married sister of our dad. The information on the grave produced the name of her husband, ages at death and date of death of both relatives, enabling us to source birth and death certificates. Sometimes visiting cemeteries in towns, villages or cities where your ancestor lived is a worthwhile trip.

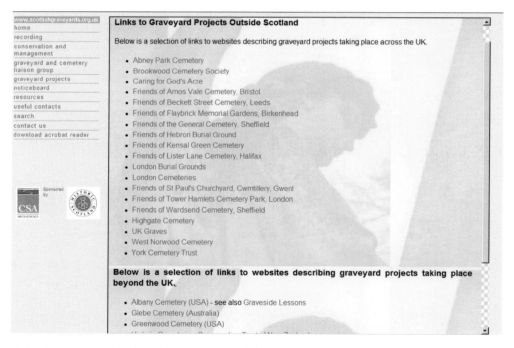

Links to graveyard projects in the UK and abroad.

Genealogical informational websites & links

GENUKI

This is a must-view site aimed at everyone. The information it provides to the family historian is invaluable.

United Kingdom
and Ireland

Contents
& Search

UK & Ireland
Genealogy

Guidance for
First-Time Users
of These Pages

Guidance for
Potential Contributors
to These Pages

Enter this large collection of genealogical information pages for England, Ireland, Scotland, Wales, the Channel Islands, and the Isle of Man.		
Getting started in genealogy	Frequently Asked Questions (FAQs)	Researching UK and Irish genealogy from abroad
World genealogy, newsgroups and bulletin boards, etc.	Recent changes to these pages	Upcoming UK & Ireland Genealogical events (GENEVA)

For the latest GENUKI server status see www.genuki.info which gives news of past, present and (where possible) future incidents that may prevent or hinder your access to parts of GENUKI.

To report errors found in these pages, please use this list of GENUKI maintainers in order to find the appropriate email address.

Note: The information provided by GENUKI must not be used for commercial purposes, and all specific restrictions concerning usage, copyright notices, etc., that are to be found on individual information pages within GENUKI must be strictly adhered to. Violation of these rules could gravely harm the cooperation that GENUKI is obtaining from many information providers, and hence threaten its whole future. GENUKI is a registered trademark.

GENUKI website, http://www.genuki.org.uk. Note there is guidance available for first-time users.

England   Contents & Search   Devon Towns & Parishes   Information related to all of Devon

UK & Ireland
Genealogy   **DEVON**

"A county of England, reaching from the Bristol to the English Channel, and bounded by Cornwall, and Somersetshire, and Dorsetshire. It is 69 miles in length, and 60 in breadth, and is divided into 31 hundreds. It is very hilly, and abounds in huge granite rocks, some of whose peaks are above 1500 feet in height. The highland is covered with wide moors, of which Dartmoor is the most extensive. But in the valleys and lower ground the soil is fertile. Its rivers are the Exe, the Culm, the Dart, the Tamar, the Otter, &c. Some parts of its coasts are composed of lofty cliffs, but at others there is a beautiful sandy shore. The air and climate are so mild and salubrious that invalids often retire to its sea-ports for the winter. Limestone, granite, some building-stone, and a species of wood-coal are found here, as well as some kinds of variegated marble. It produces corn, &c. and fruit trees, especially apples, whence much cider is made. Its fisheries also are of value. Exeter is its chief city. Population, 533, 460. It sends 22 members to parliament." (From *Barclay's Complete and Universal English Dictionary, 1842.*)

NOTE 1: The Devon Search Facility can be used to search all the GENUKI/Devon pages kept at the University of Newcastle for particular words and phrases, and the Online Gazetteer of Devon to identify which town or parish a place is located in. There is also a FAQ (Frequently Asked Questions) file for these Devon pages, and a What's New page listing major recent additions. The mailing list associated with GENUKI/Devon is DEVON-L (now co-sponsored by the Devon FHS), and Devon surnames are listed within Graham Jaunay's On-line English Names Directory. For information related to specific families or individuals see Genealogies, and Biographies.

NOTE 2: Volunteers are sought for the Devon Pre-1841 Census Transcription Project, the Devon 1841 Census Transcription Project, the Devon 1861 Census Transcription Project, the Devon Book Indexing Project, and the Devon Online Parish Clerks scheme.

INFORMATION RELATED TO ALL OF DEVON

- Almanacs
- Archives and Libraries
- Bibliography
- Biography
- Cemeteries
- Census
- Chronology
- Church History
- Church Records

- History
- Jewish History
- Land and Property
- Language and Languages
- Manors
- Maps
- Merchant Marine
- Military History
- Names, Geographical

Information about Devon on GENUKI.

I clicked on 'Enter this large collection . . .' and selected England, then narrowed my search to the county of Devon.

INFORMATION RELATED TO ALL OF DEVON

- Almanacs
- Archives and Libraries
- Bibliography
- Biography
- Cemeteries
- Census
- Chronology
- Church History
- Church Records
- Civil Registration
- Correctional Institutions
- Court Records
- Description and Travel
- Directories
- Emigration and Immigration
- Encyclopedias and Dictionaries
- Folklore
- Gazetteers
- Genealogy
- Heraldry
- History
- Jewish History
- Land and Property
- Language and Languages
- Manors
- Maps
- Merchant Marine
- Military History
- Names, Geographical
- Names, Personal
- Newspapers
- Occupations
- Periodicals
- Poorhouses, Poor Law, etc.
- Probate Records
- Schools
- Societies
- Taxation
- Voting Registers

GENUKI holds a wide variety of information and lists the categories for each county as above.

The collection of resources for Devon is exhaustive and I'm sure you won't be disappointed if you visit this wonderful site yourself.

Cyndi's List

As with Genuki, Cyndi's List is another fabulous general information site for the family historian.

Home page of Cyndi's List, http://www.cyndislist.com

Search results for 'England'; as you can see the categories are extensive.

Browse Cyndi's List:
- Main Index
- Topical Index
- Alphabetical Index
- "No Frills" Index
- Text-Only Index

Search:
- Search or Browse

Browse New Links

Submit a New Link

Mailing List
- Browse Archives
- Search Archives
- RSS Archives

About Cyndi's List

What is *Cyndi's List*?

Are You New to Genealogy?

FAQ (Frequently Asked Questions)

Make *Cyndi's List* Your Homepage!

Create a Link to *Cyndi's List*

Internet Stuff You Need To Know

U.K. - Military

Category Index
- Battles, Battlefields & Military Sites
- General Resource Sites
- Finding Old Comrades
- Historical Military Conflicts, Events or Wars
- Libraries, Archives & Museums
- Mailing Lists, Newsgroups & Chat
- Medals, Awards & Tributes
- People & Families
- Professional Researchers, Volunteers & Other Research Services
- Publications, Software & Supplies
- Records: Military, Pension, Burial
- Regimental Rosters & Histories
- Rolls of Honour & War Memorials
- The Royal Navy
- Societies & Groups

Related Categories
- General U.K. Sites
- Channel Islands
- England
- England - Counties Index
- Ireland & Northern Ireland
- Isle of Man
- Scotland
- Scotland - Counties Index
- Wales / Cymru
- Wales / Cymru - Counties Index

- Canada - Military
- Military Resources Worldwide
- Military - World War I: The Great War
- Military - World War II
- U.S. - Civil War ~ The War for Southern Independence
- U.S. - Military

Battles, Battlefields & Military Sites

- The Battle of Culloden
- The Battle of Falkirk (1746)
- Culloden - The Jacobites
- Roman Military Sites in Britain
- Waterloo 1815 Le centre du Visiteur, The Visitors Center

General Resource Sites

Alex Chirnside's Military History Page

Choosing a category will narrow your search to the specifics, as in the above example for 'military'.

Maps

My little collection of old maps also gave me additional information about the localities in which my ancestors lived, and details of who owned local businesses. I purchased *The Godfrey Edition* maps at the FRC but you can buy them online via their online shop, http://www.alangodfreymaps.co.uk/

Another great Internet resource is http://www.old-maps.co.uk.

Home page of www.old-maps.co.uk

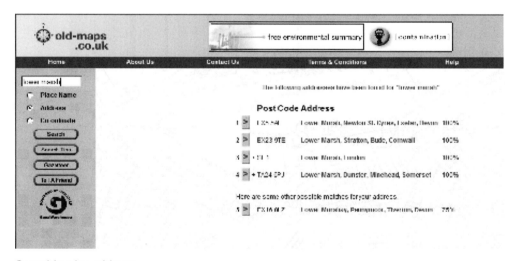

Searching by address.

I searched for the address that Martino Marelli was living at during the 1890s. After selecting the third option for London, I was taken to an old map of the area. Although the example below is small, on the site you can enlarge the image for a clearer view. The site has an exhaustive selection of maps available.

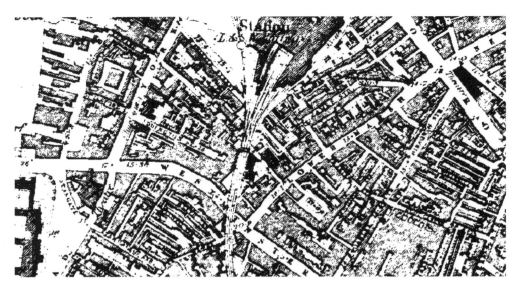

Old map of Lower Marsh, London.

From this page I was able to click the icon to find a modern-day map, coutesy of Mapquest, Inc., of the same district, meaning that part, if not all, of Lower Marsh still exists. The site showed that Lower Marsh Road is next to what is now Waterloo Station.

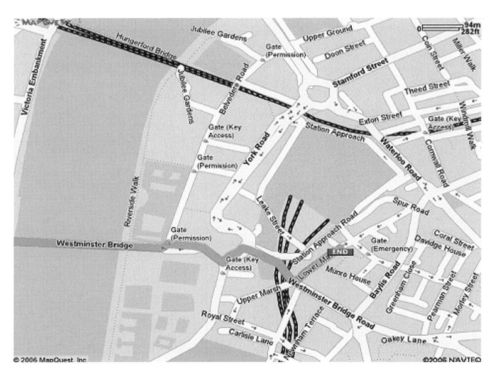

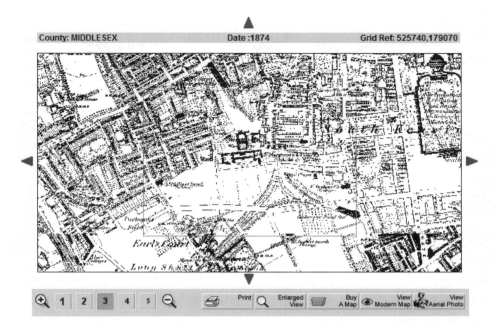

The above view will show the various options available with this site.

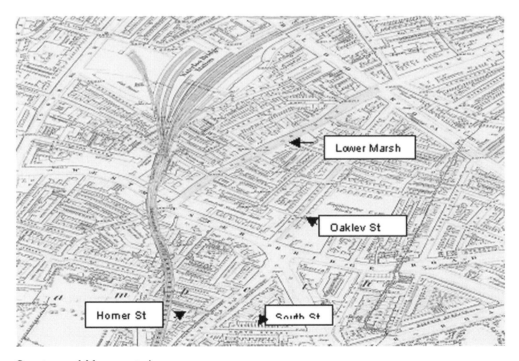

Courtesy of Mapquest, Inc.

Unfortunately, the map from this site did not reproduce well but I purchased a copy of a map for the same area from Alan Godfrey Maps, The Off Quay Building, Foundry Lane, Newcastle NE6 1LH, see top map above. The map is an Old Ordnance Survey Map of Waterloo and Southward dated 1872. I was delighted to find four addresses on this map where ancestors lived.

Mapquest

To look for modern-day maps of locations in which your ancestors lived, Mapquest is also a great favourite of mine.

Seaching on Mapquest, http://www.mapquest.co.uk

One day we will take our camera and visit the various locations where our ancestors lived and take pictures for posterity.

Family history magazines and Internet guide

A lifeline during my research has been family history magazines and Internet guidebooks for genealogists. All of the magazines provide an unbelievable array of information relating to family history, plus masses of tips, including using the Internet, and informing you of new sites coming online. Articles about the workhouses, Victorian occupations, the military, Victorian travel, industry, history of surnames, court assizes and poorhouses have helped me to understand my ancestors in a way that names and dates alone could not do.

Here are my favourite magazines which are all also available at most newsagents:

Family Tree and Family History, http://www.family-tree.co.uk

Your Family Tree, http://www.yourfamilytreemag.co.uk

Among other interesting pieces of information, this website has it's own forum http://www.forum.yourfamilytreemag.co.uk/

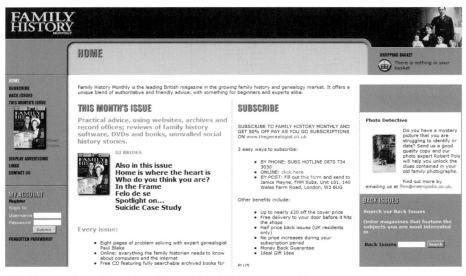

Family History Monthly, http://www.familyhistorymonthly.com

Ancestors Magazine, http://www.ancestorsmagazine.co.uk

Ancestors Magazine is the monthly family history magazine of the National Archives. It contains 64 pages of news and expert advice. This magazine can also be found online at http://www.nationalarchives.gov.uk/shop/ancestors.htm.

While browsing through the index of articles on Ancestors Magazine's website, I noticed that Peter Christian has an Internet column.

FAMILY HISTORY FROM THE EXPERTS

ANCESTORS

| Home | Issue Index | Subscribe | Back Issues | Links | Contact Us |

Index of Articles Issues

Issue 1		April/May 2001	
1a		News from the PRO	4-6
1b	Margaret Brennand	1901 Census project	10-11
1c	Jane Garmendia	PROCAT: the new PRO online catalogue	12-13
1d	David Hey	Heathcote: the story of a family name	15-16
1e	Nick Barratt	House history: how to become your own house detective	18-22
1f	Stephen Harwood	'Watch the birdie and say cheese'	25-27
1g	Peter Christian	The Internet section	29-31
1h	Peter Christian	Military genealogy on the Internet	32-35
1i	Keith Steward	Awudu Katsena, artillery carrier and later sergeant, North Nigeria Regiment	37-42
1j	Stella Colwell	Veni, vidi, vici!	44-46
1k	Ann Morton	Assize Courts	48-51
1l	Amanda Bevan	Wills before 1858: the prerogative court of Canterbury	53-57
1m	Roger Nixon	Resources at the PRO	62-64

Two articles by Peter Christian are on this website and definitely worth viewing.

Peter Christian has written a series of must-have books relating to genealogy and the Internet.

♦ *The Genealogist's Internet*, Third Edition (PRO Publications, 2003)
♦ *Web Publishing for Genealogy* (Genealogical Pub. Co., 2000)
♦ *Finding Genealogy on the Internet* (D. Hawgood, 2002)

I hope this chapter has opened your mind about how to research about the lives of your ancestors and get to know them a little better than you do now.

8

Recording & storing your family history

When I first started researching and collecting data about my ancestors I stored everything in one large file and drew trees by hand causing no end of problems simply because with every new piece of information acquired my family tree grew in height and width.

There are many software packages available for recording your family history and it would be unfair of me to try to tell you their capabilities as I am not an expert. I chose Family Tree Maker because it suited my requirements and continues to do so, but before I start explaining more about Family Tree Maker, here are three of the many family history software packages available on the Internet.

A selection of software for family historians

Legacy Family Tree, http://www.legacyfamilytree.com

My History, http://www.my-history.co.uk

family tree software in the 21st century

Click to view larger picture

Version 3 Now Released

"the best genealogy package just got better"
Family Tree Magazine, July 2006

Family Historian is a new kind of family tree program with a new and different design philosophy. To learn more about it, see Features or take the Tour of Family Historian and read What the Reviewers Have Said...

Version 3 includes a wealth of new features and improvements to existing features. See What's New in Version 3 to learn more.

To learn about the ideas behind the design of Family Historian see Design Goals & Philosophy.

Family Historian and the BBC...	UK television viewers will be familiar with the BBC's hit genealogy series: *Who Do You Think You are?* But did you know that the makers of the program use *Family Historian*?

Family Historian, http://www.family-historian.co.uk

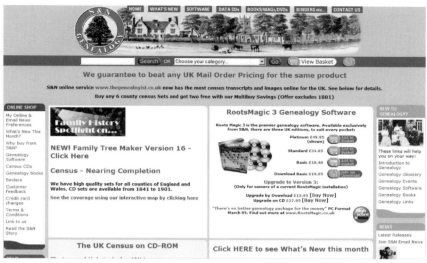

S&N Genealogy, http://www.genealogysupplies.com

For all items including software, data CDs and stationery, S&N Genealogy is always the first site I visit, and usually where my search ends.

Family Tree Maker

If you visit this site you can study the online overview of Family Tree Maker, http://www.familytreemaker.com. By clicking on 'Overview' you will be given the option to take a product tour or purchase online.

Copyright © 1998–2006 MyFamily.com Inc. and its subsidiaries.
Family Tree Maker overview.

We are now going to review my copy of *Family Tree Maker* and the way that I use this product. The next image you see will be the family page for my husband Brian and his parents. Brian's father is highlighted by clicking on the two names above, Albert and Lilian, and we will be taken up one level to the next generation.

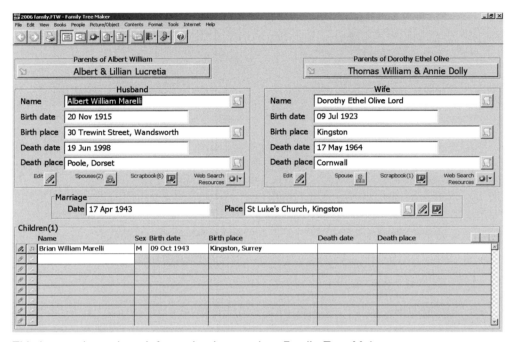

This image shows how information is stored on Family Tree Maker.

Now the software will bring up the parents of Albert William Marelli, and by clicking on Martino and Amy or Frederick and Susan we can go up another generation. We can also view any of Albert William's siblings by clicking the arrow next to their name (see opposite).

If you look at the names of the key individuals highlighted, Albert Marelli and Lilian Lucretia Chappell, you will see a scroll icon next to their name, birthplace and death place.

. The scroll icon also has a little black triangle in the corner which means I have obtained an original source. If we look at the sources for Lillian Chappell you can see that, although I have recorded the exact date of and place of her death, I obviously have not yet added the source information as there is no small black triangle.

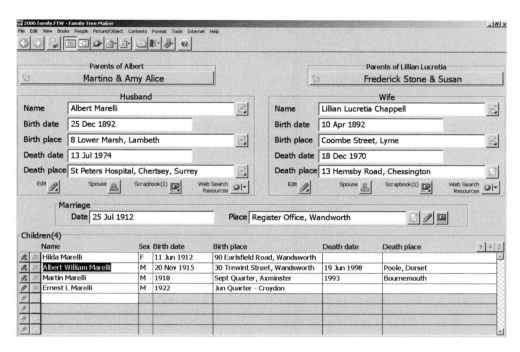

By clicking on the source icon we are taken to another screen.

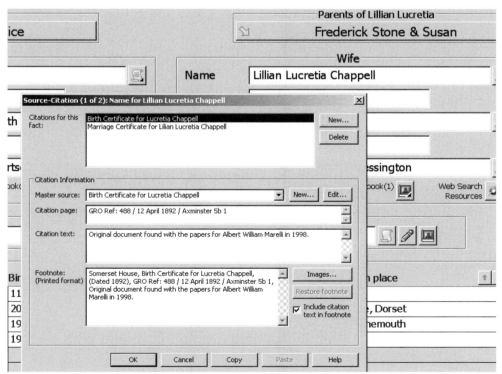

Source citation screen.

The source dialog box allows me to create, edit and add source information.

A source can be any number of things – Census records, Civil Registration details, Wills, manorial records, church records, gravestones, newspaper articles, and so on.

Each individual recorded in your software also has their own notes screen. Below the death place is an edit icon with a pencil, .

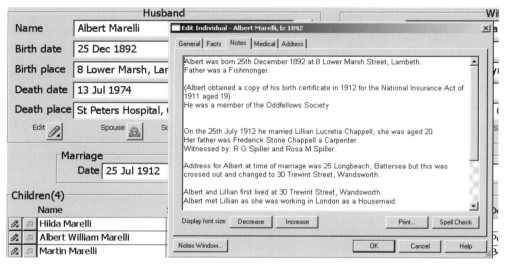

The notes screen is very handy when you are compiling the information, especially in the early days

Next to the edit icon is the spouse icon . This is where you can add second marriages and choose the preferred spouse, direct line, for your tree. You can also attach names of the children of this marriage. The advantage of this software is that you can edit and move individuals if originally attached to the wrong parents.

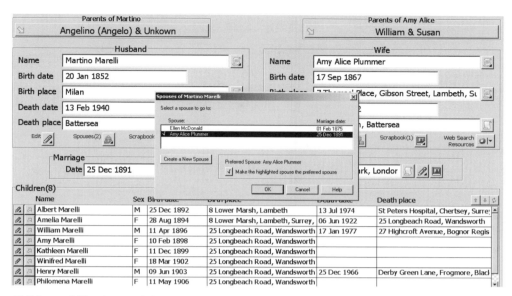

Children of Martino and Amy.

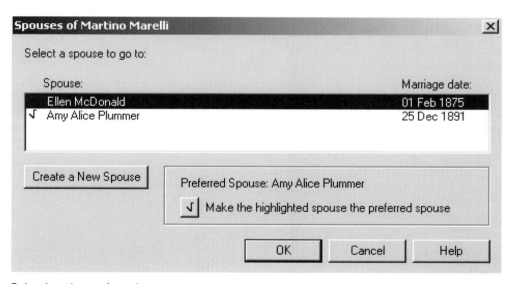

Selecting the preferred spouse.

If you want to sort children entered in the wrong order by birth, you can do so by selecting the 'people' menu at the top of the screen. This feature means that you can add siblings at any time, and sort them as you go.

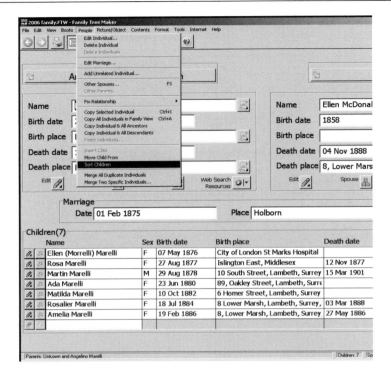

We now have all the children in the correct birth order after using the 'sort children' option.

If you have scanned photos or other documents of your ancestors you can import them into their own personal scrapbook 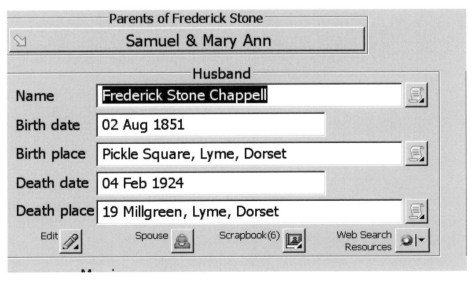.

Click on the scrapbook icon, third from left.

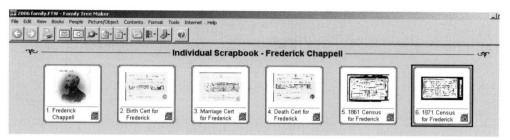

The contents of the scrapbook for Frederick Chappell.

Images can be added easily by right-clicking on a blank box. Later I will show you another wonderful feature of scrapbooks.

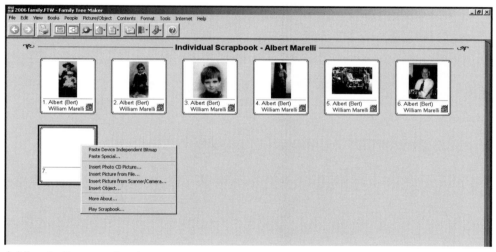

Adding to the scrapbook.

We are now going to look at creating trees from the information you have keyed into your family history database. When you have decided whose tree you are going to create, you can look for the names of those that will appear for quick reference by clicking on this ⌐ icon.

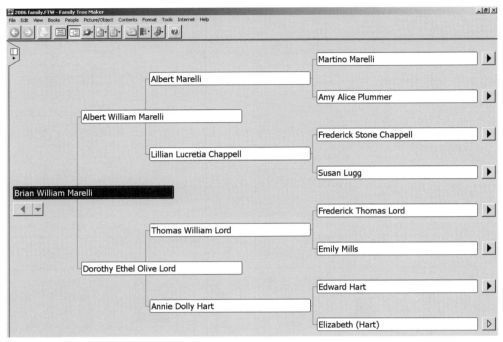

Creating your family tree.

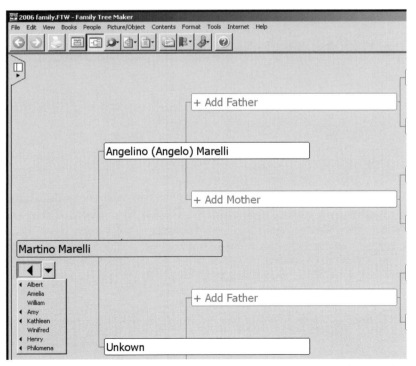

Clicking on any of the arrow to the right of screen will take you further back.

You can also access spouses, parents and siblings or the whole index of a person, and by clicking on an individual by name, you will be taken to the edit screen of your chosen ancestor.

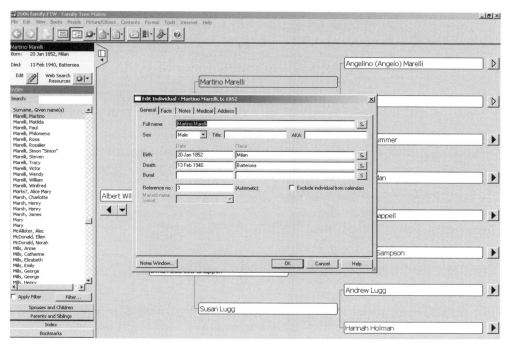

Here you can update/add the individual's date of birth, place of death etc.

Producing trees with Family Tree Maker

By clicking on the tree icon at the top of our screen a list of the tree types available to create appear. Below you will find images of the different types available.

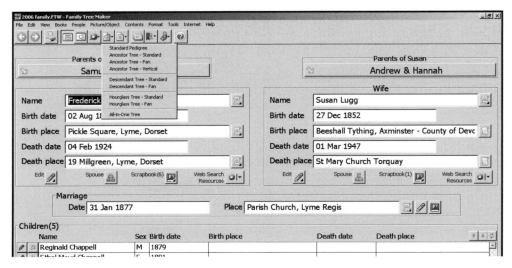

Choosing the type of family tree.

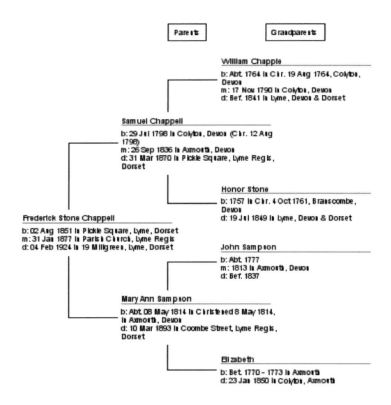

Standard pedigree tree.

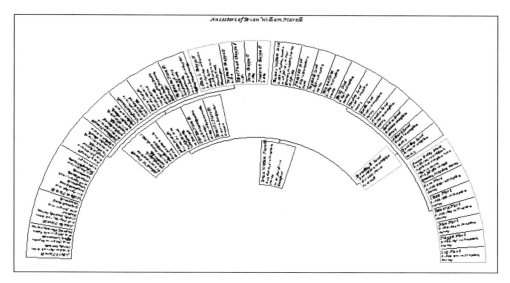

Ancestor tree fan.

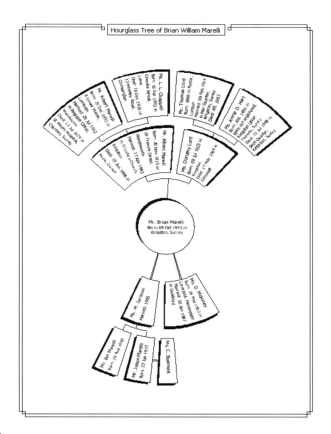

Hourglass tree.

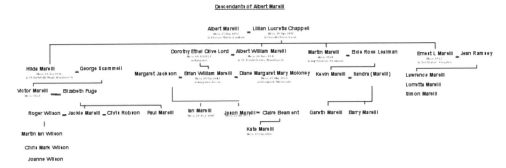

Descendant tree (this is just a small section as it's too large to view).

> Family Tree Maker allows you to move branches within the tree layout, copy the tree, convert it to another software package, convert it to a drawing or PDF and edit the tree's layout.

There is a number of features available when designing your tree for print. A right click of your mouse will bring them up.

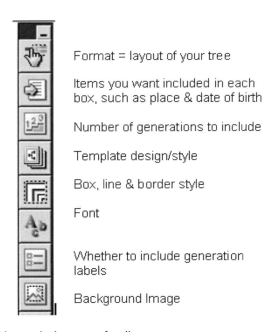

Format = layout of your tree

Items you want included in each box, such as place & date of birth

Number of generations to include

Template design/style

Box, line & border style

Font

Whether to include generation labels

Background Image

Options available when printing your family tree.

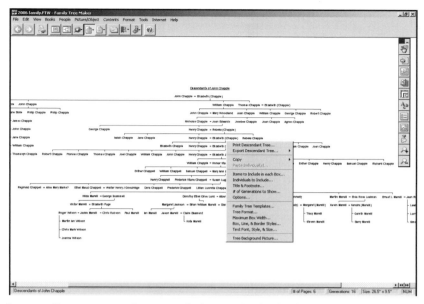

The software allows you to choose and change the look of your tree instantly.

I will now go through the process of changing the look of a tree.

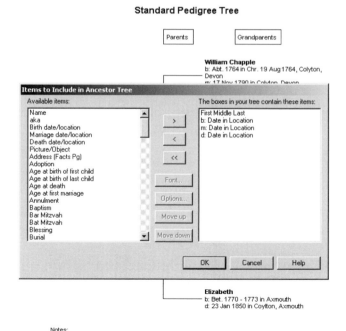

Here you can select the category of information to appear against each individual

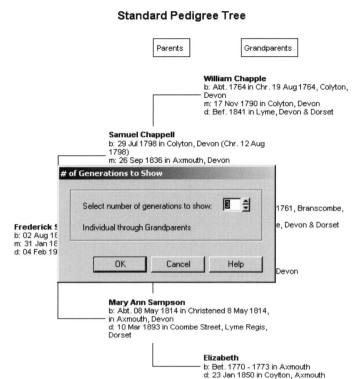

Here you can select the number of generations to show on the tree.

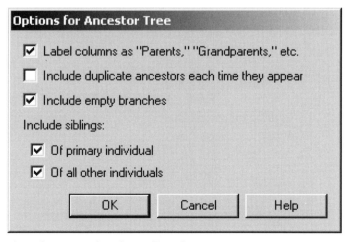

The software also gives you the above 5 options.

Below is a sample ancestor tree with siblings added. The top of this tree has been cropped for viewing purposes.

Samuel Chappell

b: 29 Jul 1798 in Colyton, Devon (Chr. 12 Aug 1798)
m: 26 Sep 1836 in Axmouth, Devon
d: 31 Mar 1870 in Pickle Square, Lyme Regis, Dorset

Esther Chappell

b: 17 Dec 1792 in Colyton, Devon
m:
d:

William Chappell

b: 15 Aug 1795 in Colyton, Devon
m:
d: 15 Jan 1846 in Lyme, Devon & Dorset

Henry Chappell

b: 09 Jun 1803 in Colyton, Devon
m:
d:

Frederick Stone Chappell

b: 02 Aug 1851 in Pickle Square, Lyme, Dorset
m: 31 Jan 1877 in Parish Church, Lyme Regis
d: 04 Feb 1924 in 19 Millgreen, Lyme, Dorset

Honor Stone

b: 1757 in Chr. 4 Oct 1761, Branscombe, Devon
d: 19 Jul 1849 in Lyme, Devon & Dorset

Henry Chappell

b: Feb 1837 in Chr. 26 Feb, Axmouth, Devon
m:
d:

John Sampson

b: Abt. 1777
m: 1813 in Axmouth, Devon
d: Bef. 1837

Mary Ann Sampson

b: Abt. 08 May 1814 in Christened 8 May 1814, in Axmouth, Devon
d: 10 Mar 1893 in Coombe Street, Lyme Regis, Dorset

Elizabeth

b: Bet. 1770 - 1773 in Axmouth
d: 23 Jan 1850 in Colyton, Axmouth

Ancestor tree with siblings added.

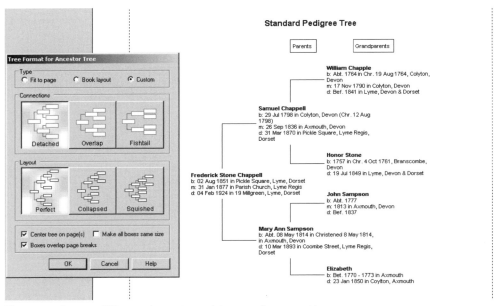

You can choose different layouts and types of connections.

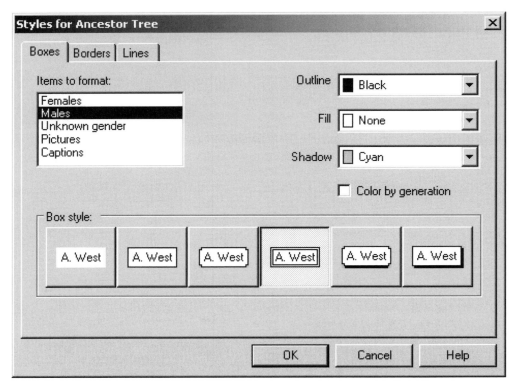

Colours and borders can be applied to identify information in the tree, e.g. applying cyan to all boxes where female ancestors appear.

Standard Pedigree Tree

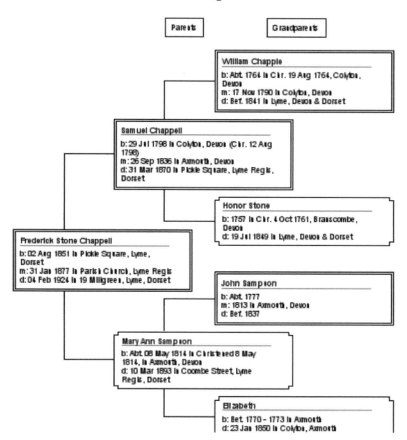

Here male and female ancestors are printed with different box styles.

Displaying backgrounds or photographs in your family tree

You may want to give your family tree a special feel, if presenting as a gift. There is a number of standard backgrounds that come with this software which can be applied to your tree.

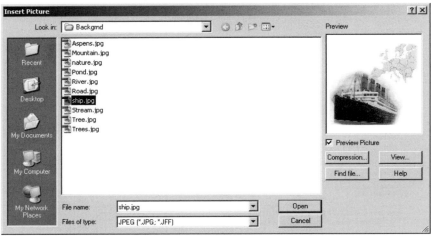

Standard available backgrounds.

But, you can also browse your own pictures (perhaps ones you have found through archives) for a particular image, edit it, and then insert it into the background of your tree.

There are several edit options available to you to make it look perfect.

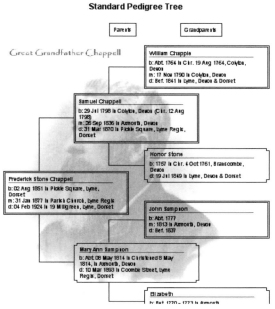

Standard Pedigree Tree

The finished family would print with the image in the background.

It is also possible to print a tree and add an object or image as part of the information you require to appear in each individual box. It is most likely to be a photograph of the individual.

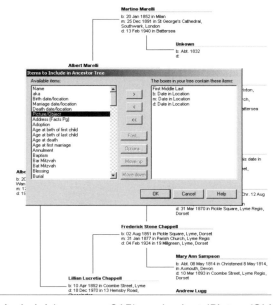

Go back to 'items to include' (see page 215), and select 'Picture/Object'.

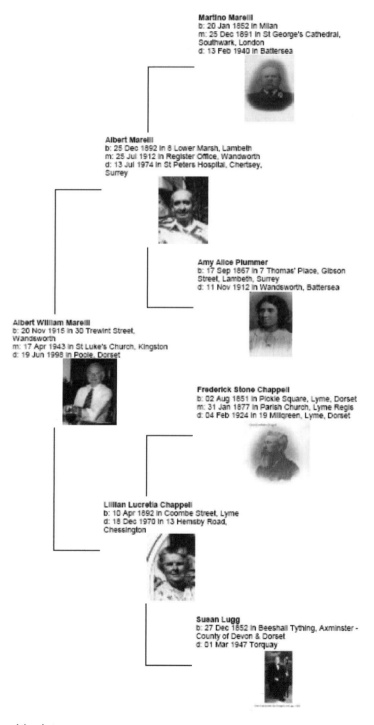

Martino Marelli
b: 20 Jan 1852 in Milan
m: 25 Dec 1891 in St George's Cathedral,
Southwark, London
d: 13 Feb 1940 in Battersea

Albert Marelli
b: 25 Dec 1892 in 8 Lower Marsh, Lambeth
m: 25 Jul 1912 in Register Office, Wandworth
d: 13 Jul 1974 in St Peters Hospital, Chertsey,
Surrey

Amy Alice Plummer
b: 17 Sep 1867 in 7 Thomas' Place, Gibson
Street, Lambeth, Surrey
d: 11 Nov 1912 in Wandsworth, Battersea

Albert William Marelli
b: 20 Nov 1915 in 30 Trewint Street,
Wandsworth
m: 17 Apr 1943 in St Luke's Church, Kingston
d: 19 Jun 1998 in Poole, Dorset

Frederick Stone Chappell
b: 02 Aug 1851 in Pickle Square, Lyme, Dorset
m: 31 Jan 1877 in Parish Church, Lyme Regis
d: 04 Feb 1924 in 19 Millgreen, Lyme, Dorset

Lillian Lucretia Chappell
b: 10 Apr 1892 in Coombe Street, Lyme
d: 18 Dec 1970 in 13 Hemsby Road,
Chessington

Susan Lugg
b: 27 Dec 1852 in Beeshall Tything, Axminster -
County of Devon & Dorset
d: 01 Mar 1947 Torquay

Family tree with pictures.

I have created an hourglass tree showing three generations of my mother Peggy.

Hourglass tree of Lilian Margaret Reynolds.

I scanned a photograph of her and added it into my pictures file so that when I browsed for images I could input it as a background of the above tree.

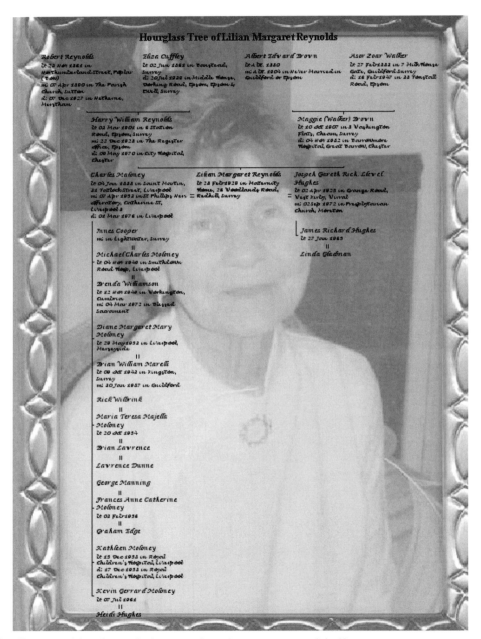

Family tree with a framed photograph makes a very special gift.

Personally, I love this feature for creating family trees.

Reports

There is a variety of reports available to print within Family Tree Maker. Click on ▐▀▌, on the top menu.

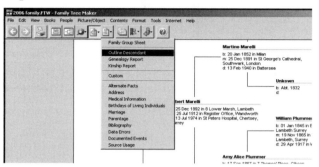

The drop-down menu shows the three types of reports.

Let's take a look at the type of reports available, all of which you can customise to suit your own requirements. What type of report is most suitable will depend on the information you want to gather, but these reports can be useful for checking and cross-referencing information.

Descendants of Frederick Stone Chappell

```
1 Frederick Stone Chappell b: 02 Aug 1851 in Pickle Square, Lyme, Dorset d: 04 Feb 1924 in 19 Millgreen, Lyme, Dorset

  +Susan Lugg b: 27 Dec 1852 in Beeshall Tything, Axminster - County of Devon & Dorset m: 31 Jan 1877 in Parish Church, Lyme
  Regis d: 01 Mar 1947 in St Mary Church Torquay

  ...... 2 Reginald Chappell b: 1879

  ...... 2 Ethel Maud Chappell b: 1881

  .......... +Mr Goodridge

  ...... 2 Dora Chappell b: 1885

  ...... 2 Frederick Chappell b: 1889

  ...... 2 Lillian Lucretia Chappell b: 10 Apr 1892 in Coombe Street, Lyme d: 18 Dec 1970 in 13 Hemsby Road, Chessington

  .......... +Albert Marelli b: 25 Dec 1892 in 8 Lower Marsh, Lambeth m: 25 Jul 1912 in Register Office, Wandworth d: 13 Jul 1974 in St
  Peters Hospital, Chertsey, Surrey

  ............ 3 Hilda Marelli b: 11 Jun 1912 in 90 Earlsfield Road, Wandsworth

  ............... +George Scammell m: Dec 1928

  ................. 4 Victor Marelli b: 1921

  .................... +Elizabeth Fuge

  ...................... 5 [1] Jackie Marelli

  ......................... +Roger Wilson

  ...................... *2nd Husband of [1] Jackie Marelli:
  ......................... +Chris Robson

  ...................... 5 Paul Marelli

  ............... 3 [3] Albert William Marelli b: 20 Nov 1915 in 30 Trewint Street, Wandsworth d: 19 Jun 1998 in Poole, Dorset

  .................. +Dorothy Ethel Olive Lord b: 09 Jul 1923 in Kingston m: 17 Apr 1943 in St Luke's Church, Kingston d: 17 May 1964 in
  Cornwall

  ................. 4 [2] Brian William Marelli b: 09 Oct 1943 in Kingston, Surrey

  .................... +Margaret Jackson m: 1965

  ...................... 5 Ian Marelli b: 20 Aug 1969

  ...................... 5 Jason Marelli b: 22 Jan 1972

  ......................... +Claire Beament

  .................. *2nd Wife of [2] Brian William Marelli:
  .................. +Diane Margaret Mary Moloney b: 29 May 1953 in Liverpool, Merseyside m: 30 Jan 1987 in Guildford

  ............... *2nd Wife of [3] Albert William Marelli:
  ............... +Nora Kennedy m: 1967 in Reigate Hill

  ................. 4 Richard Marelli (Kennedy)
```

Outline descendant report.

Descendants of Frederick Stone Chappell

Generation No. 1

1. Frederick Stone[11] Chappell (Samuel[10], William[9] Chapple, Henry[8], Henry[7], Henry[6], Henry[5], Nicholas[4], John[3], William[2], John[1]) (Source: (1) Diane Marelli/ GRO, Death Certificate for Frederick Stone Chappell, GRO: 318, March Quarter, 1924, Axminster 5b 1, Nov 2001, States Frederick Stone Chappell as Father., (2) GRO Ref 59, Axminster X18, Sept Quarter 1851, Birth Certificate for Frederick Stone Chappell, GRO, GRO Ref 59, Axminster X 18, Sept Quarter 1851., (3) Original Document, *Marriage Certificate for Lilian Lucretia Chappell & Albert Marelli*, (GRO Ref 191, Wandsworth 1d 1567).) was born 02 Aug 1851 in Pickle Square, Lyme, Dorset (Source: GRO Ref 59, Axminster X 18, Sept Quarter 1851, Birth Certificate for Frederick Stone Chappell, GRO.), and died 04 Feb 1924 in 19 Millgreen, Lyme, Dorset (Source: Diane Marelli/ GRO, Death Certificate for Frederick Stone Chappell, GRO: 318, March Quarter, 1924, Axminster 5b 1, GRO: 318, March Quarter, 1924, Axminster 5b 1.). He married **Susan Lugg** (Source: (1) Birth Certificate for Susan Lugg, December 2001, Acquired from Family Records London., (2) Original Document, *Marriage Certificate for Lilian Lucretia Chappell & Albert Marelli*, (GRO Ref 191, Wandsworth 1d 1567).) 31 Jan 1877 in Parish Church, Lyme Regis (Source: Marriage Certificate for Frederick Stone Chappell & Susan Lugg, Nov 2001, Acquired from Family Records London.), daughter of Andrew Lugg and Hannah Holman. She was born 27 Dec 1852 in Beeshall Tything, Axminster - County of Devon & Dorset, and died 01 Mar 1947 in St Mary Church Torquay.

Notes for Frederick Stone Chappell:
Painter

The gap between Henry and Frederick is about 15 years but Census confirms this as true.

More About Frederick Stone Chappell:
General: 1881, Pickle Square, Lyme Regis, Dorset

More About Susan Lugg:
General: from Hawkchurch, Dorset, England

Children of Frederick Chappell and Susan Lugg are:

2	i.	Reginald[12] Chappell, born 1879.
3	ii.	Ethel Maud Chappell, born 1881. She married Mr Goodridge.
4	iii.	Dora Chappell, born 1885.
5	iv.	Frederick Chappell, born 1889.
+ 6	v.	Lillian Lucretia Chappell, born 10 Apr 1892 in Coombe Street, Lyme; died 18 Dec 1970 in 13 Hemsby Road, Chessington.

Generation No. 2

6. Lillian Lucretia[12] Chappell (Frederick Stone[11], Samuel[10], William[9] Chapple, Henry[8], Henry[7], Henry[6], Henry[5], Nicholas[4], John[3], William[2], John[1]) (Source: (1) Somerset House, *Birth Certificate for Lucretia Chappell*, (Dated 1892), GRO Ref: 488 / 12 April 1892 / Axminster 5b 1, Original document found with the papers for Albert William Marelli in 1998., (2) Original Document, *Marriage Certificate for Lilian Lucretia Chappell & Albert Marelli*, (GRO Ref 191, Wandsworth 1d 1567), GRO: 191, Wandsworth 1d 1567 Sept 1912, Original certificate found with the papers for Albert William Marelli in 1998.) was born 10 Apr 1892 in Coombe Street, Lyme (Source: Copy for Birth Certificate, *Birth Certificate for Lilian Lucretia Chappell*, (GRO Ref: 488 / 12 April 1892 / Axminster 5b 1).), and died 18 Dec 1970 in 13 Hemsby Road, Chessington. She married **Albert Marelli** (Source: The Oddfellows Society, *Birth Certificate for Albert Marelli*, Original copy of Birth Certificate dated 20th May 1912 which was obtained for purposes of National Insurance Act of 1911. Document found in the papers of his son Albert William Marelli in 1998.) 25 Jul 1912 in Register Office, Wandworth (Source: Original Document, *Marriage Certificate for Lilian Lucretia Chappell & Albert Marelli*, (GRO Ref 191, Wandsworth 1d 1567).), son of Martino Marelli and Amy Plimmer. He was born 25 Dec 1892 in 8 Lower Marsh, Lambeth (Source: The Oddfellows Society, *Birth*

Genealogy report.

Name	Birth date	Relationship with Frederick Chappell
	Kinship of Frederick Stone Chappell	
(Chapple), Elizabeth	1555	Wife of the 7th great-granduncle
(Chapple), Elizabeth	Abt. 1675	3rd great-grandmother
(Chapple), Elizabeth	Abt. 1700	2nd great-grandmother
(Chapple), Rebeka	Abt. 1645	4th great-grandmother
(Holman), Sarah	Abt. 1797	Grandmother of the wife
Bolle, Jane	1585	Wife of the 1st cousin 8 times removed
Chappell, Esther	17 Dec 1792	Aunt
Chappell, Frederick Stone	02 Aug 1851	Self
Chappell, Henry	09 Jun 1803	Uncle
Chappell, Henry	Feb 1837	Brother
Chappell, Samuel	29 Jul 1798	Father
Chappell, William	15 Aug 1795	Uncle
Chapple, Agnes	1625	5th great-grandaunt
Chapple, Ann	07 Aug 1767	Grandaunt
Chapple, Anthony	1550	7th great-granduncle
Chapple, Betty	01 Apr 1769	Grandaunt
Chapple, Elizabeth	1698	2nd great-grandaunt
Chapple, Esther	07 Dec 1770	Grandaunt
Chapple, Frances	1729	Great-grandaunt
Chapple, George	1582	6th great-granduncle
Chapple, George	Abt. 1642	4th great-granduncle
Chapple, Henry	Abt. 1645	4th great-grandfather
Chapple, Henry	Jun 1670	3rd great-grandfather
Chapple, Henry	1700	2nd great-grandfather
Chapple, Henry	Abt. 1744	Great-grandfather
Chapple, Henry	01 Mar 1773	Granduncle
Chapple, Isaac	1705	2nd great-granduncle
Chapple, Isaiah	1660	3rd great-granduncle
Chapple, James	1612	2nd cousin 7 times removed
Chapple, Jane		2nd cousin 7 times removed
Chapple, Jane	1665	3rd great-grandaunt
Chapple, Jesebee	1618	5th great-grandaunt
Chapple, Joan	1577	6th great-grandaunt
Chapple, Joan	1621	5th great-grandaunt
Chapple, Joan	1708	2nd great-grandaunt
Chapple, Joan	1712	2nd great-grandaunt
Chapple, Joel	1734	Great-granduncle
Chapple, John		2nd cousin 7 times removed
Chapple, John	1551	7th great-granduncle
Chapple, John	1584	6th great-grandfather
Chapple, John	1587	1st cousin 8 times removed
Chapple, John	Abt. 1739	Great-granduncle
Chapple, Mary	06 Dec 1766	Grandaunt
Chapple, Nicholas	1615	5th great-grandfather
Chapple, Philip	1587	1st cousin 8 times removed

Kinship report.

You can also print off a list of all the sources you have collected, or not yet collected, as the case may be.

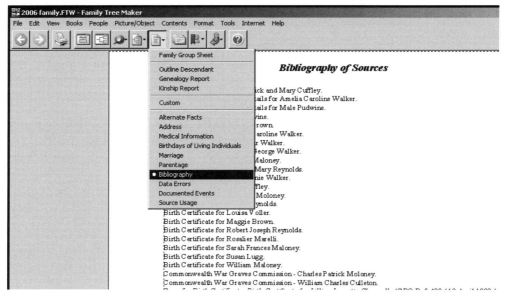

To gather all your sources select 'Bibliography'.

Charting Companion for Family Tree Maker

Charting Companion by Progeny is an add-on for the latest version of Family Tree Maker in which you can view, customize, print and publish generations of your family tree. It works by using the data in Family Tree Maker and providing many more options.

Charting Companion for Family Tree Maker
Ver 1.0
Copyright 1997-2005 by Progeny Software, Inc. All rights reserved.

Unfortunately, none of the diagrams you are about to see will be in colour, but hopefully you will get the general idea of this software package. I am going to build an hourglass tree for Albert William Marelli. I have closed down Family Tree Maker and logged into Charting Companion. My first step was to select his name from the index.

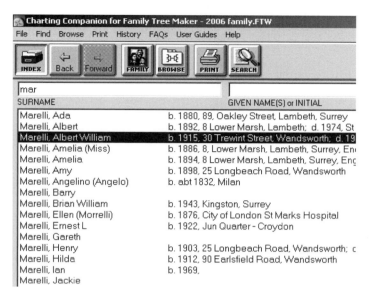

Step 1: Choose the name of the ancestor. The index information is grabbed from your FTM family file.

Next choose the tree style I want to create:

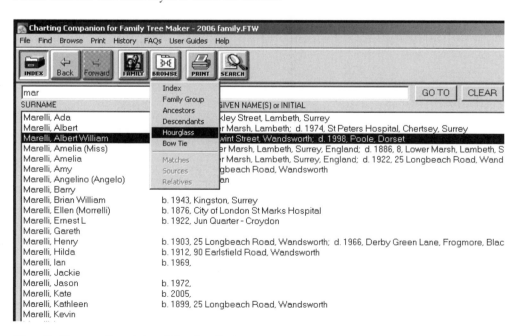

Step 2: Choose the style of the family tree.

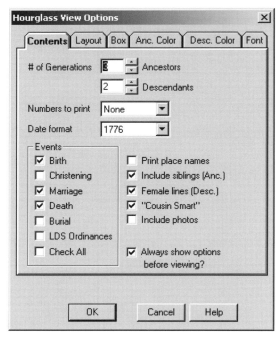

Step 3: The software provides several view options.

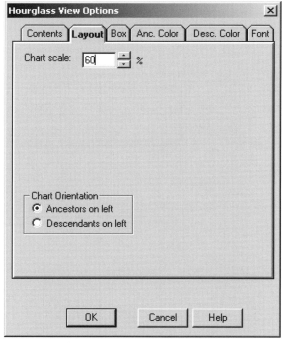

Sept 4: Select the type of layout. If the family tree is extensive, it is worth considering scaling down the chart by the percentage option.

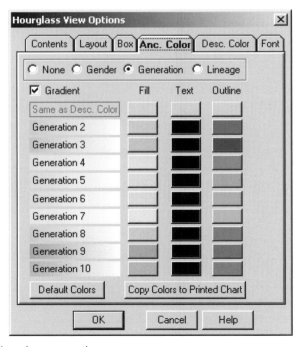

Step 5: Select the type of boxes for display.

Step 6: Select colour by generation.

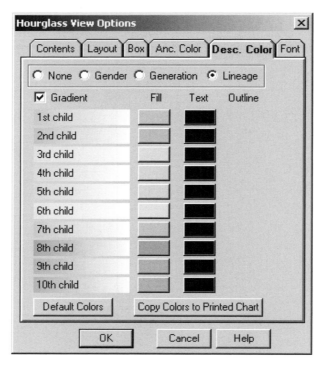

Step 7: You can select to colour by lineage.

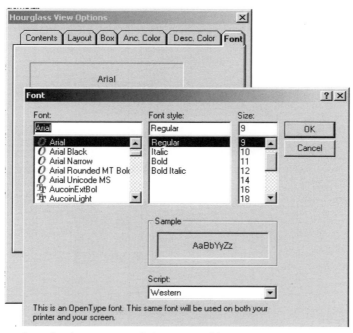

Step 8: Finally select the font; ensure it is not too big.

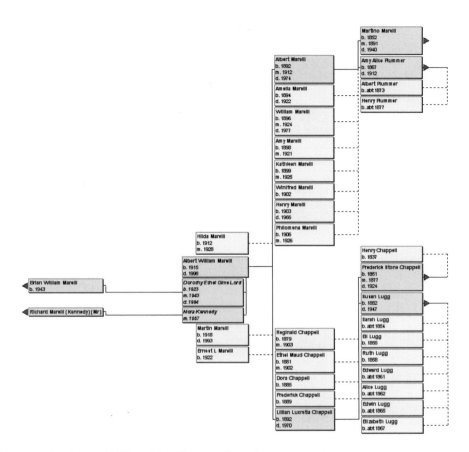

Family tree for Albert William Marelli using Charting Companion.

The software also provides a variety of charts which are useful because they provide a different way of looking at the same data.

Bow Tie generation colour chart.

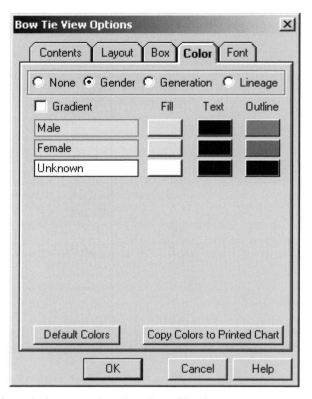

Various options for printing your data in a Bow Tie chart.

Bow Tie gender colour chart.

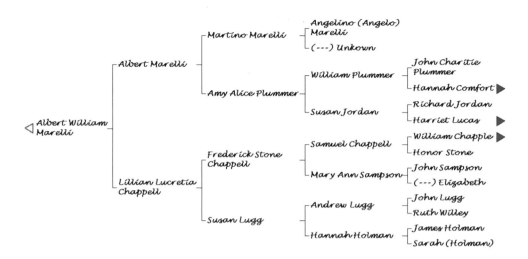

Ancestor chart.

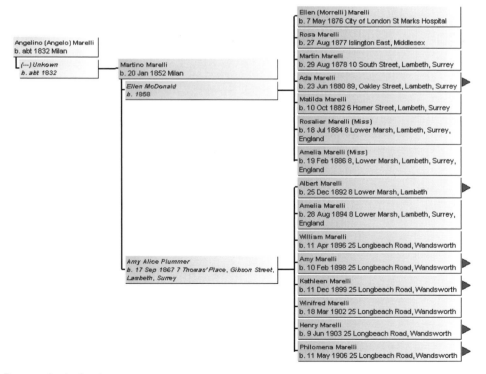

Descendant chart.

The arrows on the above charts indicate further generations.

Family Tree Maker, the Internet and your family history page

Besides the more expected features of FTM you can also launch your family history on to the Internet and create your own family history web page. Not everyone has or wants a website, but there is an easy solution to getting your family history published on the Internet through FTM. Back in the main FTM family file I am going to select the Internet menu at the top of the main screen:

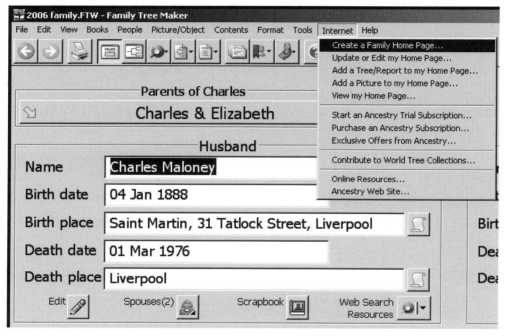

Select the Internet menu in FTM.

By selecting 'Create a Family Home Page' you will be taken into wizard that will guide you through the easy process of creating a family home page.

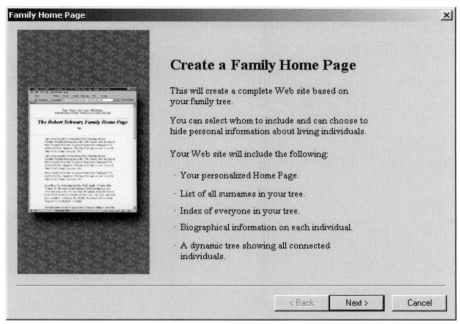

The wizard will create a family home page for you.

I already have my own website but decided to create a family history page to enhance my Internet profile. I followed the instruction wizard easily and all my data was uploaded for me to produce the following page:

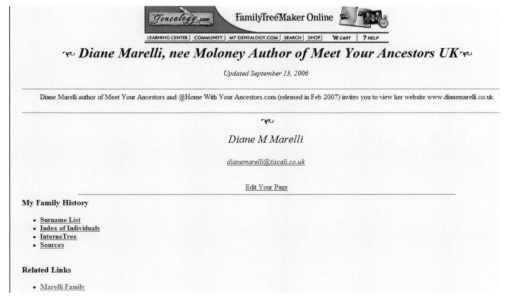

The created web page.

To the left of the screen is the list of what has been imported from FTM to my newly created family page. By clicking on 'Surname list', viewers can examine the following:

Diane Marelli, nee Moloney Author of Meet Your Ancestors UK:
Surname List

(Bristow), (Canning), (Chapple), (Cuffley), (Hart), (Holman), (Jordan), (Kennedy), (Knight), (Lord), (Marelli), (Reynolds), (Swann), (Taylor), (Uins), (Walker), (Whibley), (Willis), Alice, Antrobus, Argent, Armstrong, Audrey, Bailey, Baker, Ball, Bates, Bayley, Beament, Biggs, Bolle, Bonsey, Bridger, Bristow, Brown, Bryant, Bunting, Catchpole, Chappell, Chapple, Cheeseman, Chilman, Chitty, Clements, Cobbett, Cockran, Collins, Comfort, Comforte, Cook, Cooper, Coulson, Crabb, Crawley, Croft, Cuffley, Cufley, Culleton, Davey), Davies, Daws, Dibben, Downs, Doyle, Duke, Dunne, Edge, Edwards, Elizabeth, Emma, Esther, Evans, Ewen, Ewins, Fairweather, Farncombe, Francis, Fuge, Gerrish, Gertie, Gladman, Goodridge, Gosling, Griffiths, Harding, Harrison, Hart, Hayward, Hill, Holman, House, Huggett, Hughes, Irvine, Jackson, James, Jones, Jordan, Joy, Kelly, Kennedy, Knight, Lawrence, Lealman, Lee, Lepage, Lock, Lord, Lucas, Lugg, Lyne, Maloney, Manning, Marelli, Marks?, Marsh, Mary, McAllister, McDonald, Mills, Misnmack, Moloney, Mulaney, Oliver, Pearson, Perrin, Philpott, Phyllis, Pilkington, Plummer, Polly, Pudwine, Radford, Ramsey, Rapley, Reynolds, Richards, Richardson, Robson, Ross, Ryan, Sampson, Sanger, Saunders, Scammell, Scott), Simmonds, Slaughter, Spiller, Staley, Stepney, Stone, Stripp, Strudwick, Susannah, Swann, Tarbuck, Taylor, Thomas, Thorne, Timms, Todd, Tudor, Turner, Unkown, Vallar, Voller, Walker, Webber, Wheatley, Whibley, Wilbrink, Willey, Williamson, Wilson, Wincup/Cuffley, Winter, Wood, Woodland

For a complete list of individuals on the site, go to the Index of Individuals.

Created with Family Tree Maker Find out how!

The web page lists everyone I have researched.

By clicking on a chosen surname above or selecting the index of individuals you or viewers can examine complete families:

(Bristow)

(Bristow), Alice(b. Abt. 1838, d. 22 Oct 1914)

(Canning)

(Canning), Jane(b. Abt. 1783, d. date unknown)

(Chapple)

(Chapple), Elizabeth(b. 1535, d. 1587)
(Chapple), Elizabeth(b. 1555, d. 1595)
(Chapple), Elizabeth(b. Abt. 1675, d. 1741)
(Chapple), Elizabeth(b. Abt. 1700, d. date unknown)
(Chapple), Rebeka(b. Abt. 1645, d. 1680)

(Cuffley)

(Cuffley), Eliza(b. 1807, d. 11 Jan 1892)
(Cuffley), Fanny(b. 1851, d. date unknown)
(Cuffley), Lucy(b. 1838, d. date unknown)
(Cuffley), Maria(b. 1830, d. date unknown)
(Cuffley), Sarah(b. 1844, d. date unknown)

(Hart)

(Hart), Elizabeth(b. Abt. 1831, d. Aft. 1881)
(Hart), Elizabeth(b. 1867, d. date unknown)

(Holman)

(Holman), Sarah(b. Abt. 1797, d. Abt. 1845)

The software provides the basic details you have gathered.

Or, by clicking on the menu 'InterneTree' for a chosen name, you or viewers can produce a tree:

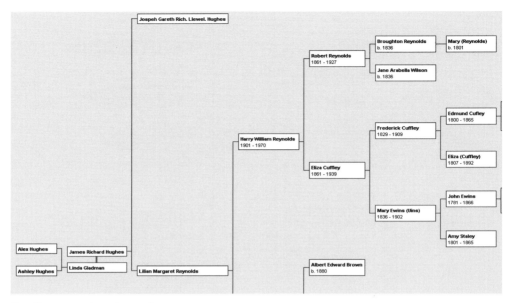

Family tree using the web page.

Also by clicking on a name on the above tree such as Lilian Margaret Reynolds, my mum, a picture of her taken from my FTM file appears for me and others to enjoy:

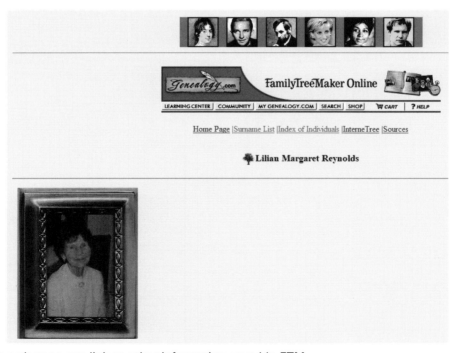

The web page can link to other information saved in FTM.

Also, if you have researched and recorded actual sources in FTM that confirm your findings, these to can be made available to other interested parties:

List of sources gathered.

If you change or update information in FTM, you can very easily update/add that information to your web page. Go to the Internet menu at the top and select 'Update or Edit my Home Page'. A wizard will take you through the simple steps to update your family page. Excellent stuff!

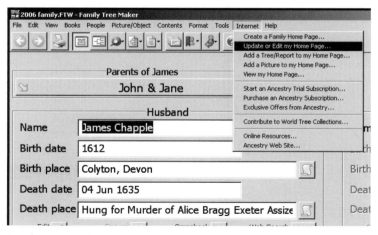

Updating your home page.

I think you will agree FTM offers a wonderful resource which makes publishing your family history on the Internet a simple yet effective process.

9

Follow-up to live exercise: researching with limited information

Where we left off

As you will remember (see page 129), I placed an order for the following:

♦ Denzil Garbett's birth certificate
♦ Certifitcate of Edgar Garbett's marriage to Ellen Cousins
♦ Edgar Garbett's birth certificate
♦ Ellen Cousins's birth certificate

The date is now 10th September and I've just phoned the GRO because only the birth certificates arrived as expected on the 26th September. I was pleasantly surprised by the response I received from the GRO. The person I spoke to was understanding, able to trace my order easily and went out of his way to solve the problem there and then. Unfortunately, he couldn't solve the problem but has put in an urgent request that my order be looked into as it was for a birthday gift. It is worth noting that in all the years I have used the services of the GRO I have never had a problem.

Below is the tree where I had left off without evidence that my research was correct:

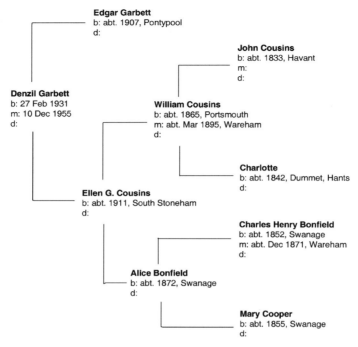

Edgar Garbett
b: abt. 1907, Pontypool
d:

John Cousins
b: abt. 1833, Havant
m:
d:

Denzil Garbett
b: 27 Feb 1931
m: 10 Dec 1955
d:

William Cousins
b: abt. 1865, Portsmouth
m: abt. Mar 1895, Wareham
d:

Charlotte
b: abt. 1842, Dummet, Hants
d:

Ellen G. Cousins
b: abt. 1911, South Stoneham
d:

Charles Henry Bonfield
b: abt. 1852, Swanage
m: abt. Dec 1871, Wareham
d:

Alice Bonfield
b: abt. 1872, Swanage
d:

Mary Cooper
b: abt. 1855, Swanage
d:

Standard pedigree tree for the Garbett and Cousins family.

Arrival of certificates

Here are the birth certificates for Edgar Garbett, Denzil Edgar Garbett and Ellen Eliza Georgina Cousins.

Birth certificate for Edgar Garbett.

CERTIFIED COPY OF AN ENTRY OF BIRTH

GIVEN AT THE GENERAL REGISTER OFFICE

Application Number COL526598

	REGISTRATION DISTRICT			Southampton					
1931	BIRTH in the Sub-district of **Southampton Eastern**				in the	**County of Southampton C.B.**			

Columns:-

No.	When and where born	Name, if any	Sex	Name and surname of father	Name, surname and maiden surname of mother	Occupation of father	Signature, description and residence of informant	When registered	Signature of registrar	Name entered after registration
139	Twenty-seventh February 1931 98 St Denys Road M.O.	Denzil Edgar	Boy	Edgar Garbett	Ellen Eliza Georgina Garbett formerly Cousins	General Labourer of 6a Aberdeen Road M.O.	E E G Garbett mother 6a Aberdeen Road Southampton	Seventh April 1931	H R Hardy Registrar	

CERTIFIED to be a true copy of an entry in the certified copy of a Register of Births in the District above mentioned.

Given at the GENERAL REGISTER OFFICE, under the Seal of the said Office, the 23rd day of August 2006

BXCB 907421

Birth certificate for Denzil Edgar Garbett.

CERTIFIED COPY OF AN ENTRY OF BIRTH

GIVEN AT THE GENERAL REGISTER OFFICE

Application Number COL526598

	REGISTRATION DISTRICT			South Stoneham					
1911	BIRTH in the Sub-district of **South Stoneham**				in the	**County of Southampton**			

Columns:-

No.	When and where born	Name, if any	Sex	Name and surname of father	Name, surname and maiden surname of mother	Occupation of father	Signature, description and residence of informant	When registered	Signature of registrar	Name entered after registration
33	Twenty-seventh September 1911 St Loughton Road South Stoneham R.S.	Ellen Eliza Georgina	Girl	William Cousins	Alice Cousins formerly Bonfield	Ships Fireman Mail Service	A Cousins Mother 81 Empress Road Southampton	Seventh November 1911	Alfred Charles Miller Registrar	

CERTIFIED to be a true copy of an entry in the certified copy of a Register of Births in the District above mentioned.

Given at the GENERAL REGISTER OFFICE, under the Seal of the said Office, the 23rd day of August 2006

Birth certificate for Ellen Eliza Cousins.

Garbett family tree

Our tree with the extra information taken from the above birth certificates now looks like this:

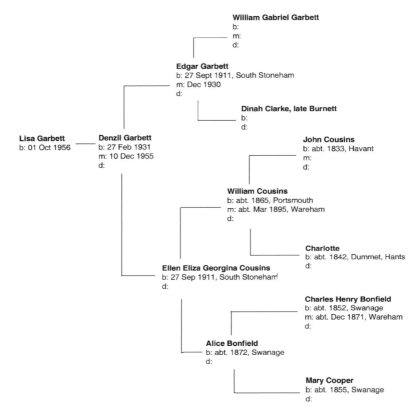

Garbett family tree updated.

Denzil's birth certificate confirmed that Edgar Garbett and Ellen Cousins were his parents. Edgar's birth certificate gave me the names of Denzil's grandparents and Lisa's great grandparents William Gabriel Garbett and Dinah Clarke; late Burnett told me that this was Dinah's second marriage. Ellen's birth certificate gave me the names of her parents, William Cousins and Alice Bonfield, confirming my early unconfirmed research.

While waiting for the marriage certificate for Ellen Cousins and Edgar Garbett, I decided to order the marriage certificate for William Gabriel Garbett to Dinah Burnett, née Clarke, to even out the above branches. I found it in the December quarter of 1899.

Marriage certificate for William G. Garbett to Dinah Burnett.

With this additional information I went straight back to verify my Census data. My findings are correct, even without the marriage certificate that is yet to arrive.

The missing marriage certificate

The certificate arrived two days after my call, as promised. The certificate confirms the early information taken from the birth certificates – so I definitely have the right marriage for Edgar and Ellen. Looking at the witnesses I see there is an Edith Ellen Cousins, which I presume could be a sibling because of her second name Ellen.

Certificate of marriage for Edgar Garbett to Ellen Cousins.

The final result

A further search of the Census provided me with the name of Ellen's mother, Harriet. I also carried out a search for Dinah Clarke's mother, Mary. Within a short period of time I had achieved the following results, completing much of the detail in the family tree.

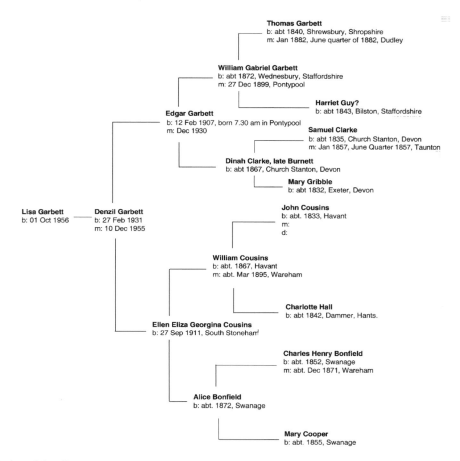

Updated family tree.

I followed the same process for Lisa's maternal ancestry and feel duty-bound to report that I did find an error in my unqualified research taking one branch of her history into completely the wrong direction. However, the certificates put me back on track and with the help of the Census she is now the proud owner of her own family history including sources to verify her ancestry.

The moral of this story is:

♦ If patient, wait for evidence before moving on another generation
♦ If impatient, go for it but be prepared for error

Personally, I always go for the latter.

Summary

The aim of this book is to launch you into family history and the capabilities within your grasp through the use of the Internet, but it should not be viewed as a definitive guide. All the information within this book comes from my own genuine experiences while learning about and researching my own family history over the past nine years.

Naturally, not everyone has access to the Internet or wants it, and initially all my research was carried out at establishments such as The Family Records Centre in London, The National Archives in Kew, The Surrey History Centre in Woking, The Society of Genealogists in London, all of which are detailed in my first book *Meet Your Ancestors,* currently being updated for release in Spring 2007.

If you read this book or my first book, then you are interested in family history. If you hate computers, have time issues or live out of reach of family history establishments, why not employ a researcher to help get you started, like me?

I would be also interested to hear from other researchers who believe they have a family link with any of the families noted in my books. I can be contacted via my website www.dianemarelli.co.uk.

The internet is a valuable resource but only when followed up with original documentation such as the Census, Church Records or Civil Registration. You may not be in a position to purchase the above when you suspect you have found your ancestors, but remember without original documentation you hve not verified your source. You do not have to order every piece of documentation but try to purchase key records that should provide you with enough information to let you know you are on the right track.

Appendix I: Quick website guide

Chapter 1-6

♦ Registration Districts in England and Wales (1837–1974) Genuki: http://www.fhsc.org.uk/genuki/reg/

♦ Ancestry.co.uk: http://www.ancestry.co.uk

♦ Find my past: http://www.findmypast.com

♦ General Register Office: http://www.gro.gov.uk

♦ GENUKI BRITISH ISLES GENEALOGY GENUKI Contents and Site Map: http://www.genuki.org.uk/contents

♦ The Church of Jesus Christ of Latter Day Saints: http://www.familysearch.org

♦ The Society of Genealogy: http://www.sog.org.uk

♦ Author website: http://www.dianemarelli.co.uk

♦ Chappell Family Tree Site and others: http://www.stevenjones.me.uk

Chapter 7

♦ The Newspaper Detectives (transcription of 19th century *Surrey Advertiser*): http://www.newspaperdetectives.co.uk

♦ The British Library Online: www.uk.olivesoftware.com

- The National Archives: http://www.nationalarchives.gov.uk

- The Old Bailey: http://www.oldbaileyonline.org

- The Commonwealth War Graves Commission: http://www.cwgc.org

- Genes Reunited http://www.genesreunited.co.uk

- Genealogy Quest: http://www.genealogy-quest.com/glossaries/diseases1.html

- The Hall Genealogy Website: http://www.rmhh.co.uk

- The Victorian Dictionary: http://www.victorianlondon.org

- The Canal Museum: http://www.canalmuseum.org.uk/ice/index.html

- The Weald of Kent: http://thesussexweald.org

- The Surrey History Centre: http://www.surreycc.gov.uk/surreyhistorycentre

- Historical Directories: http://www.historicaldirectories.org/hd/index.asp

- Cemsearch UK: http://www.cemsearch.co.uk

- Scottish Graveyards and UK Links: http://www.scottishgraveyards.org.uk

- UK and Ireland Genuki Home Page: http://www.genuki.org.uk

- Cyndi's List: http://www.cyndislist.com

- Old Maps: http://www.old-maps.co.uk

- Alan Godfrey Maps: http://www.alangodfreymaps.co.uk

- Map Quest: http://www.mapquest.co.uk

- Family Tree Magazine and Practical Family History: http://www.family-tree.co.uk

- Your Family Tree Magazine: http://www.yourfamilytreemag.co.uk

- Family History Monthly: http://www.familyhistorymonthly.com

- Ancestors Magazine: http://www.ancestorsmagazine.co.uk

- Ancestors Magazine and The National Archives:
  http://www.nationalarchives.gov.uk/shop/ancestors.htm

- Peter Christian Internet Guides to Family History: http://www.spub.co.uk

Chapter 8

- Legacy Family Tree Software: http://www.legacyfamilytree.com

- My History Software: http://www.my-history.co.uk

- Family Historian Software: http://www.family-historian.co.uk

- Family Tree Maker Software: http://www.familytreemaker.com

Chapter 9

- S & N Genealogy: http://www.genealogysupplies.com

Appendix 2: My family surnames

B	BONSEY BRISTOW BROWN BROWN BROWN	**J**	JACKSON JONES JORDAN	**S**	SAMPSON SANGER SCAMMELL SIMMONDS SLAUGHTER SPILLER STRIPP SWANN
C	CHAPPELL CHAPPLE COMFORT COMFORTE COOPER- MOLONEY CRAWLEY CUFFLEY CUFLEY CULLETON	**K**	KELLY	**T**	TAYLOR THOMAS TIMMS TODD TUDOR TURNER
D	DAVIES DAWS DIBBEN DUNNE	**L**	LAWRENCE LEE LORD LUCAS LUGG	**U**	UINS
E	EDGE EVANS EWEN EWINS	**M**	MALONEY MANNING MARELLI MARSH MCALLISTER MCDONALD MISNMACK MOLONEY	**V**	VALLAR VOLLER
G	GOODRIDGE GOSLING GRIFFITHS	**O**	OLIVER	**W**	WALKER WILBRINK WILSON WINCUP/CUFFLEY WOOD
H	HARRISON HART HAYWARD HOLMAN HOUSE HUGGETT HUGHES	**P**	PEARSON PERRIN PHILPOTT PILKINGTON PLUMMER PODEVIN PUDVINE PUDWINE		www.dianemarelli.co.uk 'History is fascinating but never more so
I	IRVINE	**R**	RADFORD RADFORD REYNOLDS RICHARDS ROBSON ROSS RYAN		than when it's your own'

A–Z of surnames from the family file of Diane Marelli.

Appendix 3: Family history & genealogical societies

England

BEDFORDSHIRE
Bedfordshire FHS
CONTACT: Mrs Anne Simmonds, PO Box 214, Bedford MK42 9RX
e: bfhs@bfhs.org.uk
w: www.bfhs.org.uk

BERKSHIRE
Berkshire FHS
CONTACT: The Secretary, Berkshire FHS, Yeomanry House, 131 Castle Hill, Reading, RG1 7TJ
e: secretary@berksfhs.org.uk
w: www.berksfhs.org.uk

BUCKINGHAMSHIRE
Buckinghamshire FHS
CONTACT: The Secretary, c/o PO Box 403, Aylesbury, Buckinghamshire HP21 7GU
e: society@bucksfhs.org.uk
w: www.bucksfhs.org.uk

CAMBRIDGESHIRE
Cambridgeshire FHS
CONTACT: David Wratten, 43 Eachard Road, Cambridge CB3 0HZ
e: secretary@cfhs.org.uk
w: www.cfhs.org.uk

Cambridge University H&GS
CONTACT: c/o Crossfield House, Dale Road, Stanton, Bury St Edmunds, Suffolk
IP31 2DY
e: mlm39@hermes.cam.ac.uk
w: www.cam.ac.uk/societies/cuhags

Fenland FHS
CONTACT: Judy Green, Rose Hall, Walpole Bank, Walpole St.Andrew, WISBECH
PE14 7JD
e: judy.green@farming.me.uk
w: www.fenlandfhs.org.uk

CHANNEL ISLANDS
Channel Islands FHS
CONTACT: Mrs P A Neale, Secretary, PO Box 507, St Helier, Jersey JE4 5TN
w: user.itl.net/~glen/AbouttheChannelIslandsFHS.html

La Société Guernesiaise (FH Section)
CONTACT: The Secretary, Family History Section of La Société Guernesiaise,
PO Box 314, Candie, St Peter Port, Guernsey, GY1 3TG
w: www.societe.org.gg/sections/familyhistorysec.htm

CHESHIRE
The FHS of Cheshire
CONTACT: Mike Craig, 10 Dunns Lane, Ashton, Chester, CH3 8BU
e: info@fhsc.org.uk
w: www.fhsc.org.uk

North Cheshire FHS
CONTACT: Mrs Rhoda Clarke, 2 Denham Drive, Bramhall, Stockport, Cheshire
SK7 2AT
e: r.demercado@ntlworld.com
w: www.ncfhs.org.uk

CORNWALL
Cornwall FHS
CONTACT: The Administrator, 5 Victoria Square, Truro, Cornwall TR1 2RS
e: secretary@cornwallfhs.com
w: www.cornwallfhs.com

CUMBERLAND
Cumbria FHS
CONTACT: Mrs S Dench, 279 Newtown Road, Carlisle, Cumbria CA2 7LS
w: www.cumbriafhs.com

Furness FHS
CONTACT: Miss J Fairbairn, 64 Cowlarns Road, Barrow-in-Furness, Cumbria
LA14 4HJ
e: julia.fairbairn@virgin.net
w: www.furnessfhs.co.uk

DERBYSHIRE
Derbyshire FHS
CONTACT: Mr Dave Bull, Bridge Chapel House, St Mary's Bridge, Sowter Rd,
Derby DE1 3AT
w: www.dfhs.org.uk

Chesterfield & District FHS
CONTACT: D Rogers, Correspondence Secretary, 2 Highlow Close, Loundsley
Green, Chesterfield, Derbyshire S40 4PG
e: mail@cadfhs.org.uk
w: www.cadfhs.org.uk

DEVON
Devon FHS
CONTACT: The Secretary, Devon FHS, PO Box 9, Exeter, Devon EX2 6YP
e: secretary@devonfhs.org.uk
w: www.devonfhs.org.uk

DORSET
Dorset FHS
CONTACT: Dorset FHS, Treetops Research Centre, Suite 5 Stanley House,
3 Fleets Lane, Poole, Dorset, BH15 3AJ
e: contact@dorsetfhs.org.uk
w: www.dorsetfhs.org.uk

Somerset & Dorset FHS
CONTACT: The Secretary, PO Box 4502 Sherborne DT9 6YL
e: society@sdfhs.org
w: www.sdfhs.org

DURHAM
Northumberland & Durham FHS
CONTACT: Mrs Frances Norman, 23 Monkton Avenue, Simonside, South Shields,
Tyne & Wear NE34 9RX
e: frances@fnorman.fsnet.co.uk
w: www.ndfhs.org.uk

Cleveland, N. Yorkshire & S. Durham FHS
CONTACT: Mr A. Sampson, 1 Oxgang Close, Redcar, Cleveland TS10 4ND
w: http://www.clevelandfhs.org.uk/

ESSEX
Essex SFH
CONTACT: Mrs A Church, Windyridge, 32 Parsons Heath, Colchester, Essex CO4 3HX
e: secretary@esfh.org.uk
w: www.esfh.org.uk

East of London FHS
CONTACT: Ian Whaley, 46 Brights Avenue, Rainham, Essex RM13 9NW
e: eolfhs@btopenworld.com
w: www.eolfhs.org.uk

Waltham Forest FHS
CONTACT: Mr B.F. Burton, 49 Sky Peals Rd, Woodford Green, Essex IG8 9NE

GLOUCESTERSHIRE
Bristol & Avon FHS
CONTACT: Margaret Smith, 7 Henleaze Park Drive, Bristol, BS9 4LH
e: secretary@bafhs.org.uk
w: www.bafhs.org.uk

Gloucestershire FHS
CONTACT: Alex Wood, 37 Barrington Drive, Hucclecote, Gloucestershire GL3 3BT
e: gfhs@blueyonder.co.uk
w: http://www.gfhs.org.uk

HAMPSHIRE
Hampshire Genealogical Society
CONTACT: Mrs. Sheila Brine, 3 Elaine Gardens, Lovedean, Waterlooville, Hants. PO8 9QS
e: secretary@hgs-online.org.uk
w: www.hgs-online.org.uk

Isle of Wight FHS
CONTACT: Mrs Brenda Dodgson, 9 Forest Dell, Winford, Sandown, I.O.W, PO36 0LG
e: brendave@dodgson9.freeserve.co.uk
w: www.isle-of-wight-fhs.co.uk

HEREFORDSHIRE
Herefordshire FHS
CONTACT: Brian Prosser, 6 Birch Meadow, Gosmore Road, Clehonger, Hereford, HR2 9RH
e: prosser_brian@hotmail.com
w: http://www.rootsw.com/~ukhfhs/

HERTFORDSHIRE
Hertfordshire FHS
CONTACT: Mrs Amelia Cheek, 38 Roselands Avenue, Hoddesdon, Herts
EN11 9BB
e: secretary@hertsfhs.org.uk
w: www.hertsfhs.org.uk

Letchworth & District FH Group
CONTACT: Mrs Helen Fitzgibbons, 2 Cross Street, Letchworth Garden City, Herts,
SG6 4UD
e: hfitz45@ntlworld.com
w: www.letchworthgardencity.net/LDFHG/Index.html

Royston & District FHS
CONTACT: Mrs Kay Curtis, "Baltana" London Road, Barkway, Nr Royston, Herts
SG8 8EY
e: kay.tails@virgin.net
w: www.roystonfhs.org

HUNTINGDONSHIRE
Huntingdon FHS
CONTACT: Mrs C. Kesseler, 42 Crowhill, Godmanchester, Huntingdon, Cambs
PE29 2NR
e: secretary@huntsfhs.org.uk
w: www.huntsfhs.org.uk

ISLE OF MAN
Isle of Man FHS
CONTACT: Mrs Priscilla Lewthwaite, Pear Tree Cottage, Lhergy Cripperty,
Union Mills, Isle of Man IM4 4NF

ISLE OF WIGHT
Isle of Wight FHS
CONTACT: Mrs Brenda Dodgson, 9 Forest Dell, Winford, Sandown, I.O.W, P036
0LG
e: brendave@dodgson9.freeserve.co.uk
w: www.isle-of-wight-fhs.co.uk

KENT
Kent FHS
CONTACT: Mrs Kristin Slater, Bullockstone Farm, Bullockstone Road, Herne,
Kent CT6 7NL
e: kristn@globalnet.co.uk
w: www.kfhs.org.uk

Folkestone & District FHS
CONTACT: Mrs Janet Powell, Kingsmill Down, Hastingleigh, Ashford, Kent.
TN25 5JJ
e: secretary@folkfhs.org.uk
w: www.folkfhs.org.uk

North West Kent FHS
CONTACT: Mrs Vera Bailey, 58 Clarendon Gardens, Stone, Dartford, Kent
DA2 6EZ
e: secretary@nwkfhs.org.uk
w: www.nwkfhs.org.uk

Tunbridge Wells FHS
CONTACT: Roy Thompson, 5 College Drive, Tunbridge Wells, Kent TN2 3PN
e: roythompson@mailsnare.net
w: www.tunwells-fhs.co.uk

Woolwich & District FHS
CONTACT: Mrs Edna Reynolds, 54 Parkhill Road, Bexley, Kent DA5 1HY
e: FrEdnaFHS@aol.com

LANCASHIRE
Cumbria Family History Society
Ulpha, 32 Granadas Road
Denton, Manchester, M34 2LJ

General Register Office
Certificate Services Section
PO Box 2
Southport
PR8 2JD
T: 0845 603 7788

Lancashire FH & Heraldry Soc
CONTACT: Joyce Monks, 21 Baytree Road, Clayton le Woods, PR6 7JW
e: secretary@lfhhs.org.uk
w: www.lfhhs.org.uk

Manchester & Lancashire FHS
CONTACT: Judith Sellers, c/o M&LFHS, Clayton House, 59 Piccadilly, Manchester
M1 2AQ
e: office@mlfhs.org.uk
w: www.mlfhs.org.uk

Furness FHS
CONTACT: Miss J. Fairbairn, 64 Cowlarns Road, Barrow-in-Furness, Cumbria
LA14 4HJ
e: julia.fairbairn@virgin.net
w: www.furnessfhs.co.uk

Lancashire Parish Register Society
CONTACT: Alan Kenwright, 19 Churton Grove, Shevington Moor, Wigan, Lancs
WN6 0SZ
e: akenwright@yahoo.com
w: www.lprs.org.uk

Lancaster FH Group
CONTACT: Mrs P. Harrison, 116 Bowerham Road, Lancaster LA1 4HL
e: secretary@lfhg.org
w: www.lfhg.org

Liverpool & SW Lancs FHS
CONTACT: Mr David Guiver, 11 Bushbys Lane, Formby, Liverpool L37 2DX
e: DavidGuiver@aol.com
w: www.liverpool-genealogy.org.uk

North Meols FHS
CONTACT: Jane Scarisbrick, 6 Millars Place, Marshside, Southport, PR9 9FU
e: jane.scarisbrick@virgin.net
w: www.nmfhssouthport.co.uk

Ormskirk & District FHS
CONTACT: ODFHS, PO Box 213 Aughton, Ormskirk, Lancs. L39 5WT
e: secretary@odfhs.org.uk
w: www.odfhs.org.uk

Wigan F&LHS
CONTACT: John Wogan, 678 Warrington Road, Goose Green, Wigan,
Lancashire WN3 6XN
e: johnwogan@blueyonder.co.uk
w: www.ffhs.org.uk/members/wigan.htm

LEICESTERSHIRE
Leicestershire & Rutland FHS
CONTACT: Mrs Joan Rowbottom, 37 Cyril Street, Leicester, LE3 2FF
e: secretary@lrfhs.org.uk
w: www.lrfhs.org.uk

LINCOLNSHIRE
Lincolnshire FHS
CONTACT: Brenda Coulson, 57 Lupin Road, Lincoln, LN2 4GB
e: secretary@lincolnshirefhs.org.uk
w: www.lincolnshirefhs.org.uk

Isle of Axholme FHS
CONTACT: Norma Neill (Secretary), 'Colywell', 43 Commonside, Westwoodside,
Doncaster DN9 2AR
e: secretary@axholme-fhs.org.uk
w: www.axholme-fhs.org.uk

LONDON/MIDDLESEX AREA
East of London FHS
CONTACT: Ian Whaley, 46 Brights Avenue, Rainham, Essex RM13 9NW
e: eolfhs@btopenworld.com
w: www.eolfhs.org.uk

East Surrey FHS
CONTACT: ESFHS, 119 Keevil Drive, London, SW19 6TF
e: secretary@eastsurreyfhs.org.uk
w: www.eastsurreyfhs.org.uk

Guild of One-Name Studies
CONTACT: c/o Hon Sec, Box G, 14 Charterhouse Buildings, Goswell Road,
London EC1M 7BA
e: guild@one-name.org
w: www.one-name.org
T: 0800 011 2182

Hillingdon FHS
CONTACT: Mrs G. May, 20 Moreland Drive, Gerrards Cross, Bucks SL9 8BB
e: Gillmay@dial.pipex.com
w: www.hfhs.co.uk

International Society for British Genealogy & Family History
Kathleen W. Hinckley, CGRS Business Manager
International Society for British Genealogy & Family History
PO Box 350459 Westminster, CO 80035-0459
e: isbgfh@yahoo.com
w: http://www.isbgfh.org

London Westminster & Middlesex FHS
CONTACT: Mr & Mrs Pyemont, 57 Belvedere Way, Kenton, Harrow, Middlesex
HA3 9XQ
w: www.lnmfhs.dircon.co.uk

North West Kent FHS
CONTACT: Mrs Vera Bailey, 58 Clarendon Gardens, Stone, Dartford, Kent
DA2 6EZ
e: secretary@nwkfhs.org.uk
w: www.nwkfhs.org.uk

Society of Genealogists
14 Charterhouse Buildings
Goswell Road
London EC1M 7BA
T: 0207 251 8799

Waltham Forest FHS
CONTACT: Mr B.F. Burton, 49 Sky Peals Rd, Woodford Green, Essex IG8 9NE

West Middlesex FHS
CONTACT: Tony Simpson, 32 The Avenue Bedford Park, Chiswick, London
W4 1HT
e: secretary@west-middlesex-fhs.org.uk
w: www.west-middlesex-fhs.org.uk

Westminster & Central Middlesex FHS
Woolwich & District FHS
CONTACT: Mrs Edna Reynolds, 54 Parkhill Road, Bexley, Kent DA5 1HY

NORFOLK
Norfolk FHS
CONTACT: Mr Edmund G Perry, Kirby Hall, 70 St Giles Street, Norwich, NR2 1LS
e: nfhs@paston.co.uk
w: www.norfolkfhs.org.uk/)

Mid-Norfolk FHS
CONTACT: Mrs Kate Easdown, Secretary MNFHS, 47 Greengate, Swanton Morley,
Dereham, Norfolk, NR20 4LX
e: keasdown@aol.com
w: www.mnfhs.freeuk.com

NORTHAMPTONSHIRE
Northamptonshire FHS
CONTACT: Mr Keith Steggles, 22 Godwin Walk, Ryehill, Northampton NN5 7RW
e: secretary@northants-fhs.org
w: www.northants-fhs.org

Peterborough & District FHS
CONTACT: Mrs Margaret Brewster, 111 New Road, Woodston, Peterborough
PE2 9HE
e: meandmygarden@hotmail.com
w: www.peterborofhs.org.uk

NORTHUMBERLAND

Northumberland & Durham FHS
CONTACT: Mrs Frances Norman, 23 Monkton Avenue, Simonside, South Shields,
Tyne & Wear NE34 9R
e: frances@fnorman.fsnet.co.uk
w: www.ndfhs.org.uk

NOTTINGHAMSHIRE

Nottinghamshire FHS
CONTACT: Stuart Mason, 26 Acorn Bank, West Bridgford, Nottingham NG2 7DU
e: secretary@nottsfhs.org.uk
w: www.nottsfhs.org.uk

Mansfield & District FHS
CONTACT: Miss B.E. Flintham, 15 Cranmer Grove, Mansfield, Notts, NG19 7JR

OXFORDSHIRE

Oxfordshire FHS
CONTACT: Mrs J. Kennedy, 19 Mavor Close, Woodstock, Oxford OX20 1YL
e: secretary@ofhs.org.uk
w: www.ofhs.org.uk

RUTLAND

Leicestershire & Rutland FHS
CONTACT: The Secretary, c/o 51 New Street, Barrow Upon Soar, Leicestershire
LE12 8PA
e: secretary@lrfhs.org.uk
w: www.lrfhs.org.uk

SHROPSHIRE

Shropshire FHS
CONTACT: Mrs D. Hills, Redhillside, Ludlow Road, Church Stretton, Shropshire
SY6 6AD
e: secretary@sfhs.org.uk
w: www.sfhs.org.uk

SOMERSET

Bristol & Avon FHS
CONTACT: Margaret Smith, 7 Henleaze Park Drive, Bristol BS9 4LH
e: secretary@bafhs.org.uk
w: www.bafhs.org.uk

Somerset & Dorset FHS
CONTACT: The Secretary, PO Box 4502, Sherborne DT9 6YL
e: society@sdfhs.org
w: www.sdfhs.org

Weston-super-mare FHS
CONTACT: Brian Airey, 125 Totterdown Road, Weston Super Mare BS23 4LW
e: secretary@wsmfhs.org.uk
w: www.wsmfhs.org.uk

STAFFORDSHIRE
Birmingham & Midland SGH
CONTACT: Mrs Jackie Cotterill, 5 Sanderling Court, Kidderminster DY10 4TS
e: gensec@ bmsgh.org
w: www.bmsgh.org

Burntwood FH Group
CONTACT: Jennifer Lee, 8 Peakes Road, Rugeley, Staffs WS15 2LY.
e: jennifer.lee@care4free.net
w: www.geocities.com/bfhg1986

SUFFOLK
Felixstowe FHS
CONTACT: Mrs J.S. Campbell, 7 Victoria Road, Felixstowe, Suffolk IP11 7PT

Suffolk FHS
CONTACT: Mrs P Marshall, 2 Flash Corner, Theberton, Leiston, Suffolk IP16 4RW
e: admin@suffolkfhs.org.uk
w: www.suffolkfhs.org.uk

SURREY
East Surrey FHS
CONTACT: ESFHS, 119 Keevil Drive, London SW19 6TF
e: secretary@eastsurreyfhs.org.uk
w: www.eastsurreyfhs.org.uk

Surrey History Centre
130 Goldsworth Road
Woking
Surrey GU21 6ND
T: 01483 518737

The National Archives
Kew
Richmond
Surrey
TW9 4DU
T: 020 8876 3444

West Surrey FHS
CONTACT: Mrs Ann Sargeant, 21 Sheppard Road, Basingstoke, Hants RG21 3HT
e: secretary@wsfhs.org
w: www.wsfhs.org

SUSSEX
Eastbourne & District (Family Roots) FHS
CONTACT: Mr John Crane, 8 Park Lane, Hampden Park, Eastbourne BN21 2UT
e: johnandval.crane@tiscali.co.uk
w: www.eastbournefhs.org.uk

Hastings & Rother FHS
CONTACT: Linda Smith, 355 Bexhill Road, St Leonards-on-Sea, East Sussex
TN38 8AJ
e: enquiries@hrfhs.org.uk
w: www.hrfhs.org.uk

Sussex FHG
CONTACT: Mrs Val Orr, 54 Heron Way, Horsham, Sussex RH13 6DL
e: secretary@sfhg.org.uk
w: www.sfhg.org.uk

Tunbridge Wells FHS
CONTACT: Roy Thompson, 5 College Drive, Tunbridge Wells, Kent TN2 3PN
e: roythompson@mailsnare.net
w: www.tunwells-fhs.co.uk

WARWICKSHIRE
Birmingham & Midland SGH
CONTACT: Mrs Jackie Cotterill, 5 Sanderling Court, Kidderminster DY10 4TS
e: gensec@ bmsgh.org
w: www.bmsgh.org

Coventry FHS
CONTACT: Angela Crabtree, Barton Fields Cottage, 1 Barton Fields, Ecton,
Northants NN6 0BF
e: gen-sec@covfhs.org
w: www.covfhs.org

Nuneaton & North Warwickshire FHS
CONTACT: Peter Lee, PO Box 2282, Nuneaton, Warwickshire CV11 9ZT
e: Nuneatonian2000@aol.com
w: www.nnwfhs.org.uk

Rugby FHG
CONTACT: Mr John A. Chard, Springfields, Rocheberie Way, Rugby CV22 6EG
e: j.chard@ntlworld.com
w: www.rugbyfhg.co.uk

Warwickshire FHS
CONTACT: Chairman, 44 Abbotts Lane, Coventry CV1 4AZ
e: chairman@wfhs.org.uk
w: www.wfhs.org.uk

WESTMORLAND
Cumbria FHS
CONTACT: Mrs S. Dench, 279 Newtown Road, Carlisle, Cumbria CA2 7LS
w: www.cumbriafhs.com

WILTSHIRE
Wiltshire FHS
CONTACT: Mrs Diana Grout, 42 Stokehill, Hilperton, Trowbridge, Wiltshire
BA14 7TJ
e: secretary@wiltshirefhs.co.uk
w: www.wiltshirefhs.co.uk

WORCESTERSHIRE
Birmingham & Midland SGH
CONTACT: Mrs Jackie Cotterill, 5 Sanderling Court, Kidderminster DY10 4TS
e: gensec@ bmsgh.org
w: www.bmsgh.org

Malvern FH Society
CONTACT: Betty Firth, Apartment 5, Severn Grange, Northwick Road, Bevere,
Worcester WR3 7RE
e: betty.firth@virgin.net
w: www.mfhs.org.uk

YORKSHIRE
East Yorkshire FHS
CONTACT: Mrs M. Oliver, 12 Carlton Drive, Aldbrough, East Yorkshire HU11 4SF
e: secretary@eyfhs.org.uk
w: www.eyfhs.org.uk

London Group of Yorkshire FHSs
CONTACT: Ian Taylor, 1 Waverley Way, Carshalton Beeches, Surrey SM5 3LQ
e: ian-taylor@blueyonder.co.uk
w: www.genuki.org.uk/big/eng/YKS/Misc/FHS/

Yorkshire Archaeological Society FH Section
CONTACT: Mrs J Butler, Secretary, c/o YAS, Claremont, 23 Clarendon Road, Leeds
LS2 9NZ
e: secretary@yorkshireroots.org.uk
w: www.yorkshireroots.org.uk

Yorkshire - East Riding
City of York & District FHS
CONTACT: Mrs Mary Varley, Ascot House, Cherry Tree Avenue, Newton-on-Ouse,
York YO30 2BN
e: secretary@yorkfamilyhistory.org.uk
w: www.yorkfamilyhistory.org.uk

Yorkshire - North Riding
Cleveland, N. Yorkshire & S. Durham FHS
CONTACT: Mr A. Sampson, 1 Oxgang Close, Redcar, Cleveland TS10 4ND
w: http://www.clevelandfhs.org.uk/

YORKSHIRE – WEST RIDING
Barnsley FHS
CONTACT: Gail Woodhead, 4 Cranford Gardens, Royston, Barnsley S71 4SP
e: secretary@barnsleyfhs.co.uk
w: www.barnsleyfhs.co.uk

Bradford FHS
CONTACT: Carol Duckworth, 5 Leaventhorpe Avenue, Fairweather Green,
Bradford BD8 0ED
e: secretary@bradfordfhs.org.uk
w: www.bradfordfhs.org.uk

Calderdale FHS (incorporating Halifax & District)
CONTACT: Anne Whitaker, 13 Far View Illingworth, Halifax, West Yorkshire
e: secretary@cfhsw.co.uk
w: www.cfhsw.co.uk

Doncaster & District FHS
CONTACT: Mrs M. Staniforth, 5 Breydon Avenue, Cusworth, Doncaster, South
Yorkshire DN5 8JZ
e: secretary@doncasterfhs.co.uk
w: www.doncasterfhs.co.uk

Harrogate & District FHS
CONTACT: Mrs Wendy Symington, 18 Aspin Drive, Knaresborough, N Yorks
HG5 8HH

Huddersfield & District FHS
CONTACT: Alan Stewart-Kaye, 63 Dunbottle Lane, Mirfield, West Yorkshire
WF14 9JJ
e: secretary@hdfhs.org.uk
w: www.hdfhs.org.uk

Keighley & District FHS
CONTACT: Mrs S. Daynes, 2 The Hallowes, Shann Park, Keighley, W. Yorks
BD20 6HY
w: http://www.keighleyfamilyhistory.org.uk

Morley & District FH Group
CONTACT: Mrs Carol Sklinar, 1 New Lane, East Ardsley, Wakefield WF3 2DP
e: carol@morleyfhg.co.uk
w: www.morleyfhg.co.uk

Pontefract & District FHS
CONTACT: Mrs Glynis Tate, Eadon House, Main Street, Hensall, Goole
DN14 0QZ
e: secretary@pontefractfhs.org.uk
w: www.pontefractfhs.org.uk

Ripon Historical Society & FHG
CONTACT: Mrs Mary Moseley, 42 Knox Avenue, Harrogate, N. Yorks HG1 3JB
w: www.yorksgen.co.uk/rh/rh1.htm

Rotherham FHS
CONTACT: Brian Allott, Secretary Rotherham FHS, 36 Warren Hill, Rotherham,
South Yorkshire S61 3SX
e: secretary@rotherhamfhs.co.uk
w: www.rotherhamfhs.co.uk

Selby FHS
CONTACT: Marilyn Newall, Keswick House, Kelfield Road, Riccall, York
YO19 6PG
e: m_newall@hotmail.com
w: www.geocities.com/selbyfamilyhistory/

Sheffield & District FHS
CONTACT: Mrs Diane Maskell, 5 Old Houses, Piccadilly Road, Chesterfield S61
0EH
e: secretary@sheffieldfhs.org.uk
w: www.sheffieldfhs.org.uk

Wakefield & District FHS
CONTACT: Kathy Wattie, Secretary Wakefield & District FHS, 12 Malting Rise,
Robin Hood, Wakefield, W. Yorks WF3 3AY
e: secretary@wdfhs.co.uk
w: www.wdfhs.co.uk

Wharfedale FHG
CONTACT: Mrs Susan Hartley, 1 West View Court, Yeadon, Leeds LS19 7HX
e: hon.secretary@wfhg.org.uk
w: www.yorksgen.co.uk/wfhg/wfhg.htm

Association of Family History Societies of Wales
CONTACT: Geoff Riggs, Peacehaven, Badgers Meadow, Pwllmeyric, Chepstow,
Mon NP16 6UE
e: secretary@fhswales.info
w: www.fhswales.info

Ireland

Genealogical Soc of Ireland
CONTACT: Mr Michael Merrigan, Hon. Secretary, 11 Desmond Avenue,
Dun Laoghaire, Co. Dublin, Ireland
e: GenSocIreland@iol.ie
w: http://welcome.to/GenealogyIreland

Irish FHS
CONTACT: c/o The Secretary, PO Box 36, Naas, Co Kildare, Ireland
e: ifhs@eircom.net
w: http://welcome.to/GenealogyIreland

Irish Genealogical Research Society
CONTACT: Peter Manning, 18 Stratford Avenue, Rainham, Gillingham, Kent
ME8 0EP
e: info@igrsoc.org
w: www.igrsoc.org

North of Ireland FHS
CONTACT: G M Siberry, c/o Graduate School of Education, The Queen's
University of Belfast, 69 University Street, Belfast NI BT7 1HL
e: enquiries@nifhs.org
w: www.nifhs.org

Scotland

The Scottish Association of Family History Societies
Aberdeen and North East Scotland Family History Society
The Hon. Secretary, The Family History Shop,
164 King Street, Aberdeen AB24 5BD
T: 01224 646323, Fax: 01224 639096
e: enquiries@anesfhs.org.uk
w: www.anesfhs.org.uk/

Alloway & Southern Ayrshire Family History Society
The Hon. Secretary, c/o Alloway Library,
Doonholm Road, Ayr KA7 4QQ
e: asafhs@mtcharlesayr.fsnet.co.uk
w: http://www.asafhs.co.uk

Anglo Scottish Family History Society
Clayton House
59 Piccadily, Manchester M1 2AQ

Association of Scottish Genealogists and Researchers in Archives (ASGRA)
The Hon. Secretary, 93 Colinton Road, Edinburgh EH4 1ET
e: hazelweir@sea-insite.org.uk
w: www.asgra.co.uk

Borders Family History Society
Hon. Secretary, Ronald Morrison
Buchan Cottage, Duns Castle
Duns TD11 3NW
w: www.bordersfhs.org.uk

Caithness Family History Society
Hon Secretary, Mr Sandy Gunn
9 Provost Cormack Drive, Thurso
Caithness KW14 7ES
e: sandy.gunn@btinternet.com
w: www.caithnessfhs.org.uk

Central Scotland Family History Society
The Hon. Secretary, 11 Springbank Gardens
Dunblane FK15 9JX
w: www.csfhs.org.uk/

Dumfries and Galloway Family History Society
The Hon. Secretary, Family History Centre,
9 Glasgow Street, Dumfries DG2 9AF
e: secretary@dgfhs.org.uk
w: www.dgfhs.org.uk

East Ayrshire Family History Society
The Hon. Secretary c/o The Dick Institute,
Elmbank Ave, Kilmarnock KA1 3BU
e: enquiries@eastayrshirefhs.org.uk
w: www.eastayrshirefhs.org.uk/

Fife Family History Society
The Hon. Secretary, Glenmoriston,
Durie Street Leven, Fife KY8 4HF
e: wadmin@fifefhs.org
w: www.fifefhs.org

Glasgow & West of Scotland Family History Society
The Hon. Secretary, Unit 13, 32 Mansfield Street,
Glasgow G11 5QP
w: www.gwsfhs.org.uk/

Highland Family History Society
The Hon. Secretary, c/o Reference Room
Public Library, Farraline Park
Inverness IV1 INH
e: jdurham@highlandfhs.org.uk
w: www.highlandfhs.org.uk

Lanarkshire Family History Society
Hon. Secretary, 26A Motherwell Business Centre
Coursington Road, Motherwell, Lanarkshire ML1 1PW
e: info@lanarkshirefhs.org.uk or society@lanarkshirefhs.org.uk
w: www.lanarkshirefhs.org.uk

Largs and North Ayrshire Family History Society
c/o Largs Library, 18 Allanpark Street
Largs KA30 9AG
w: http://www.largsnafhs.org.uk/home.htm

Orkney Family History Society
Hon. Secretary, Orkney FHS.,
Orkney Library & Archive
44 Junction Road, Kirkwall
Orkney KW15 1HG

Renfrewshire Family History Society
The Hon. Secretary, PO Box 9239, Kilmacolm PA13 4WZ
w: www.renfrewshirefhs.co.uk

SCOTSLOT
Chairman: Mrs Elizabeth van Lottum
16 Bloomfield Road, Harpenden
Herts AL5 4DB

Shetland Family History Society
The Hon. Secretary, 6 Hillhead,
Lerwick, Shetland ZE1 0EJ
e: secretary@shetland-fhs.org.uk
w: www.shetland-fhs.org.uk

Tay Valley Family History Society covering the former Counties of Angus, Fife,
Kinross & Perth
The Hon. Secretary, Research Centre,
179-181 Princes Street, Dundee DD4 6DQ
T: 01382 461845
e: tvfhs@tayvalleyfhs.org.uk
w: www.tayvalleyfhs.org.uk

The Genealogy Society of Utah
Family History Support Office
185 Penns Lane, Sutton Coalfield
West Midlands B75 1JU
w: www.familysearch.org/

The Heraldry Society of Scotland
The Hon Secratary
22 Craigentinny Crescent
Edinburgh EH7 6QA
e: c.napier@napier.aol.com.uk
w: www.heraldry-scotland.co.uk

The Lothian Family History Society
The Hon. Secretary, c/o Lasswade High School Centre,
Eskdale Drive, Bonnyrigg,
Midlothian EH19 2LA
e: lothiansfhs@hotmail.com
w: www.lothiansfhs.org.uk

The Scottish Genealogy Society
The Hon. Secretary, Library and Family History Centre,
15 Victoria Terrace, Edinburgh EH1 2JL
T: 0131 220 3677
e: sales@scotsgenealogy.com
w: www.scotsgenealogy.com

Troon @ Ayrshire Family History Society
The Hon. Secretary, c/o M.E.R.C. Troon Public Library,
South Beach, Troon, Ayrshire KA10 6EF
e: info@troonayrshirefhs.org.uk
w: www.troonayrshirefhs.org.uk

West Lothian Family History Society
Hon. Secretary, 23 Templar Rise,
Livingstone EH54 6PJ
e: honsec@wlfhs.org.uk
w: www.wlfhs.org.uk

Wales

ANGLESEY
Gwynedd FHS
CONTACT: J. Bryan Jones, Secretary Gwynedd FHS, 7 Victoria Road, Old Colwyn,
Conwy LL29 9SN
e: bryan.jones8@btinternet.com
w: www.gwyneddfhs.org

BRECONSHIRE (OR BRECKNOCKSHIRE)
Powys FHS
CONTACT: Keith Morgan, Drefach, Siluria, Walton, Presteigne, Powys DL8 2RE
e: kmor@kmor.wanadoo.co.uk
w: www.rootsw.com/~wlspfhs/

CAERNARVONSHIRE
Gwynedd FHS
CONTACT: J. Bryan Jones, Secretary Gwynedd FHS, 7 Victoria Road, Old Colwyn,
Conwy LL29 9SN

CARDIGANSHIRE
Cardiganshire FHS
CONTACT: Menna H. Evans, Cardiganshire FHS, Adran Casgliadau, c/o National
Library of Wales, Aberystwyth, Ceredigion SY23 3BU
e: sec@cgnfhs.org.uk
w: www.cgnfhs.org.uk

Dyfed FHS
CONTACT: Mrs Beti Williams, 12 Elder Grove, Llamgunnor, Carmarthen,
Carmarthenshire SA31 2LQ
e: secretary@dyfedfhs.org.uk
w: www.dyfedfhs.org.uk

CARMARTHENSHIRE
Dyfed FHS
CONTACT: Mrs Beti Williams, 12 Elder Grove, Llamgunnor, Carmarthen,
Carmarthenshire SA31 2LQ
e: secretary@dyfedfhs.org.uk
w: www.dyfedfhs.org.uk

DENBIGHSHIRE & FLINTSHIRE
Clwyd FHS
CONTACT: Mrs A. Anderson, The Laurels, Dolydd Road, Cefn Mawr, Wrexham
LL14 3NH
w: www.clwydfhs.org.uk

GLAMORGAN
Glamorgan FHS
CONTACT: Mrs R. Williams, 93 Pwllygath Street, Bridgend CF 36 6ET
e: secretary@glamfhs.org
w: www.glamfhs.org

MERIONETHSHIRE
Gwynedd FHS
CONTACT: J. Bryan Jones, Secretary Gwynedd FHS, 7 Victoria Road, Old Colwyn,
Conwy LL29 9SN

MONMOUTHSHIRE
Gwent FHS
CONTACT: Hon. Secretary, 11 Rosser St, Wainfelin, Pontypool NP4 6EA
e: secretary@gwentfhs.info
w: www.gwentfhs.info

MONTGOMERYSHIRE
Powys FHS
CONTACT: Keith Morgan, Drefach, Siluria, Walton, Presteigne, Powys DL8 2RE
e: kmor@kmor.wanadoo.co.uk
w: www.rootsw.com/~wlspfhs/

Montgomeryshire GS
CONTACT: Mrs Sue Harrison-Stone, Cambrian House, Brimmon Lane, Newtown,
Montgomeryshire, Powys SY16 1BY
e: sue_powys@hotmail.com
w: home.freeuk.net/montgensoc

PEMBROKESHIRE
Dyfed FHS
CONTACT: Mrs Beti Williams, 12 Elder Grove, Llamgunnor, Carmarthen, Carmarthenshire SA31 2LQ
e: secretary@dyfedfhs.org.uk
w: www.dyfedfhs.org.uk

RADNORSHIRE
Powys FHS
CONTACT: Keith Morgan, Drefach, Siluria, Walton, Presteigne, Powys DL8 2RE
e: kmor@kmor.wanadoo.co.uk
w: www.rootsw.com/~wlspfhs/

Australia

Australasian Federation of Family History Organisations Inc
CONTACT: PO Box 3012, Weston Creek, ACT 2611 Australia
E: secretary@affho.org
w: www.affho.org/

Australian Institute of Gen Studies Inc
CONTACT: PO Box 339, Blackburn, Victoria 3130
e: info@aigs.org.au
w: www.aigs.org.au

Blue Mountains Family History Society
CONTACT: Mrs Suzanne Voytas, Secretary, Blue Mountains FHS Inc, PO Box 97, Springwood, New South Wales 2777
e: exploretree@yahoo.com.au
w: www.rootsw.com/~nswbmfhs/activities.htm

Botany Bay FHS Inc
CONTACT: Botany Bay FHS Inc, PO Box 1006, Sutherland, New South Wales 1499
e: botanybayfhs@yahoo.com.au
w: http://au.geocities.com/bbfhs

Cape Banks FHS Inc
CONTACT: PO Box 67, Maroubra, New South Wales 2035
e: hazelb@compassnet.com.au
w: www.capebanks.org.au

Cairns & District FHS Inc
CONTACT: Mrs Beverley O'Hara, PO Box 5069, Cairns, Queensland 4870
e: rondac@ozemail.com.au
w: cwpp.slq.gld.gov.au/cdfhs

Central Queensland FH Association Inc
CONTACT: CQFHA, PO Box 6000, Rockhampton Mail Centre, Queensland 4701
e: cqfha@hotmail.com
w: www.rootsw.com/~auscqfha

Central Coast FHS Inc
CONTACT: PO Box 4090, East Gosford, New South Wales 2250
e: secretary@centralcoastfhs.org.au
w: www.centralcoastfhs.org.au

Dubbo & District FHS Inc
CONTACT: PO Box 868, Dubbo, New South Wales 2830
e: ddfhs_2000@yahoo.com.au
w: au.geocities.com/ddfhs_2000

Genealogical Soc of the Northern Territory Inc
CONTACT: Mrs June Tomlinson, PO Box 37212, Winnellie, Northern Territory
0821

Genealogical Soc of Queensland Inc
CONTACT: PO Box 8423, Woolloongabba, Queensland 4102
e: gsq@gsq.org.au
w: www.gsq.org.au

Gold Coast Family History Society Inc
CONTACT: PO Box 2763, Southport, Queensland 4215
e: annmorse@ozemail.com.au
w: members.ozemail.com.au/~annmorse/nerang.html

Illawarra FHG
CONTACT: Mrs K. Alexander, PO Box 1652, South Coast Mail Centre, Wollongong,
New South Wales 2521
w: www.rootsw.com/~ausifhg/

Lithgow & District FHS Inc
CONTACT: PO Box 516, Lithgow, New South Wales 2790
e: ldfhs@lisp.com.au
w: www.lisp.com.au/~ldfhs

Maryborough District FHS Inc
CONTACT: PO Box 408, Maryborough, Queensland, 4650
e: mdfhs@satcom.net.au
w: www.satcom.net.au/mdfhs

Moruya & District Historical Society Inc
CONTACT: PO Box 259, Moruya, New South Wales 2537

Nepean FHS Inc
CONTACT: PO Box 81, Emu Plains, New South Wales 2750

Newcastle FHS Inc
CONTACT: The Secretary, NFHS Inc, PO Box 189, Adamstown,
New South Wales 2289
w: www.ozemail.com.au/~ahgw/nfhs

Orange FHS
CONTACT: PO Box 930, Orange, New South Wales 2800

Queensland FHS Inc
CONTACT: PO Box 171, Indooroopilly, Brisbane, Queensland 4068
e: info@qfhs.org.au
w: www.qfhs.org.au

Richmond-Tweed FHS
CONTACT: The Secretary, PO Box 817, Ballina, New South Wales 2478

South Australian Gen & Her Soc Inc
CONTACT: Mr Dale Johns, GPO Box 592, Adelaide, South Australia 5001
e: info@saghs.org.au
w: www.saghs.org.au

Soc of Australian Genealogists
CONTACT: Richmond Villa, 120 Kent Street, Observatory Hill, Sydney,
New South Wales 2000
e: info@sag.org.au
w: www.sag.org.au

Scottish Ancestry Group, Genealogical Society of Victoria Inc.
Hon. Secretary, Level 6, 179 Queen Street, Melbourne,
Victoria 3000, Austailia
e: gsv@gsv.org.au
w: www.gsv.org.au

Scottish Interest Group, Genealogical Society of Queensland Inc.
Hon. Secretary, P.O. Box 8423 Woolloongabba,
Queensland, 4102, Australia
e: gsq@gsq.org.au
w: www.gsq.org.au

Scottish Interest Group, Western Australian Genealogical Society
6/48 May Street, Bayswater, 6053, Western Australia
e: genealogy@wags.org.au
w: www.wags.org.au

Shoalhaven FHS
CONTACT: Robyn Burke, P.O. Box 591, Nowra New South Wales 2541, Australia

Society of Australian Genealogists
Richmond Villa, 120 Kent Street, Sydney, NSW 2000, Australia
e: info@sag.org.au
w: www.sag.org.au

South Australia Genealogy & Heraldry Society Inc
Hon.Secretary, PO Box 592, Adelaide, SA 5001, Australia
e: admin@saghs.org.au
w: www.saghs.org.au

Tasmanian FHS Inc
formerly Genealogical Society of Tasmania, prior to 01APR2001
CONTACT: Mrs Betty Bissett, PO Box 191, Launceston, Tasmania 7250
e: secretary@tasfhs.org
w: www.tasfhs.org/

The Genealogical Soc of Victoria Inc
CONTACT: 6th Floor, 179 Queen Street, Melbourne, Victoria 3000
e: gsv@gsv.org.au
w: www.gsv.org.au

The Heraldry & Genealogy Soc of Canberra Inc
CONTACT: GPO Box 585, Canberra, Australian Capital Territory 2601
e: hagsoc@hagsoc.org.au
w: www.hagsoc.org.au

Tweed Gold Coast FH & Heritage Association
CONTACT: PO Box 266, Tweed Heads, New South Wales 2485
e: tweedfhs@hotmail.com
w: www.geocities.com/twintownsfamilyhistory/

Wagga Wagga & District FHS
CONTACT: PO Box 307, Wagga Wagga, New South Wales 2650, Australia
e: rivtron@bigpond.com
w: www.wsg.net.au/wagga

Western Australian Gen Soc Inc
CONTACT: Unit 6, 48 May Street, Bayswater, Western Australia 6053
e: genealogy@wags.org.au
w: www.wags.org.au

Canada

Alberta Family Histories Soc
CONTACT: 712-16 Avenue NW, Calgary, Alberta, Canada T2M 0J8
e: afhs@afhs.ab.ca
w: www.afhs.ab.ca

Alberta Genealogical Soc
CONTACT: #116, 10440-108 Avenue, Edmonton, Alberta T5H 3Z9
e: agsoffice@compusmart.ab.ca
w: http://abgensoc.ca/

British Isles Family History Society of Greater Ottawa
P.O. Box 38026, Ottawa, Ontario, K2C 3Y7, Canada
e: queries@bifhsgo.ca
w: www.bifhsgo.ca

Ontario Gen.Society (Kingston Branch)
CONTACT: The Corresponding Secretary, Post Office Box 1394, Kingston, Ontario,
K7L 5C6, Canada
w: http://w.ctsolutions.com/ogskingston/

Ontario Gen.Society (Toronto Branch)
CONTACT: Paul Jones, Ontario Genealogical Society, Toronto Branch, Box 518,
Station K, Toronto, Ontario, M4P 2G9, Canada
e: pauljones@rogers.com
w: http://www.torontofamilyhistory.org

Quebec FHS
CONTACT: PO Box 1026, Postal Station Pointe Claire, Quebec H9S 4H9
e: admin@qfhs.ca
w: www.qfhs.ca

Saskatchewan Genealogical Soc
CONTACT: 2nd Floor, 1870 Lorne Street, P.O. Box 1894, Regina, Saskatchewan
S4P 3E1
w: www.saskgenealogy.com

The British Columbia Gen Soc
CONTACT: PO Box 88054, Lansdowne, Richmond, British Columbia V6X 3T6
e: bcgs@bcgs.ca
w: www.bcgs.ca/

Victoria Genealogical Soc
CONTACT: PO Box 43021, RPO Victoria North, Victoria, BC V8X 3G2
e: vgs@victoriags.org
w: www.victoriags.org

New Zealand

New Zealand FHS Inc
CONTACT: Mrs J. Lord, PO Box 13301, Armagh, Christchurch
e: reasearch@xtra.co.nz

New Zealand Society of Genealogists Inc.
P.O. Box 8795, Symonds Street, Auckland 1035, New Zealand
e: nzsg-contact@genealogy.org.nz
w: www.genealogy.org.nz

United States

British Isles FHS - USA
CONTACT: Secretary, 2531 Sawtelle Blvd, PMB 134, Los Angeles, CA 90064-3124, USA
w: www.rootsw.com/~bifhsusa

Federation of Genealogical Societies
CONTACT: PO Box 200940, Austin, TX 78720-0940, USA
e: fgs-office@fgs.org
w: www.fgs.org

Genealogical Society of Pennsylvania
CONTACT: 215 S. Broad St, 7th Floor, Philadelphia PA 19107-5325, USA
e: gsppa@aol.com
w: www.genpa.org

International Society for British Genealogy & Family History
CONTACT: PO Box 350459, Westminster, CO 80035-0459, USA
e: isbgfh@yahoo.com
w: www.isbgfh.org

Santa Barbara County Gen Soc
CONTACT: PO Box 1303, Goleta, CA 93116-1303, USA
e: sbcgs@msn.com
w: http://www.cagenw.com/santabarbara/sbcgs/

Other Societies

Anglo-German FHS
CONTACT: Mr Peter Towey, 20 Skylark Rise, Woolwell, Plymouth, Devon PL6 7SN

Anglo-Italian FHS
CONTACT: Elaine Collins (Chairman) 3 Calais Street, London SE5 9LP
e: chairman@anglo-italianfhs.org.uk
w: www.anglo-italianfhs.org.uk

British Association for Cemeteries in S. Asia
CONTACT: Mr T. Wilkinson MBE, 76½ Chartfield Avenue, London SW15 6HQ

British Record Society
CONTACT: Mrs C. Busfield, Stone Barn Farm, Sutherland Road, Longsdon, Staffs
ST9 9QD
e: britishrecordsociety@hotmail.com
w: http://britishrecordsociety.org.uk

Catholic FHS
CONTACT: Mrs Margaret Bowery, 9 Snows Green Road, Shotley Bridge, Consett,
Co. Durham DH8 0HD
w: www.catholic-history.org.uk/cfhs/index.htm

Genealogical Society of Utah (UK)
CONTACT: Mr G. D. Mawlam, 185 Penns Lane, Sutton Coldfield, West Midlands
B76 1JU

The Institute of Heraldic & Genealogical Studies
CONTACT: Mr J. Palmer, Northgate, Canterbury, Kent CT1 1 BA
e: ihgs@ihgs.ac.uk
w: www.ihgs.ac.uk

Jewish Genealogical Society of Great Britain
CONTACT: Mr A Winner, PO Box 13288, London N3 3WD
e: enquiries@jgsgb.org.uk
w: www.jgsgb.org.uk/

Krans-Buckland Family Association
CONTACT: Mrs J. Buckland, PO Box 1025, North Highlands, California 95660-1025
e: jkbfa@sbcglobal.net

Pedigree Users Group
CONTACT: Malcolm Austen, 11 Corn Avill Close, Abingdon, Oxford OX14 2ND
e: chairman@pugw.org.uk
w: www.pugw.org.uk

Quaker FHS
CONTACT: Mrs Liz Butler, 3 Sheridan Place, Hampton, Middlesex TW12 2SB
e: info@qfhs.co.uk
w: www.qfhs.co.uk

Railway Ancestors FHS
CONTACT: Mr Jeremy Engert, Lundy, King Edward St, Barmouth, Gwynedd
LL42 1NY
w: www.railwayancestors.fsnet.co.uk

Romany & Traveller FHS
CONTACT: Mrs J. Keet-Black, 6 St.James Walk, South Chailey, East Sussex
BN8 4BU
w: www.rtfhs.org.uk

Society of Genealogists
CONTACT: 14 Charterhouse Buildings, Goswell Road, London EC1M 7BA
e: genealogy@sog.org.uk
w: www.sog.org.uk

The Association of Genealogists and Researchers in Archives (AGRA)
CONTACT: Mr David Young, 29 Badgers Close, Horsham, West Sussex RH12 5RU
e: agra@agra.org.uk
w: www.agra.org.uk

The Families in British India Society
CONTACT: Mr Peter Bailey, Sentosa, Godolphin Rd, Weybridge, Surrey KT13 0PT
w: www.fibis.org

Index